Geoff Lemon has covered cricket since 2010, for outlets including the ABC, BBC, *Wisden Almanack*, *The Guardian*, *The Cricketer*, *The Saturday Paper* and ESPNcricinfo. He has worked on radio and television in Australia, England, New Zealand, South Africa, India, Sri Lanka, the Caribbean, Ireland and the UAE, and hosts cricket podcast *The Final Word*. His writing outside sport appears in *Best Australian Stories*, *The Monthly* and *Meanjin*. His books include essay collection *The Sturgeon General Presents*, collaborative novel *Willow Pattern*, and poetry collection *Sunblind*. His last book, *Steve Smith's Men*, was named Wisden Book of the Year, MCC & Cricket Society Book of the Year, Cricket Writers' Club Book of the Year, and was shortlisted for *The Telegraph* Cricket Book of the Year and the Mark & Evette Moran Nib Literary Award.

THE COMEBACK SUMMER

THE COMEBACK SUMMER

WHEN SMITH AND STOKES GOT THE MAGIC BACK

GEOFF LEMON

Hardie Grant

BOOKS

Published in 2020 by Hardie Grant Books, an imprint of Hardie Grant Publishing

Hardie Grant Books (Melbourne)
Building 1, 658 Church Street
Richmond, Victoria 3121

Hardie Grant Books (London)
5th & 6th Floors
52–54 Southwark Street
London SE1 1UN

hardiegrantbooks.com

 A catalogue record for this book is available from the National Library of Australia

The Comeback Summer
ISBN 978 1 74379 715 0

10 9 8 7 6 5 4 3 2 1

Cover design by Luke Causby
Edited by Michael Epis
Typeset in 11/18 pt Sabon LT Std by Kirby Jones
This book draws on a range of the author's writing published by *The Guardian* and the ABC between 25 May and 16 September 2019, and his 'England v Australia 2019 Review' for *Wisden Cricketers' Almanack 2020*.
Printed in UK

Hardie Grant acknowledges the Traditional Owners of the country on which we work, the Wurundjeri people of the Kulin nation and the Gadigal people of the Eora nation, and recognises their continuing connection to the land, waters and culture. We pay our respects to their Elders past, present and emerging.

Contents

Chapter 1

Safe Harbour

DRUMMOYNE OVAL IS a long, long way off Broadway. Not the actual road in Sydney named Broadway, although it's not on that either. It's the cricket ground version of visiting suburban parents. Quiet, sedate, the kind of joint where they're pretty rich but would only ever call themselves 'comfortable'. It's lush – Moreton Bay figs sprawling out limbs like drunken uncles, oaks and eucalypts on parade, the oval sunk into parkland, bounded by a neat little scoreboard and a neat little pavilion. All grassy banks and sea air. It's right on the harbour, that nourishing swathe of water that makes property prices shoot with endless vitality towards the light. A short skip down the shoreline is Malcolm Turnbull's waterside residence, and he used to pop in for official visits as prime minister to see the Governor-General's XI.

In October 2019, Steve Smith was the only former national leader hanging out at Drummoyne. A year and a half since being sacked as Australian captain, he had spent most of the second day of a Sheffield Shield match making a typically bloody-minded hundred for New South Wales, content to stay in the rhythm of a long slow innings on a low bland pitch. On resuming the following morning he had been knocked over by Shane Warne's new favourite bowler, a young Tasmanian named Riley Meredith, who had bent a delivery at pace towards the leg stump. With the stride that Smith takes across his crease to face up, the ball had somehow hooped back between his legs to hit timber.

He would have felt some disappointment, but the surroundings didn't exactly reflect intensity. In contrast, his previous 18 months had been full on. The first year had been spent in the wilderness, suspended from the cricket world that was all he had known since adolescence, after players under his command were caught sandpapering the ball during a Test against South Africa in Cape Town. The strength of anger and bleakness of disappointment from a broad section of Australians had surprised almost everyone. First fell Smith, his deputy David Warner, junior batsman Cameron Bancroft, then their coach Darren Lehmann. An investigation into the team's cheating was smothered even as a broader 'cultural review' was commissioned, which later returned damning results. Half a dozen senior administrators eventually followed the players out the door.

Smith was banned from all Australian national and domestic teams for a year. His 2018 Indian Premier League contract got cancelled, and he was unlikely to be welcomed by the England & Wales Cricket Board, Cricket Australia's close ally. He spent his suspension wandering the world like a banished rōnin, assuaging shame through T20 service to regional shōguns like the Toronto Nationals, Barbados Tridents and Comilla Victorians. In early 2019 he needed an elbow operation and months of rehabilitation before his international comeback started in May.

In most of these experiences he was paired with Warner, reluctant partners in fate. Their returns were just in time for the World Cup and the Ashes in England, where deeply partisan crowds were never going to let the sins of their biggest rival pass unremarked.

What followed has a strong case for being the most extraordinary single season that cricket has seen. Against that fevered backdrop, story after story escalated in absurdity, and central throughout were the characters of Smith, Warner and England all-rounder Ben Stokes. He too had a reputation to rebuild, and inevitably each of their sporting comebacks was framed in terms of personal redemption.

I followed those stories up and down England, watching some games from the commentary box and some from the boundary line, some from transit between other matches and some from down among the crowds. All summer, the spent-cordite smell of excitement lingered in the nostrils. There were my stories too from covering such a season, the details not visible from an audience view. The concept of spiritual restoration deserved the light of the examination table. The ideas in this book were forming before the season was done, and they're the stories it will try to tell.

At Drummoyne on that October afternoon, memories of England felt like a distant dream. Only weeks earlier Smith had been in an Ashes cauldron, facing up against a dark Dukes ball under gloomy skies, lost in the booze-basted roar of English voices in their thousands. Now he was back home and padded up for New South Wales with a crowd in the dozens. For a player of his level it was a modest opportunity, but it was also something he had been barred from doing for so long. Now he was through to the other side. And on this side, things couldn't have been more relaxed. A gentle sunny Sunday, the shade of the overarching trees, a press conference held on the grass by the boundary with half a dozen journos yawning and holding out dictaphones.

When Smith had led the national team his media appearances usually projected antipathy, even toward the small pack of touring reporters who travelled the same miles as he did and generally were more fair and nuanced than distant newsrooms. He would be edgy or defensive about perceived insinuations, or flatly deny obvious problems. Right up until he was sacked, he deployed a trademark smirk while brushing off suggestions that his team had a behavioural problem.

Now, though, he was chill as a sponsor's Zooper Dooper. He greeted each of us and smiled readily. He was open about recent exhaustion. 'Emotionally, physically, mentally. All of the above,' he said of his Ashes comedown. 'I was pretty knackered by the end of it. I worked pretty hard, I spent a lot of time out in the middle. I didn't have a great deal of time off the field, if that sort of makes sense? It was a long campaign, with the World Cup as well. It was good to have a couple of weeks off and then get back home for New South Wales. So, all smooth rolling from here.'

He looked like a man who'd had a weight lifted. He was home, and far enough past his career resumption that it might soon cease to be a talking point. He was a guaranteed pick for three Australian teams, with a satisfyingly full but low-profile home summer ahead. There was the pleasure of being back where he wanted to be, and the sense that after the tumult, things might be returning to Steve Smith's version of normal.

Chapter 2

Into the Wilderness

WHEN DAVID WARNER lit the fuse on the ball-tampering story in March 2018, nobody could have imagined the explosion to come. Hansie Cronje's match-fixing exposé in 2001 and Bodyline in 1933 were the only cricket stories that compared. Even in Cape Town on the evening itself, after Steve Smith admitted to cheating in pursuit of reverse swing, those of us reporting at the ground didn't anticipate the intensity of public anger. The offence was scuffing a cricket ball, not consorting with criminals or endangering lives. But its dishonesty and hypocrisy, after decades of Australian players lecturing others while exhausting their own goodwill, meant that supporters blew up even more than opponents.

Having written a book about Australian cricket's failings in that era, I won't repeat the detail. Those failings cumulatively created the anger, and the anger demanded a response. The standard demerit points or a missed match were not going to do.

Cricket Australia had to come up with something that wouldn't destroy the country's two best batsmen but would salvage public regard for the sport.

A year's ban was a decent choice. It sounded solid, a weight in your palm. Nine months for Cameron Bancroft – the one with the sandpaper down his jocks – made it clear that the senior players were more culpable. It gave Bancroft part of the next home summer to ease his return while the others would miss the whole thing. After all, most Australians wouldn't pay attention to cricket between March and November, so if Smith and Warner appeared during that next season it would seem like they'd never been away. Nor could CA risk a situation where gun batsmen were smashing runs in the Big Bash League while the Test team was struggling without them. Sports administration is like ophthalmology: it's all about the optics and the nerve.

Before the players could disappear from view they had to offer penance. A day in the stocks, with camera flashes instead of rotten fruit. Smith delivered his apology straight off the plane from Johannesburg, only taking the time to change into a suit before sitting in front of a press conference of massed news media rather than familiar cricket reporters. He broke down in sobs as he spoke of having let down his parents. His father, Peter, placed a consoling hand on his son's shoulder. Even so soon, a lot of hard hearts softened.

Warner waited a couple more days. There were hints that he resented being blamed, on the understanding that tampering was common and everyone in his team benefited. Perhaps he was swayed by how well Smith's contrition was received, but Warner's didn't hit the same spot. His voice cracking in distress sounded less believable, though his tears looked real enough. His image was ironically not helped by having celebrity PR agent Roxy Jacenko accompany his wife Candice in the audience, nor by his statement and answers all using the same vague phrasing of 'accepting responsibility for my part in what happened in Cape Town'. It would take another five days for him to accept his punishment, waiving his right to appeal. Smith and Bancroft also dodged detail, but without the repetition that lawyers had drilled into Warner. Already the pricklier character, he came out of the process with far less sympathy.

Without cricket, you wondered what Smith and Warner would do. They were pathway boys, on the treadmill since joining New South Wales teenage teams. They had developed their talents early and been in national colours for the best part of a decade. Suddenly they were on their own. No training, no physio, no time in the nets, unless the neighbourhood kids had a bowl. The IPL's masters had no problem signing Ben Stokes while he awaited trial after a street brawl, but the sin of ball-tampering was too great. The Indian board cancelled contracts worth a couple of million Aussie dollars apiece.

Smith wisely got out of Dodge, heading to New York City where cricket was an unlikely conversation starter. He needed to process his humiliation. Warner grabbed a custom-decorated hardhat and joined the construction work on his new house in the 'locals only' area of southern beachside Sydney. In a new look for him, he kept his head down. Aside from a cameo on Channel Nine's commentary of a One-Day International from England in June, he made no public appearances or attempts to improve his image. He seemed to have been well advised that the best thing he could do was make sure people didn't have to think about him for a while.

By the end of June the teammates were both on the other side of the world to play in the auspicious Global T20 Canada competition, a new league involving almost no Canadians, set up in the hope of selling television rights by some opaque beneficiaries who would go on to fail at staging the many-times-cancelled Euro T20 Slam. Smith suited up for the Toronto Nationals, Warner for the Winnipeg Hawks, among five teams named for parts of Canada that those teams would never visit, alongside the thrillingly presented 'Cricket West Indies B Team', at a tournament played entirely at King City, Ontario.

The banishment was already symbolic, in the way that sinners go into the wilderness and reconnect with God. But the outer reaches of the cricket world didn't get more distant than a paddock miles north of Toronto, between a swamp and some crop fields on York Regional Road 40, at a ground with no stands, a few houses backing onto it, and a pitch so worn that you could roll into the divots and hide. Players who weeks earlier had been running the team with the biggest reputation in the world were now ring-ins for franchises whose names would die on the first breath, in a smash-and-grab tournament whose subsequent year would see players go on strike for not being paid. Try fronting up like Warner to make 1, 4, 1, 6 and 0 in your first five hits for Winnipeg and see how optimistic you are about the road back.

Warner's first venture onto an Australian field was with Bancroft in a Darwin 50-over competition in July. Playing penitent, he crept to 93 from 139 balls against some proper club bowling. Extravagance might have been poorly received. But the immediate disgrace part of the arc was done by then, a conclusion marked when Australia's most outhouse-worthy newspaper published a supposed scoop of Smith having a beer alone in a New York bar. The paper got panned. The only strangeness in the story was the same as ever: that Steve Smith doing ordinary tasks gives the impression that he's a benign alien trying to blend in without quite understanding what humans are up to.

Smith had an opportunity, beyond sport cliche. A chance to escape the professional grind. In his apology he had identified a failure of his leadership. Even as a captain he had not really led, but had reflected the people around him: their ideas, their desires, their standards. There was no strong sense of his own thoughts beyond prevailing wisdom. Having been so long immersed in cricket, even he didn't know who he was outside it.

There was a ready example in Jobe Watson, another former captain who was banned for a year. He had led Australia Football League club Essendon, where officials had ordered players to take injections that were later ruled to have breached drug codes. Like Smith, Watson took off for New York, but not on his way north to keep his kicking skills primed for the Edmonton Wombats in the Alberta Footy League. He stayed in New York to work in a cafe, embracing the anonymity of being just another bearded Australian barista in a checked flannel. He returned having popped his head out of the bubble, with a better sense of the world around him, and became a better leader as a result.

A lack of breadth and worldliness was foremost among Smith's shortcomings. His cricket lifestyle had created that problem, but also gave him the contacts and cash to dissolve any barrier to addressing it. The world is full of places where nobody has heard of cricket, where he could hop off a bus as a guy called Steve. There was a life of Forrest Gumpian possibility out there: picture Australia's greatest post-war batsman hauling in a fresh catch on a fishing trawler, hiking through bear country to plant radio trackers, assisting on an excavation of a Maya city. Imagine Steve with New York at his back and a dream of the shining Pacific ahead, embarking on a cross-country road trip with an unlikely ally wherein they would discover both America and themselves.

But no. After that beer, he batted on. Not for ego and probably not for cash, but because it was all he had ever known. He passed up a new world for a familiar orbit: throwdowns and dressing rooms and a top bunch of blokes. Both he and Warner went on to the Caribbean Premier League, then the Bangladesh version, either side of playing local cricket in Sydney the next home summer. The pause was only a springboard for the resumption.

As the players spent 2018 pondering their public perception, CA had to follow suit. The immediate Cape Town fallout changed nothing. Every person in a senior position with questions to answer hung on to his (and yes, his) job. No-one bar the three players was held responsible for the ball-tampering embarrassment, as though the idea, the brashness, the gall, the stupidity, had sprung up spontaneously and independently of the influences and systems and mentors that surrounded the team at the cost of many millions of dollars.

Coach Darren Lehmann was irretrievably compromised by his team's cheating but had to make his own decision to quit after Sutherland kept backing him. Lehmann said he knew nothing of the plot, though it was curious that none of the banned players included him in their apologies even though according to their stories they had cost an innocent man his job. But the cost wasn't high, as CA immediately moved Lehmann to coach at the academy in Brisbane until his contract ran out, at which point Fox Sports popped him in a commentary box for a season. He was soon welcomed back to coaching with the Brisbane Heat and in England's new competition The Hundred, the destruction of the Australian team not harming his credentials. Pro cricket is a very small club.

In June 2018 Sutherland got to set his own exit, saying he would retire at some point in the next 12 months. High-performance manager Pat Howard set a date following the next Ashes. CA conducted a performative farce of searching for their next CEO, claiming they were scouring the world for the best talent before settling on the bloke in the next office, Kevin Roberts. It was the same as the worldwide search for the men's coach, which had picked the next-in-line Justin Langer. Sutherland pulled the pin sooner rather than later, handing over in October 2018 so that Roberts could be in the job before the annual general meeting. Sutherland got the farewells that you'd expect after 17 years at the top.

That left chairman David Peever. His trademark style of high-handedness and corporate coldness had not won admirers, but he wielded power nonetheless. He had spent a long time trying to nudge Sutherland off the plank, and having installed his preferred man in Roberts, he decided that his own presence for another term was just what the game needed. Australia's state cricket associations technically make that call, but they're dependent on CA's revenue tap and none wished to risk its flow. Peever was given three more years by unanimous vote.

The problem was that Peever's board had been sitting on information. Six months earlier, in the immediate Cape Town aftermath, CA had promised an independent review into the entire organisation's corporate culture. The results arrived a few days before the AGM. CA had funded the process, but if Peever had expected a gloss job then he was quickly deflated. Dr Simon Longstaff and his Ethics Centre gave a politely devastating assessment.

Initially it stayed with the board. There were murmurs about not releasing the report at all, citing it as CA property, but having publicly talked it up when it was commissioned this wasn't sustainable. In the end its release was held back until four days after the AGM. Peever saw no problem with asking the state associations to secure his tenure before they were allowed to scrutinise the administration he had led.

The report landed with a splash. The Ethics Centre described an organisation that operated with a carelessness and lack of regard for consequence mirrored in the men's team. 'The most common description of CA is as "arrogant" and "controlling". The core complaint is that the organisation does not respect anyone other than its own. Players feel that they are treated as commodities. There is a feeling amongst some state and territory associations that they are patronised.'

The attempt to suppress the report matched that description to the letter, and members of the state associations were incensed. Peever still didn't get it, making noises of acceptance while in effect dismissing the report as 'in some instances, difficult to agree with'. A disastrous interview on the ABC's 7.30 program sealed his fate. A flushed Peever blinked and dragged out his words like he'd been roused from a nap, trying to evade questions in the most visible slow-motion. Interviewer Leigh Sales took him apart as neatly and expertly as a line worker at the chicken factory.

'How can the very same people who presided over the flourishing of this toxic culture now be the ones to change it, particularly when as the report explains, you're the only people who couldn't identify the problems?' she asked. That's not a question that anyone could answer well, but he didn't even try, wandering off on obfuscatory tangents.

Peever's closing line was the clincher. 'We have had a hiccup in South Africa and we are taking the opportunity to learn the lessons of that so that we can make the game even stronger.'

After all the angst, all the shame, all the upset, nobody was going to tolerate the cause of the whole disaster being diminished to a 'hiccup'. At last some administrators showed something other than compliance. Cricket New South Wales has clout where others might not, and its chair John Knox told Peever that he no longer had its support. That made Peever's national position untenable, and other states would likely follow. Less than a week after the vote in his favour, Peever was sent to live on a farm where he would have lots of room to run around.

This left a test for Roberts: new in the job, there as Peever's man, but his backer was gone and he was tied to the failings of the old regime. He had been second in charge to Sutherland and the lead negotiator in 2017's disastrous pay war with the players. Framing himself as a fresh new choice would take more than giving Malibu Stacy a new hat. Within a week, Roberts pulled the trigger on two of his top executives. High-performance boss Howard would not get his chosen farewell, and broadcast rights manager Ben Amarfio, whose bizarre behaviour and treatment of colleagues had repeatedly made the papers, was escorted from the building. Howard was congratulated for his successes in CA's press release. His colleague got a single line: 'Ben Amarfio has left the business today.'

There was little public explanation of why those two had to go, but journalists were briefed about a euphemistic need to improve workplace culture. One relevant link was that a section of the review had been redacted, containing accounts of bullying and other unacceptable behaviour. Given these were personal recollections rather than testimony, they couldn't be published without the risk of defamation suits, but they were enough footing for the new CEO to give a concrete demonstration of change.

Former captain Mark Taylor resigned from the board the same week, saying he was worn out after a fraught couple of years. So the tally was Lehmann, Sutherland, Peever, Howard, Amarfio, Taylor: all but the coach had milked another six months, but in the end there was a substantial renovation at the top. Roberts made an effort to drop his former invisibility cloak and build a less antagonistic relationship with the press. In general, CA from late 2018 appeared a more cheerful and responsive operation, and a losing home summer against India was met with refreshing humility.

Moving into that summer, Warner continued to bank the value of shutting up. He was playing local cricket at Randwick Petersham, while Smith turned out for Sutherland Cricket Club alongside former national teammate Shane Watson. Playing grade cricket was a good look. It spoke of humility, community, an earthy connection with real life. It also says a bit about Watson that the Big Rig was still excited to get the shirt off and get involved at that level. An earlier Test player, Mike Whitney, was now Randy Pete's president and praised Warner generously. 'He has gone way above my personal expectation about training and playing, coming down and spending time with all of our grades, our Under–21s, our Green Shield side, our Under–16 side. I couldn't have asked him to do any more.'

But if Warner was mounting a hearts-and-minds campaign, someone in Smith's camp wanted hearts and wallets. In the week leading up to Christmas, people were surprised to hear Smith on the telly. First came audio grabs from his sobbing apology nine months earlier, coupled with the sound of cameras flashing. To make sure the point was adequately laboured, this was laid over 15 seconds of him staring into a clubhouse mirror, literally taking a good hard look at himself.

'I was in a pretty dark space,' his voice intoned. 'It made me realise what other people go through and what they need to get through those difficult times.' Now he was in a classroom with a group of teenage boys nodding as they soaked up his wisdom. 'It was just about being upfront and honest and taking responsibility,' he told them, despite never having given more than a sketch of what happened at Cape Town. The footage returned to the rooms, now filling with players. 'It's nice to be back at the club. I just love being in a contest.' Smith was in the middle, batting, sprinting between wickets in rollercoaster GoPro footage. 'I've certainly had some difficult days, but it's ok to be vulnerable. Everyone makes mistakes,' he said over more runs and some coaching with kiddies. 'I want to come back better than I was.' The emotive music peaked, and in vivid red on a background of black came the message we were waiting for: Vodafone?

Yep. This inspirational short film was an ad. With months yet to serve on the ban that had brought about his newfound insight, he was using that ban to sell phones. The sales pitch needed a grassroots image – small grounds, unsponsored shirts, cheerful rooms. They needed to show you the big name sitting with ordinary folk, an inspiration in progress.

It was tone-deaf beyond belief. Smith's problem in South Africa had been letting those around him make bad decisions. This was more of the same. Not coincidentally he soon popped up for his first press conference since the one at Sydney Airport that Vodafone had found so useful. He said the ad was about supporting a mental health charity whose logo appeared for one passing second on the back of some guy's shirt. He said a portion of his fee would go to the charity, but didn't know how much or in aid of what.

'It's ok to make a mistake, and it's ok to make a quid, but it's not ok to make a quid from a mistake,' wrote an incredulous Greg Baum in *The Age*. 'Smith has commodified repentance, putting it on the same mutually advantageous level as his previous commercial endorsements, unless you happen to believe that all these years, Smith has had a financially disinterested vocation for razor blades and breakfast biscuits.'

With attention elsewhere, Bancroft enjoyed relative quiet. Unlike Smith, he did take himself away from the game. He travelled to Broome, Brisbane, Melbourne, saw relatives, did charity work, and spent so much time at yoga that he ended up becoming an instructor. This factoid got over-reported in the press, as did the Spanish lessons that probably won't see him reading Cervantes in the original any time soon. But he gave self-improvement a decent go.

When Bancroft published an article in *The West Australian* on 22 December, it was affecting. The 'letter to myself' format can be naff, and the accompanying yoga photoshoot reached the stage of self-parody, but his words were honest, addressing the shell-shocked version of himself who had sat alone in a hotel room after doing his Tim the Tool Man bit. It was perceptive to write that 'The simple mistake of doing something because you were wanting to fit in had come at a huge cost.'

He put across how bewildering the intervening months had been, trying to figure out who he was. A lower profile meant less certainty. The other two had reputations that all but guaranteed them cricket employment and a shot at a national comeback. Bancroft was the emerging player who had as quickly vanished. For most of his life he had only thought about playing cricket, and now he had to accept that might be over.

It made sense for him to move slowly into public view given his ban was about to expire on 29 December, but Bancroft's next step was less successful. For starters his television interview was with Adam Gilchrist, a very pleasant man who wouldn't know a tough question if it lodged in his urethra. For credibility Bancroft needed a journalist, not a mate from the Western Australian cricket fraternity.

The producers did their subject no favours by getting him in his exercise gear so they could take layover shots of him walking the streets with his yoga mat. This meant the visual for the interview was Bancroft kicking back in a cafe wearing a singlet, looking like he'd just rolled out of bed and probably wasn't going to call you. They didn't help him by screening it on Boxing Day, the biggest day in the Australian cricket calendar. It looked like Bancroft was grabbing the spotlight that should have been on the team. Nor did he help himself by not working out his message ahead of time.

Within two minutes Gilchrist had variously euphemised with 'the incident in Cape Town', then 'the day all these events transpired', and 'the events of what led up to that unfortunate situation'. He couldn't bring himself to name the truth.

Nor could Gilchrist clarify the waffle. Take Bancroft's description of how the tampering came about: 'At the time Dave suggested to me to carry the action out on the ball given the situation we were in in the game, and I didn't know any better.' This was the line that drew most criticism: how could he say he didn't know better when every kid knows that tampering is wrong?

What Bancroft was trying to say was coded in his next line. 'Because I wanted to feel valued.' Or a moment earlier: 'I valued fitting in. You hope that fitting in earns you respect.' He meant that he hadn't known how to make a better choice, he hadn't been equipped to take the difficult option. It was the same idea as the perceptive line in his newspaper copy, but clumsily expressed. Gilchrist didn't help him, too eager to nod in kindly agreement lest any attempt at elucidation be seen as a challenge.

Only once was Bancroft explicit: 'There are people out there who are forever going to look at me and say, he's a cheat!

He's the guy that cheated, he is a cheater, and like, you know, point the finger and be really really serious about it. I know that there's going to be people like that forever.' Which again could be an important realisation, except he went on to say that it reflected their unhappiness rather than his action. 'When we see other people make mistakes, the reason they emotionally connect with us is that we've got something in our own life that actually maybe we're not proud of. Maybe it hurts us because we've actually done that in some way ourselves.'

Which is true in some cases, but also dismisses fair anger from people who feel they've had something sullied. He was deflecting criticism back onto its source, like the guy who didn't call you saying that you're only upset because of your own insecurities. Most likely it was a philosophical suggestion given to a young man to help him cope. He needed it; but it was an incomplete understanding.

Then came the parts that had no explanation, like Bancroft talking up 'being accountable for what I did' on the night of the drama by apologising to the umpires for lying, right before he left their room to lie to the media. 'The thing that I was proud of in that moment was that Steve and I wanted to be really honest and be accountable in our actions,' he said of the press conference in which both of them covered up Warner's involvement and lied about using tape on the ball rather than sandpaper.

Bancroft called that part of the story 'really interesting', because 'for me the whole issue I felt got forgotten about. The issue was that I went out with an intentional decision to tamper with the ball.' It's true that the tool was a detail, but he dodged the question of why they decided to lie about that detail, how that lie was agreed, and who knew about it. Gilchrist's summary of this hodgepodge of evasion was 'you are staring it in the eye and want to take it on'. Bravo.

As the Australian summer rolled through January, Warner was back to being his on-field self in Bangladesh, at one point deciding to bat right-handed halfway through an over from Chris Gayle and banging the next three balls for a six and two fours. Soon both he and Smith went down with an elbow injury, removing the tricky question of whether to shoehorn them into the national team halfway through an ODI series at the end of March. Instead they passed through Dubai to pay that squad an ice-breaking visit before carrying on to India for a delayed start to that year's IPL. It settled any doubt that the pair would be part of Australia's World Cup at the end of May. Warner bossed the IPL as top run-scorer, while Smith got the chance to captain a side again.

Then the exile was over in low-key fashion. It was early May at Allan Border Field as they slipped on Australian shirts for some warm-ups against New Zealand in Brisbane. More practice games in England gave them a long runway, but they needed it. The northern summer ahead was intimidating. England. World Cup. Ashes. Their return to official international cricket would be made on the longest tour in front of the least hospitable audience for the two biggest prizes in the sport.

Chapter 3

The Place That's Missing a Vowel

I F YOU'RE LOOKING for a place where misadventure could begin, you can't go past Mbargo. The nightclub's streetfront is painted a purple so bright you'll see it in your dreams. Strings of giant sequins shimmer in the breeze. Its phonically inventive name is spelt in silver letters that climb its three-storey terrace facade. Inside are strips of burning neon, a few booths, floorboards so marinated in drink that they have an ingredients list. Bristol is a student city on England's south coast crowded with music and nightlife and street art. This is Banksy's home town, and the tourism board suggests in rather strong terms that 'you would be a fool not to see his amazing work firsthand'. The same organisation describes Mbargo as 'intimate', which is fair for a place where you can catch an STI standing up. Students cram into its modest dimensions while people with names like

DJ Klaud battle for billing with £1.50 drink deals over seven sloppy nights a week. To get a sense of the story about to come, consider that it's the kind of place open until two o'clock on a Monday morning, and that at two o'clock on a Monday morning, Ben Stokes still thought it had closed too early.

The Ashes of 2017–18 had disciplinary bookends. It was after that series that Australia's two leaders went off the rails in South Africa. It was a few weeks before that Ashes tour that England's biggest star windmilled his way into his own disaster.

In the early hours of 25 September 2017, Stokes and teammate Alex Hales were barred from re-entering Mbargo after a night out on the piss. A Sunday thrashing of an abject West Indies in an ignored series at the fag-end of the season apparently required ample celebration. After arguing with the bouncer and hanging about at the door for a while, they wandered off to find a casino in the hope of more drinking. They'd barely made it around the corner before getting in the middle of a conflict between four locals. As is said on the internet, it escalated quickly.

The 26 September reporting was bloodless. Withholding names, police stated that a man 'was arrested on suspicion of causing actual bodily harm' while another went to hospital with facial injuries. England's director of cricket Andrew Strauss separately confirmed that Stokes was the arrestee, adding that he had been released without charge and that Hales had gamely offered to 'help police with their enquiries'. Administrators had a good chance of hiding behind that investigation, and the next day Stokes was named in the upcoming Ashes squad as expected. But that night the video emerged.

Bristol student Max Wilson had shot it on his phone, then offered it to *The Sun*. What he thought was playing hardball was actually lowball: his opening price of £3000 was snapped up by a tabloid that would have paid ten times that. *The Sun* went on to make a mint by syndicating the rights worldwide.

From a window above the fray, the vision showed six men on the street below performing the muddled choreography of a melee. One was right at the centre of it. One was waving a bottle, one dipped in and out, one tried to calm it. Two others floated around the edges. The central figure was unmistakable: red hair burning even in the streetlight as he launched into a series of blows against two of the men, falling to grapple with them on the ground, then following both across the street, swinging punches the whole way. Hales trailed behind, repeatedly and impotently shouting 'Stokes! Stop! Stokes! Enough!'

The ECB could fudge issues that existed only in thickets of legalese, but not those captured in moving colour. Stokes was stood down from the next West Indies match, then suspended indefinitely. It emerged that he had broken his hand during the fight, something he'd done twice before while punching objects in dressing rooms.

The response in Australia was fierce: Stokes was a thug, a lowlife, a selection that would disgrace England. It was not entirely coincidental that a ban for England's best player would be handy for the Aussie team, but there was also a cultural split. In England, plenty of people still minimise pub fights as lads letting off steam. In Australia, heavy media coverage as a succession of young men were killed had inverted that tolerance. The discourse now saw any punch as potentially deadly and accordingly reckless. This was more poignant in a cricket context given that David Hookes, the dashing Test batsman and state coach, was killed in 2004 by a pub bouncer's fist.

The PR situation was bad for Stokes as details emerged of the injuries to the men he'd hit, and that one was a young war veteran and father. Stokes wasn't officially removed from the Ashes squad through October but stayed behind when his teammates left, hoping for police to dismiss the matter in time for a late dash to Australia. His annual contract was renewed on the due date in case that came to pass. Then 29 October brought a twist in the tale.

'Ben Stokes praised by gay couple after defending them from homophobic thugs,' ran the headline. Kai Barry and Billy O'Connell had emerged. Not entirely out of nowhere: while Stokes had made no public comment, this story in his defence had initially been leaked to TV host Piers Morgan after the fight, as soon as the video appeared. Police body-camera footage played in court would later show that Stokes had given the same story to the arresting officer on the night. But no-one knew the identities of the fifth and sixth men in the video, and police appeals had turned up nothing.

It was *The Sun* again with the breakthrough. Kai and Billy were perfect for a readership not keen on nuance. 'We couldn't believe it when we found out they were famous cricketers. I just thought Ben and Alex were quite hot, fit guys,' said Kai, who was memorably described as a 'former House of Fraser sales assistant'. The paper had the pair do a full photo shoot: layering the fake tan, showing off chest waxes, mixing Ralph Lauren and Louis Vuitton into a range of outfits. Their best shot had them standing back to back, heads turned to the camera, in a mirror-image *Zoolander* moment.

Suddenly *The Sun* was the England team's best friend. 'Their claims could lead to the all-rounder being cleared over the punch-up and freed to play in the First Test in Australia next month,' it gushed, then gave a tasting platter of quotes:

'We were so grateful to Ben for stepping in to help. He was a real hero.' 'If Ben hadn't intervened it could have been a lot worse for us.' 'We could've been in real trouble. Ben was a real gentleman.'

Would it be known forever as Kai and Billy's Ashes? No. While the Bristol boys provided spin for Stokes' reputation they didn't influence the police. With charges still pending there was little choice – not given Strauss had previously sacked Kevin Pietersen for being annoying. Stokes remained suspended through the Ashes and a one-day series in Australia, and lost the vice-captaincy. It was January 2018 before the Crown Prosecution Service laid a charge.

That charge surprisingly came in as affray, a crime that can carry prison time but is classified as 'a breach of the peace as a result of disorderly conduct'. The men he had punched, Ryan Ali and Ryan Hale, faced the same count, charged as equal participants in a fight rather than Stokes being charged with assaulting them. Alex Hales was not charged, despite being seen in the video to aim several kicks when Ryan Ali was lying on the ground. Given the underwhelming standing of the offence, Stokes was cleared by the ECB to tour New Zealand, and kept playing until his trial in August 2018, which he missed a Test to attend. None of the three defendants would be convicted.

The reasoning behind the charges was never released and was attributed vaguely to 'CPS lawyers'. The service gave the case to Alison Morgan, a prosecutor of a class known as Treasury Counsel who usually handle serious criminal matters. Morgan had a scheduling clash and never ended up in court for the case, but in 2018 and 2019 she would go on to win damages and admissions of libel from *The Daily Mail*, *The Times* and *The Daily Telegraph* variously for incorrectly reporting that she had been responsible for the inadequate and inconsistent charging decisions.

Morgan's successor on the case was Nicholas Corsellis QC, who on the first day of trial was permitted by the CPS to request two assault charges be added against Stokes. 'Upon further review,' claimed a CPS statement, 'we considered that additional assault charges would also be appropriate.' This was patent nonsense from the service that eight months earlier had chosen the lesser charge. Any lawyer knows that no judge will allow new charges once a trial has begun, because the defence hasn't had time to prepare. But such a request could deflect criticism of the prosecution service by technically making the judge the one who disallows the charge.

Working through the story from the trial and the tape is complicated. You had a Ryan and a Ryan, a Hale and a Hales, a Billy and a Barry and a Ben. You had several versions of events as to who knew whom, who was drinking with whom, who had insulted whom and who had merely engaged in 'banter', a word that in modern Britain has to do an unconscionable amount of lifting. The reporting had constantly mixed up the Ryans as to who had which injury, who was in hospital, who had played which part in the fight, and whose mum had which stern words to say about it.

Let's agree that from now Ryan Ali is Ryan One, the firefighter who ended up with a fractured eye socket and a cracked tooth. Ryan Two can be Ryan Hale, the soldier who scored concussion and facial lacerations. Mr Barry and Mr O'Connell are best known per *The Sun* as Kai and Billy. In scorecard parlance we'll leave the cricketers as Stokes and Hales.

Amid the confusion, Stokes and his lawyers built his case in a straightforward way. The UK legal definition of affray is 'if a person threatens or uses unlawful violence or force towards another person, which causes another person of reasonable firmness present at the scene to fear for their safety'. That means it doesn't account for violence that harms a target, but violence that might frighten a theoretical bystander. The wiggle room for Stokes was with 'unlawful', because the charge excuses violence in defending oneself or others.

This interpretation hinged on the beginning of the video, where Ryan One waves a beer bottle about and takes a swing at Kai. The version from Stokes was that he was minding his own business walking down the street when he heard homophobic abuse. He intervened verbally and was threatened verbally by Ryan One – something that Ryan One denied but that couldn't be proved or disproved. In fear for his safety Stokes had to nullify that threat by bashing Ryan One before it went the other way. He registered Ryan Two in his peripheral vision as another possible threat, and again had only one recourse.

Stokes also had to convince the jury to disregard testimony from Mbargo's bouncer that he had been looking for a fight.

A solid lump of a man, Andrew Cunningham had not enjoyed his patron's attempts to get back into the club after the bouncer declined an offer of a bribe. 'He got a bit verbally abusive towards myself. He mentioned my gold teeth and he said I looked like a cunt and I replied, "Thank you very much." He just looked at me and told me my tattoos were shit and to look at my job.' Cunningham described these words as coming in 'a spiteful tone, quite an angry tone', and said that Stokes still seemed angry as he walked away.

These were details the doorman had nothing to gain by inventing, but each of them Stokes denied. By his own accounting he had drunk a beer at the game and three pints at his hotel, then 'potentially had some Jägerbombs' along with half a dozen vodkas at the club. He insisted that after all of this he was not drunk.

If I may take a moment here to call upon the wisdom of experience – a person who cannot definitively say whether they have had any Jägerbombs has definitely had some Jägerbombs. A Jägerbomb is an experience that does not pass one by. Further to that, a person who says they have 'potentially' done something has definitely done that thing and doesn't want to admit it. A person who has had between 15 and 24 standard drinks in one evening is shitfaced. A person who tries to bribe a bouncer £300 – three hundred quid! – to get into Mbargo – Mbargo! – is beyond shitfaced.

If Stokes admitted that he was drunk then the prosecution could say he was out of control. He claimed clear recall of assessing a threat, feeling fear and deciding to protect himself with force. He confidently denied details from the bouncer's testimony, like using the word 'cunt' or mentioning gold teeth. Yet on other details he claimed a 'significant memory blackout'. He didn't remember the punch that saw Ryan One taken away by ambulance. He didn't remember what the Ryans had said to Kai and Billy, only that those words were homophobic. With no head injury, as one of the few people who hadn't been hit, he had supposedly suffered this memory loss despite being sober.

The version from Kai and Billy was compatible but vague: they had been walking along, they 'heard … shouts' of abuse from an unspecified source, then Stokes 'stepped in' and thus they avoided possible harm. They claimed to have been bought a drink by Stokes at Mbargo, although CCTV showed them meeting outside. The overall implication from both accounts was that the cricketers had been pals with Kai and Billy, while the Ryans as per *The Sun*'s headline were a roving band of thugs.

The reality though is that the Ryans were the ones hanging out with Kai and Billy at Mbargo. Police discussed CCTV from inside the club in questioning and at trial. On that footage the four Bristolians bought drinks for one another, danced together, and Kai was noted to have variously touched Ryan Two's crotch and Ryan One's buttock. Ryan One told police that all of this was taken lightheartedly and wasn't a problem. Indeed, when the Ryans called it a night the other two left with them.

This much is clear from footage out the front of Mbargo, which shows Kai and Billy exit the club and start talking with a subdued Hales and a demonstrative Stokes, who are stuck outside. The vision was played in court to determine whether Stokes was antagonistic towards Kai and Billy, as he appears to impersonate them and to throw a lit cigarette their way.

More interesting is that after a few minutes the Ryans emerge, and all six actors in the fight video briefly form a prequel in the one frame.

Ryan Two pats Billy on the chest in friendly fashion with his right hand before clapping him on the back with his left. He moves past and does the same to Kai before leaving the shot. Ryan One stops to speak to Kai. They lean in for a moment, talking, then Kai turns and they walk out of frame together. Billy hangs around for a few seconds at the door and then looks after them and races to catch up. Stokes and Hales remain outside the club to remonstrate further with the bouncers. Whatever discord develops around the corner is between four men who left amicably together minutes earlier.

There's no way to know what caused that friction. If Ryan One did use homophobic slurs, he might have been drunkenly obnoxious for no reason. He might have had an insecure macho response to some extra flirtation. He might have thought unkindness was funny – 'banter' once again. Or he might have said something that was misunderstood, as both Ryans insisted in court that they had not used nor had the impulse to use any abusive language.

What clearly didn't happen was an attack by bigots on random passers-by. This kind of crime is regular enough that an audience understands the horror of it, and this is what was evoked by the public accounts of Stokes, Billy and Kai. All we know is that there was some verbal dispute among the Bristol locals, and that Stokes came along behind them and put himself in the middle of it. Ryan One responded to the interference aggressively and away they went.

There are plenty of reasons to look sideways at the idea that Stokes was a saviour. Foremost, neither Kai nor Billy was called upon as witnesses in court. You'd think it would be ideal to have Stokes' story backed up by those who benefited from his selflessness. But his defence team had developed the impression that the pair had shown a changeable recall of events amid a hard-partying lifestyle, and would be dismantled by the prosecution on the stand.

That raises the question of whether *The Sun* coached their quotes for the 2017 interview. Despite missing court, Kai and Billy clearly enjoyed the attention. In 2018 after the trial they did a follow-up spread in the same paper about how poor Ben had been mistreated. They got a television spot on *Good Morning Britain* and glowed about his heroism. In 2019 *The Sun* wheeled them out once more to say that Stokes should get a knighthood. In 2017 they had 'never watched cricket' but by 2019 were supposedly volunteering sentences like, 'He saved us, now he's saved the Ashes.' Whether they were paid for these appearances is not known, but the chance to be famous for a day can be lure enough.

If you find this cynical, consider that on the night in question, the Bristol boys were so deeply moved and thankful for Ben's intervention that they left him to be arrested and never attempted to find out who he was. Seconds after the video ended, an off-duty policeman reached the scene. You might think that someone grateful to a saviour would speak on his behalf. Instead, said Kai, 'it all got a bit scary so we walked off. It was too much for me and we went to Quigley's takeaway for chicken burgers and cheesy chips.' They didn't give their hero a thought for over a month while police issued multiple appeals for witnesses.

As for Stokes, he told his arresting officer that 'his friends' had been attacked. After three minutes of chat outside a nightclub, these friends were so dear to him that he has never contacted them again: not after the newspaper piece, not after the verdict. He didn't want to see how they were or thank them for their support. He didn't mention them by name in his solicitor's statement after the trial.

The Stokes defence rested on Ryan One's bottle, which he had carried out of Mbargo to finish a beer, not to use in a Sharks versus Jets amateur production. But once he turned it over to hold it by the neck it became a weapon. Intent and interpretation can change the material nature of things. Part of Stokes' justification in court was that the bottle implied that the two Ryans might have 'other weapons' hidden away. You can understand how a jury could decide that created doubt.

Not being convicted, though, doesn't give the contents of the video a big green tick. It does not, as his lawyer claimed, vindicate Stokes. Looking in detail, Ryan One is belligerent but his movements telegraph a bluff. Hales is the person he's gesturing at, but they're several metres apart when Ryan One cocks his arm ostentatiously, showing off the bottle rather than bracing to swing. He skips forward but Hales skips back and Ryan One doesn't follow. Kai stretches out an arm to impede Ryan One, who has a drunken stumble, nearly eats pavement, then staggers towards Kai and hits him in the back. That hand is still holding the bottle, but his strike is a side-arm cuff on a soft part of the body. It's all pretty tame.

This is where Stokes gets involved. Having moved across to protect Hales, he now takes three large steps to run around

Kai and booms his first punch at Ryan One. They fall to the ground and the bottle clinks away. Stokes gets to his feet to punch down at the fallen man, while Hales arrives to kick him ineffectively then runs off across the street for some unknown reason. Ice-cream van? Stokes is soon back in the grapple having his shirt pulled up to show off his Durham tan. Ryan Two steps in for the first time to pull Stokes away, prompting a couple more random punches at this new target, then Stokes trips backwards over Ryan One and sprawls in the street. Hales chooses this moment to return and aim some solid kicks at the head of the man on the ground.

Nothing so far is a triumph of moral philosophy or the pugilistic arts. But if it all stopped here, perhaps you could say it was somewhere approaching fair. Ryan One has behaved like a turnip and it's not an entirely unjust world that would give him a whack across the chops. The antagonists have disentangled, Stokes has some distance, it's time to dust off and go home. Ryan Two steps forward for this purpose with his palm raised in conciliatory style and says, 'Settle down, stop.'

So Stokes punches him.

It's roughly his fifth punch overall, and he really winds up into this one. He misses so hard that he stumbles away into the shadows of the shop awnings along the road.

Hales starts shouting for him to stop. Ryan Two backs into the street, still holding his palm up. Stokes closes on him from about five metres away, six large steps, to where Ryan Two is standing on his own. Stokes pushes him a couple of times, as Ryan Two keeps trying to placate him and saying 'Stop.' Stokes throws his sixth punch, largely missing as his target ducks.

Ryan Two keeps pulling away and reversing, into the middle of the street now. Stokes follows him, grabbing his sleeve to drag him back. By this point Ryan One has found his feet and walked around behind his friend. Both of them are in the same line of sight for Stokes, and both are backing away. Stokes aims his seventh and his eighth punches, which Ryan Two tries to deflect, as Hales walks up behind Stokes to grab him.

Stokes yanks away from his friend and switches to Ryan One instead, taking seven paces to grab him before throwing his ninth punch of the night. He grabs again; Ryan One blocks that arm and pushes himself back away from Stokes. Ryan Two again intercedes, putting himself between the two with his palms up and his arm extended.

Stokes throws his tenth punch, a right-hander at the face of Ryan Two, then shoves him backwards. Ryan Two backs away once more, four paces. Stokes follows, steadies, lines up, then launches his strongest punch yet, his eleventh, a proper right hook from a solid base, one that cracks across the man's head and gives him concussion. Ryan Two ends up flat on his back in the middle of the street, his hands still outstretched for a moment in useless protest until they twitch and drop to the blacktop.

Stokes isn't done. He once more shoves away the restraining Hales and follows Ryan One, who keeps backing away saying, 'Alright, alright, alright.' Five more paces from Stokes before another blow at the man's head. Kai and Billy are now standing over the poleaxed Ryan Two. The video ends, but seconds later Stokes will punch Ryan One hard enough to knock him out too, before off-duty cop Andrew Spure arrives on the scene to bring down the curtain. When the body-camera footage kicks in some minutes later, Stokes is in handcuffs but Ryan One is still laid out in the street. Ryan Two has regained consciousness, folded his shirt under his friend's head and is asking police for an ambulance.

'At this point, I felt vulnerable and frightened. I was concerned for myself and others.' This was how Stokes described that sequence to the court. An elite athlete with years of gym work and training to snap a bat through the line of a ball with astounding power and precision, swinging fists as hard as he can at men with none of those advantages. Punching so hard that he breaks his hand, and repeatedly shoving away a friend so he can punch some more. Frightened and threatened by two targets shouting 'Get back!' and 'Stop!'

The off-duty officer testified that Stokes 'seemed to be the main aggressor or was progressing forward trying to get to' Ryan One, who was 'trying to back away or get away from the situation'. The student who filmed the video can be heard on the tape at one stage exclaiming 'Fuck!' and testified that it was because 'I felt a little bit sorry about the lad that had been punched and it looked like he had his hands up'. That tallied with the prosecutor's depiction of 'a sustained episode of significant violence that left onlookers shocked at what was taking place'.

The defendant stuck to his strategy. 'No, my sole focus was to protect myself.' All up, in the 33 seconds of footage after he falls over, Stokes takes 35 steps forward to keep hitting two men who keep trying to get away. Not once is he hit back.

After the verdict, Stokes' solicitor positioned him as the victim. It had been 'an eleven-month ordeal for Ben ... The jury's

decision fairly reflects the truth of what happened that night ...
He was minding his own business ... It was only when others
came under threat that Ben became physically engaged. The
steps that he took were solely aimed at ensuring the safety of
himself and the others present ...' The statement was impossibly
self-righteous and self-absorbed.

If there was anyone to feel sorry for it was Ryan Hale, the
second of our two Ryans. He's the one who emerged from the
club with a friendly arm around the shoulder for Kai and Billy.
He's the one who interposed himself to end the fight, then
kept putting himself back in the firing line, trying to calm an
intimidating stranger while dodging blows. For his show of
restraint he got laid out regardless, concussed in the street, then
was issued a criminal charge equal to that of the man who hit
him, and described in national media as a violent bigot in an
untested story to support that man's defence.

Lawyers for Ryan Two made a more convincing post-trial
statement, noting that Kai and Billy, 'neither of whom were relied
upon by the prosecution or the defence team for Mr Stokes, have
taken the opportunity to speak with various media outlets about
the alleged homophobic abuse that they received in the early
hours of September 25. Mr Hale has passionately denied this
allegation throughout the course of this case,' it continued.

'It is upsetting to Mr Hale that although he was acquitted,
the accusation that he was the author of such abuse remains.
Both Mr Hale and Mr Ali were knocked unconscious by Mr
Stokes, and although Mr Stokes has been acquitted of an affray,
Mr Hale struggles with the reasons why the Crown Prosecution
Service did not treat him as a victim of an unlawful assault.'

Good question. Avon and Somerset police were the investigating force, and they were frustrated by the decision. Ryan Two was filmed clearly not hurting anyone, but police were instructed by the CPS to proceed with a charge. Hales (the cricketer) was filmed fighting but 'a decision was made at a senior level of the CPS' not to proceed. Police expected Stokes to be charged with assault but the CPS declined. It doesn't take a wild cynic to think that placing the same lukewarm charge on three men for vastly divergent behaviour might ensure that none would be convicted, even as the trial would maintain the pretence that a defendant of influential standing had not been given a free pass.

A couple of years down the line, the original interview with Kai and Billy has disappeared. All traces have been scrubbed from *The Sun* website, its social media history, and even from the Wayback Machine internet archive. Given its headline of 'homophobic thugs' and text that names Ryan Two but not Ryan One, the libel liability isn't hard to spot. Later interviews with Kai and Billy take the passive voice – they 'suffered homophobic slurs outside a Bristol nightclub'. The article that was once claimed to exonerate brave Ben Stokes now links only to a missing content page, with a picture of a dropped ice-cream cone and the phrase 'legal removal' inserted into the web URL.

In terms of consequences, Stokes missed one tour. When he resumed his career in January 2018, the Australians hadn't yet ruined theirs. Their year-long bans looked much more stringent. But the Stokes case dragged on in other ways. With no criminal liability, the Australians confessed promptly enough for the sporting world to give them the full length of the lash. Their situation was ugly but there was closure. Stokes got stuck in legal stasis, unable to be fully backed or condemned. Instead his issue was always present, a browser full of open tabs that the ECB swore they would read any day now.

Through 2018 Stokes was back but he wasn't *back*, in the sunglasses and finger-guns sense. In his return one-day series he nearly cost England a match with 39 from 73 balls in Wellington. His first Test hit was a duck as England got rolled in Auckland for 58. At Trent Bridge while Stokes was injured, England posted a world record 481 against Australia. With Stokes three weeks later at the same ground they made 268. He crawled to 50 from 103, the second-slowest any Englishman had reached that milestone in 20 years. That span covered Alastair Cook's whole career. It was apologetic batting, acting out responsibility via the scorecard. Stokes was creeping back into the team like he'd been kicked out in a blazing row and was hoping to tip-toe to the sofa.

It was December 2018 before the ECB disciplinary committee ruled on him and Hales. In a 'remarkable coincidence', wrote Simon Heffer in *The Telegraph*, 'the punishment both players faced in terms of bans from playing at international level was covered by the amount of games they had already missed when dropped by England's selectors, in the furore that followed the incident'. The verdict compounded the omissions around the case by not addressing the violence at its heart. Nor did Stokes, apologising only 'to my team-mates, coaches and support staff', and then 'to England supporters and to the public for bringing the game into disrepute'.

The implicit next step was to rebuild that reputation. It might have been easier had his court defence not meant that he wasn't game to admit any fault at all. It might have been easier if he or his advisers had been willing to change tack once the trial was done. Imagine a world where Stokes had stood outside court and apologised for overreacting, for the injuries he'd caused, and for the time and energy he had sucked out of other people's lives. That would have been a show of responsibility beyond a scorecard. When the time came around to assess forgiveness, it might have meant forgiveness was deserved.

Chapter 4

The Year of Slim Pickings

WHEN STEVE SMITH and David Warner were banned for a year they weren't the only ones hit. There was also the team they left behind. For those people who insisted that Australia's bowlers must have known about the sandpapering and had got away without punishment, the second part certainly wasn't true: those bowlers paid the price of their workload in a side that could never give them enough runs.

For some teams, shedding a captain and vice-captain might freshen them up – a chance to move in a new direction, give opportunities to emerging players. But Australia's problem even before the bans was a shortage of quality batting. Usman Khawaja, Shaun Marsh and Mitchell Marsh all promised the world but rarely delivered. Joe Burns got curtailed, Glenn Maxwell never got a shot, Matthew Renshaw and Peter Handscomb started brightly but didn't graduate. Those last four were the Johannesburg replacements after the suspensions, but none was picked in Australia's next series.

This wasn't the 1990s anymore, Toto. There was no reserve of gnarled Shield veterans. Since a spate of Test retirements in 2015, two players had carried the batting. In any conditions you would find Smith straining in all directions trying to hold things together. Warner was not a reliable source of hundreds overseas, but was a steady presence who could at least make 40s or 50s and contribute to a platform. At home he was dominant, downing visiting teams before they had a chance to think about winning. He and Bancroft left two vacancies at the top of the order above its fragile middle.

Start as you mean to go on, they say, and the makeshift Australians did. After the week of Cape Town chaos they finished their African trip with the kind of thrashing that makes your eyes water. South Africa batted for nine of the first eleven sessions before flattening their guests in 46 overs as the finale. Australian players made 16 scores in single figures. A loss wasn't surprising in the circumstances, but a margin of nearly 500 runs when the series could have been tied was a stark result.

That was the start of April. Thankfully for all of them, the national men had a break until a one-day tour of England in June. It gave Cricket Australia time to think about what was next, appoint Justin Langer as coach without a rush, and let him settle in. He had the brief of renovating Darren Lehmann's booze-enthused blokefest, where the training was hands-off, the quicks bowled 150 clicks, the bats scored seven per over, and the coaching wisdom was captured in PowerPoint slides saying 'Watch The Ball, Cunt'.

Whether Langer was a likely agent of change was questionable. He had been involved with the team that fell from grace, twice filling in as coach when Lehmann took a break. He acknowledged what had gone wrong in the preceding year but not the longer-standing behavioural problems dating back to his playing era. You wondered whether he had the appetite to tackle the tougher questions. The new captain Tim Paine did, having seen first-hand the damage in Cape Town. Paine knew how broadly his team had lost public favour, and his priority was to win it back. Langer became his ally in that cause.

The trip to England was a free hit. It was a contextless bilateral series, the games were in the middle of the Australian night, and it was up against the football World Cup. Paine and Shaun Marsh were the only remnants from South Africa. Hardly anyone back home would be watching. Just as well, you might say, given the 5–0 loss to a rampaging England that had spent three years rebuilding its one-day team into a kind of *Fury Road* war engine that could plough through anything in front of it.

Paine hadn't played an ODI between 2011 and 2018, having made his way back into Test cricket via the T20 side and a national run drought for wicketkeepers. But having named him the permanent Test captain after Joburg, CA needed the symbolism of him leading the next fixture no matter the format. Contrary to the scoreline, his team put up a fight. They made two decent scores in 304 and 310, but England piled on more. They defended 208 and 214 tenaciously, making England crawl home by three wickets and then by one. The only thrashing came on a day that none of them will care to remember, when they met pending champions at the absolute peak of their powers.

Add up 139 to Jonny Bairstow, 147 to Alex Hales, 82 to Jason Roy and 67 at double speed to Eoin Morgan, and you go a long way to a world record score. The game was at tiny Trent Bridge, where half of the field at backward square has been sliced off for a grandstand, on a pitch that offered to give batsmen a foot rub between sixes. England hit 21 of those. The total was 481. Australia's reply was somewhat less.

Through the series, Paine's desperation to make it work was palpable. You would hear him on the field geeing up his team like a husky driver. It was exemplified in Cardiff when Roy missed a ball down the leg side that bounced and hit Paine in the face, splitting his lip on the outside and driving his teeth into the inside. Just as he had refused to leave the field in Johannesburg while keeping wicket with a fractured thumb, he stayed out there this time, catching Roy one-handed a few minutes later. The sight of him spitting claret onto the grass conjured the strident declaration of The Mountain Goats: 'I am coming home to you with my own blood in my mouth / and I am coming home to you if it's the last thing that I do'.

His quantifiable returns were less impressive: 36 runs in five hits. That left no inclination to extend Paine's captaincy to T20s before a tri-series in Zimbabwe with Pakistan. Selectors thought that Paine had enough work ahead with the Test team, and Aaron Finch had already been captaining the fireworks format when Smith and Warner weren't available. Finch went and snorted out 172 runs in an innings in Harare, beating his own record for the highest international score, and out only when he did a Paul Bunyan on his own timber. It was enough to have him take over the one-day team as well from Paine.

Finch also found himself in line for a Test debut. With an underwhelming first-class record in the middle order, he had never been a contender for a baggy green. But Langer liked his leadership and experience, so by October that year Finch was lining up in Dubai. It was six months after the sandpaper series, Australia's first Test engagement since, in the giant sporting anticlimax that is the United Arab Emirates.

It's a tough tour. Desert heat and empty echoing stadiums, long before a pandemic was to blame. A much better Australian side got steamrolled there in 2014. When Pakistan bat in the UAE, the pitch looks like concrete. When Pakistan bowl they draw mysteries from its depths. So it was again: Australia losing the toss, bowling, an opening stand of 205 that lasted past the tea break. The maligned Mohammad Hafeez hadn't played a Test in two years but clattered a hundred on his return. 'I love this format,' he beamed in our boundary interview.

The second day was the same, another huge partnership, a ton this time for Haris Sohail. Pakistan made 482. Australia's new batting order had Finch at the top, Khawaja shifted up to open with him, Shaun Marsh at three, Mitch Marsh now a number four after four good games, then debutants with moderate domestic records, Travis Head and Marnus Labuschagne. This pair made a pair of ducks, the Marshes 7 and 12, and Australia followed an opening stand of 142 by losing all ten wickets for a further 60 runs.

After lunch on day four Pakistan set 462 to win or five sessions to survive. Neither was realistic. The openers survived nearly 30 overs before an avian equation where two Marsh ducks followed Finch. In his ninth Test match, the seamer Mohammad Abbas was bowling like a dream. Three wickets in seven balls for no score, as he defied the conditions and the wear on the ball to make it shimmy in the air and deck off the crease, into the right-handers for lbw decisions, away from the lefty for a nick behind.

This time Head managed to stem the collapse, reaching stumps with Khawaja. The spinners Nathan Lyon and Jon Holland spent the session in the dugout doing a crossword. No-one was expecting much. On the last day the pitch wasn't breaking up but was growing dustier and less consistent. Leg-spinner Yasir Shah held the record for reaching 200 wickets in the fewest matches, most of which had come on these Arabian grounds. Debutant off-spinner Bilal Asif had 6 for 36 in the first innings. You can't outplay spin in these conditions, you can only ride your luck the short distance it will take you.

As for Khawaja, the conditions were at the centre of a Venn diagram of his weaknesses. He averaged 25.57 outside Australia, 14.62 in Asia, and 16.2 against spin away from home. Yet over two days he found a way. Down the wicket when required, back quickly in his crease at other times. The threat was Yasir landing in the rough outside off stump and spinning it into the left-hander, with prodigious turn and natural variation in angle and bounce. Khawaja nullified this with his boldest move, reverse-sweeping anything wide outside off. He played the shot more than 20 times and nailed almost every one. The runs were irrelevant, yet Pakistan got hypnotised into placing a more defensive field, a third man taking one catcher away from the bat.

With the temperature well over 40 degrees, Khawaja thought he had heatstroke on the fifth afternoon, but batted on past tea and halfway to stumps before Yasir finally trapped him. His 141 runs were more than he had totalled in the rest of his career – nine innings – in Asia. Head and Labuschagne were long gone; Paine had been his companion for a couple of hours. A thrilling finish followed, as tailend wickets fell and Paine batted out most of the last hour with Lyon for company and the fractional batting of Holland to come. The tension cranked up every ball, until in the shadows of dusk a certain loss was saved.

Paine gestured to his rooms to dampen the response as he walked off, not wanting to be seen celebrating a match where they had largely been outplayed. But there was no denying that this effort was extraordinary. Khawaja had batted for 524 minutes – the only longer defence in history was the famous 643 minutes of England captain Michael Atherton against South Africa in 1995. No Australian team in Asia had batted longer in the fourth innings than this 139.5 overs or scored more than this 362 for 8.

Peter Siddle had bowled some heroic spells in the imposing heat. Finch made 111 for the match, Head's 72 was Khawaja's main support, and the world was introduced to the irrepressible enthusiasm of Labuschagne, buzzing around like he'd got stuck into the *Breaking Bad* props. He failed with the bat but picked up wickets with decent leg-spin. After his first, he stayed out in the heat bowling on the practice pitches right through the tea break, making sure he was landing the ball and his back foot after being warned for running on the wicket. First over after the break he nailed Babar Azam with a run out. The aim to restore pride in the team needed exactly these sorts of performances.

But the vibe didn't last in Abu Dhabi. The wicket was incongruously grassy given the Ozymandian surrounds:

'boundless and bare / The lone and level sands stretch far away'. The stadium named for king of kings Sheikh Zayed spares no expense to truck in megalitres of water a day. Labuschagne snared a freak rebound catch at short leg while spinning on his back like Michelangelo in the *Ninja Turtles* opening credits, then Lyon made use of the bounce in a hot minute that netted him four wickets in six balls. Pakistan were 57 for 5.

With a match firmly in their hands, the Australians dropped it on their toes. Pakistan captain Sarfaraz Ahmed played a gem, constantly attacking without boundaries, taking guard miles outside leg so he could carve twos off his stumps through the off side. At the other end on debut was Fakhar Zaman, known for one-day whirlwinds but here playing a more careful role. 'Safi plays spin really well, always. He was feeling comfortable, but I was not comfortable against the spinners. That's why I was blocking the ball and taking my time,' he said later. Neither quite reached a hundred as Labuschagne took three wickets, but they recovered their team's position to 282. Sarfaraz had been hurt when Mitchell Starc hit his unprotected elbow, but before stumps he dived heedless of injury to catch Khawaja's edge.

Once again, Australia was hit by Abbas. He was an unlikely destroyer, of modest appearance and modest pace. Not tall, a neat trot to the bowling crease. He had worked menial jobs while trying to make a go of first-class cricket, and didn't play for Pakistan until he was 27. Then he turned in a prolific start of 59 wickets in his first ten Tests. At that point he was on the official list of bowling averages with 15.64, fourth of all time. The three ahead of him were George Lohmann, JJ Ferris and Billy Barnes, all of whom bowled on the goat tracks of the 1880s.

His keys were accuracy and subtlety. In the movie *Speed* a bus couldn't go below 50 miles an hour or it would explode. Here, Abbas couldn't go above 80 miles an hour but blew up nonetheless. He used the thatched pitch to seam the ball in both directions. Australia were done inside 51 overs, before Pakistan pummelled weary bowlers for another 400 runs and declared. This time there would be no Khawaja miracle; he hurt his knee in the warm-up and couldn't bat. Abbas took five wickets in each innings.

Pakistan had turned 57 for 5 into a 373-run win, their biggest against Australia. The effort by the visitors was summed up by the end of a decent partnership of 37, when Starc pushed a gentle drive back at Yasir. The spinner let it run off his fingers. This wasn't a split-second thing: it rolled past Labuschagne at the non-striker's end as he stood out of his crease with his bat held up over the line. His head turned as he calmly watched the ball all the way back onto his stumps, then remembered to put his bat down.

The T20 team didn't go much better. They laboured through a mismatch against the UAE team, then got squashed three times by a Pakistan template: set 150 on wearing tracks and squeeze. Australia went in heavy on power-hitters but Finch, D'Arcy Short, Chris Lynn and Ben McDermott couldn't time a shot. Only Maxwell found a way to score. McDermott achieved the rare feat of three run-outs in a row. Australia lost 28 wickets in three innings.

On it went into November at home, losing a one-day series and a lone T20 to South Africa, drawing a T20 series with India after rain washed out a likely loss, and losing a one-day series to India in January. Finch's run of white-ball scores starting in the Emirates stretched to 1, 0, 3, 1, 5, 41, 11, 6, 27, 0, 28, 6, 6, 14, 0, 8, 0. If it was annoying reading those, imagine how it felt making them. The mental and technical strain of trying to be a red-ball opener had thrown his approach out of whack, but this streak would also see him prang his shiny new Test career.

Four Tests starting in December were India's big chance. Despite a blueblood lineage they had never won a series in Australia. No Asian team had. India had got closest. In 2004 Australia held them off at the SCG for a 1–1 draw. On the same ground in 2008 Michael Clarke's bowling and Steve Bucknor's umpiring whisked a decisive match from them with minutes to spare. In 1978, one of the grandest series of all, they lost 3–2 in the fifth. But now Virat Kohli led a slick, drilled modern side against a fragile home team. Labuschagne and Mitch Marsh were out, Marcus Harris and Handscomb were in. It wouldn't make a difference.

The start at Adelaide was one of those Test match days that sparkles. Khawaja, once a lame duck fielder, flew like a swallow to swallow Kohli at gully. India crashed to 19 for 3 only for Cheteshwar Pujara to play a stunner, getting India back into the game with his defence before subtly increasing his tempo with each wicket that fell. He was 123 by the final over, rushing a single to claim strike for the next morning. But there was Cummins, 88 overs into the day, having bowled 19 of them. He swooped, no other word for it, from mid-on towards a ball rolling wide of that position. Picked it up one-handed, dived forward to clear a path, flung his right arm under and across his torso. Fully mid-air when the ball left his hand, body horizontal, directly side-on to the stumps, one to aim at. The throw went flat, fast, and beat Pujara home by an inch.

India's 250 shouldn't have been enough, but their bowlers came out snorting and high-stepping like thoroughbreds. Ishant Sharma with a mane flowing, Jasprit Bumrah, Mohammed Shami. A sight we'd never seen: India had produced good seamers but never a pace *attack*. A full complement with more in reserve, Bhuvneshwar Kumar and Umesh Yadav offering quality on the bench. Australia wasn't equal to it. That innings produced one of those photos that will live forever: Finch with his powerful keg-on-legs build, halfway through his shot, knee bent and hips dipped, launching his home Test career with a sonic-boom of a drive, steely eyes fixed at extra cover, one stump standing behind him. The rest of his wicket looks like the bridge on the River Kwai.

After Pujara had batted again the chase was 323. Shaun Marsh produced one of those effortless innings that he occasionally conjured from mid-air, whispering one ball to the midwicket boundary so smoothly it left a trail of butter behind it. Was he *on*, we asked, for one of his logic-defying hundreds? He probably was, but a masterful passage of bowling from Bumrah switched him off. When Paine departed, Australia needed 136 with three wickets left. They edged along. Cummins had put on 31 with Paine, then 41 with Starc and 31 with Lyon before Bumrah's quality claimed him. Lyon and Hazlewood kept going, taking the target under 50, under 40. It got as low as 32 before the last man edged Ravi Ashwin's off-break to slip. Missed by that much.

Australia got one back in Perth, where the new stadium's first pitch was a belter befitting the old WACA legend. Grown as a drop-in over three years, it had grass, pace, and trampoline bounce. Both pace attacks had moments of blasting players out, but Australia shared enough runs around and Lyon took wickets while India hadn't picked a spinner. Kohli made one of his best hundreds but couldn't take a first-innings lead, and the cracked pitch meant Australia defended 278 by a distance. For a few days it was framed as a fightback but, as in the 2010–11 Ashes, a lone win in Australia's ideal conditions proved deceptive on reaching the MCG.

Pujara killed them. An achingly slow 106 from 319 balls to bat for two days, leaving the Australians to surrender six wickets to Bumrah and fold for 151. Cummins batted longer than most of the top order, then took six wickets as India hunted declaration runs, a lone hand in a loss by 137. In Sydney, Pujara batted even longer for 193, before Rishabh Pant and Ravindra Jadeja embarked on one of the most thorough demolitions of a home attack on Australian shores, flaying 204 in 37 overs on a sun-soaked afternoon. Even the SCG started cheering them, the entertainment was so pure. Australia were set 622 and had the rare indignity of following on. Rain saved another defeat, but at 2–1 up, India didn't mind.

The public response was unusually cheerful. Australians hate losing at home. It disrupts their sense of the balance of the universe. Get beaten by South Africa in Melbourne and you might just come out tomorrow morning to find that you're driving a frog to work upside-down at the suspicion factory. But the frequency of interviews on two new television broadcasters humanised visiting players more than the Nine Network had ever done, growing an affection for the geniality of Bumrah, the humility of Pujara, and even the incoherent stump-mic streams of consciousness of Pant. Home shortcomings prompted admiration, too: Australians looked especially at Pujara and wished they had a player like that.

There was a reckoning within Langer's rooms. Finch had already been punted for Sydney, replaced by Labuschagne. Senior players Khawaja and Shaun Marsh had each made one fifty in the series and the latter's time was up. His brother was gone again after coming back for Perth, as was Handscomb, who had barely made a run. In came Kurtis Patterson and Joe Burns, who both made tons during a less testing assignment against Sri Lanka in Brisbane and Canberra.

It was a banana-skin series – the sort that you should win, so you'll be flattened if you don't. The revised team dodged that result. Labuschagne made 81 in Brisbane. Jhye Richardson debuted swinging the ball both ways at pace. Khawaja failed twice then was given a second hit in Canberra with Sri Lanka 319 runs behind, against three seamers with five Tests between them who had already sent down 80 overs. You've heard about junk-time hundreds, but this was junk so pure that Keith Richards would buy the lot.

All that summer the Australians were conscious of reputation. Results aside, the season was also about the men modelling a new look. The women's team had funnily enough got on with their routine of winning games without feeling the need to be foghorns of execration while doing it. One of the few solid results of the cultural review into player behaviour was a formulation they called a Players' Pact: 'We recognise how lucky we are to play this great game. We respect the game and its traditions. We want to make all Australians proud. Compete with us. Smile with us. Fight on with us. Dream with us.' It was a bit like one of those painted ceramic plates that your aunt hangs on the wall – not unpleasant, principally decorative, pretty naff.

Some genuine wall decorations appeared too, proudly popped up online by CA executive Anthony Everard and described as 'dressing room branding'. In the withering way that only special moments on Twitter can manage, they got flamed. 'Make Australians proud,' said one slab of green and gold lettering. 'Pressure,' said another. 'Patience,' said a third. Then the coup de grace. 'Elite honesty.'

What. For those familiar with it, honesty is a pretty binary concept. You're either honest or you're not. There is no Level 70 to attain as an Honesty Mage. This wrote its own satire. The Australians, having been caught cheating, were now not just going to be honest. They were going to be *better* at honesty than everybody else. They were going to show the world what honesty really meant. This would be SAS honesty, gold-standard honesty, pure Keith Richards honesty. Australia would be custodians of the line once again.

Justin Langer had already come up with 'elite mateship', a similar advance on regular garden-variety mateship. The coach could be described as a patriot sentimentalist, a true adorer of the baggy green who probably sheds a tear whenever he's handed a 50-cent coin and sees the emu and kangaroo. He's not just ready for blood on the wattle, he's got wattle in the blood. Echoing Steve Waugh by taking his team to Gallipoli on the way to England was a classic move. His regular references to World War I soldier Albert Jacka in relation to cricketing bravery are not *reasonable* in a conventional understanding, but work in a world of inflated symbolism, where ideas become jumping castles.

It's probably fair to say, though, that if you have to advertise what good blokes you are, there may be a problem with that self-assessment. CA ended that season with a cheerful press release saying code of conduct citations were down 74 per cent, attributing that to the example set in Australian colours. It did also make you wonder just how badly everybody gobbed off the season before. The statement pumped up the national team for 'zero code of conduct charges for the first time since 2011/12'. Was there a big cardboard fist with zero fingers raised that they could use to celebrate?

Langer did offer a more realistic take. 'We can put as many words as we like out there, but it's the way we play.' Paine had managed that in Perth, where he won over fans for sassing India's batsmen and for getting quietly combative with the demonstrative Kohli while avoiding any rancour. Paine is a canny operator. He knew when stump mics would pick up his chat so he prepared lines accordingly, striking a balance between needling and humour. During the belting in Sydney, when a journalist's phone rang on the desk in front of him during a press conference, he answered and took a message. Not taking himself too seriously played well.

For all the image management, the desire was genuine. Paine had named the problem as early as his substitute stint in Johannesburg, at the heart of the fire, and repeated it after the cultural review. 'We got a little bit wrapped up in our own self-importance,' he said. 'It's not our cricket team, it's Australia's cricket team.' But there was also a sense that all this didn't count for much until the original antagonists were back in the side.

Paine's team and Finch's version also needed to sort things on the field. The dual demands were close to making Langer's head explode. It was a period of pressure that few in that job have faced. Unexpectedly, Australia and Khawaja would both find a turnaround in one-dayers, comfortably Australia's worst format in a miserable couple of years. Heading to India for five matches before the World Cup, there was no expectation of winning. Kohli had long dominated the format like no-one in its history and India's spinners dictated the tempo.

Maxwell got the India trip off to a flyer in two T20s, making a sensible 56 to chase a small score and an outrageous unbeaten 113 to chase a huge one. It was his third T20 century for Australia, something no-one else had done. The first two ODIs were lost, taking Australia's record to four wins in 28 matches. But with the series on the line, Finch broke his slump with 93 and Khawaja made his first one-day century as the two put on 193. Kohli is the best run-chaser in history, with 21 centuries in winning pursuits, but this became the fourth time he'd made a chasing ton and lost. A crazier result followed when Australia chased in Mohali, galloping after 359 thanks to a Handscomb hundred and an absurd, exhilarating 84 off 43 balls from Ashton Turner in his second game. They had needed 130 from 83 balls when Turner walked out, but he won it with seven to spare.

Winning was possible again. Australia clinched that series, only the fifth time any team had overturned a 2–0 deficit, then partially washed away bad memories of Dubai by pasting Pakistan 5–0. Admittedly it was a second-string opponent trialling players for a final few World Cup spots, containing the likes of Umar Akmal before he was suspended for getting his hog out and waving it around at a fitness session, and then banned for three years for corruption. Just another colourful time in an Akmal life.

But a win is a win when you're in need. Khawaja had never been a one-day candidate, playing 18 games in nine years. Now a streak of 13 games had brought him two hundreds, three near things, and three other half-centuries. Consistent runs had come from Shaun Marsh at first drop, Handscomb at four, and Maxwell at six. England had meticulously built for the World Cup for four years. Australia had spent a year daydreaming, two years tripping over their own feet, then with weeks to spare had found cohesion. The only problem now was accommodating the players coming back.

Chapter 5

Live from Dubai

IN THE VERY north of Brunswick, so north that you can throw stones into Coburg, runs Davies Street. It's the last outpost parallel to the boundary formed by Moreland Road, the main drag laced with tram lines where one of the ten most depressing pubs in Victoria stands on the corner, with its mock-Greek lettering and *Play School* plaster columns, its caged balcony with smokers packed in like lab chimps, and its indoor playground where you can stash the kids while you get a multi on the Superbikes, the Doggies and the fifth race from Hong Kong. Next door on Sydney Road is Gervasi supermarket, where five-foot pensioners mutter in Italian ten deep at the deli counter. These are the inner northern suburbs of Melbourne, and they might not seem like cricket country.

Brunswick was the landing place for generations of migrants after World War II: the Greeks and Italians first, then the Lebanese, Iraqis, Afghans. The surviving houses tell that

Mediterranean story, with their ornate porticos, concrete statues, laden lemon trees in front yards, olives or persimmons hanging over back fences. Students and artists followed into the homes that families left, for cheap rent a mile from the university. Gentrification came inevitably a decade or two behind, those first students reaching a wealthier age, the lemon trees growing fewer as split townhouses and low-rise apartment blocks began to crust across the suburb like psoriasis.

On Davies Street, across from the back of that supermarket, stood a house. A ramshackle one-storey thing of orange brick and timber siding and collapsing fence palings stretching into a deep suburban block, from the days when houses had miniature market gardens between the back door and the bluestone lane where nightsoil men once plied their trade.

The house was on borrowed time. On one side was a Freemasons temple, an ostentatious structure with heavy brick walls and concrete columns beneath white-painted archways evoking the compass and set-square. On the street-facing wall was a plaque informing the public of the international aims of Freemasonry, which seemed harmless enough compared to the things you read on the internet. On the other side of the house was a large block of grass and eucalypts where a church had once stood.

The house had been for the minister, presumably of whatever denomination encourages its vessels to produce hordes of children. A single hallway stretched the full length of the building. Down its flanks were doors for six bedrooms, one bathroom, another toilet, another shower, a large linen cupboard, a laundry, and a kitchen. Subsiding ground had created a drunken angle, so when you came home late from the pub you felt like a sailor on a heavy swell. It was long enough for a cricket pitch, with the slant turning the leg-break savagely from the Davies Street End but making it cut dead straight from the Garden End. Local knowledge was essential.

Under the shadow of demolition, the lease offered was six months. We lasted 11 years. There was never a second lease because the agent couldn't contact the owner. Once we worked out that the owner was greater Freemasonry, we figured that the property manager had probably died: their median age would have been 82. Every Tuesday night the old blokes would roll in with their tuxedos and aprons and briefcases, then a couple of hours later we'd hear renditions of the national anthem and Auld Lang Syne, and they'd stagger out again to pour themselves into their cars and drive home. No concerns about the local constabulary. The next morning the custodian would clink one of those double-sized recycling bins to the kerb. The international aims of Freemasonry were simpler than we'd thought. Between themselves and James Boags, the old boys all but forgot about the place next door. That also meant they couldn't put the rent up.

No surprise that it wasn't in great nick. The condition report for every room said, 'Numerous holes / marks / burns / indentations in walls / ceiling / flooring.' But the imminent wrecking ball is a lot more relaxing than dreading the first ding. We loved the looks on people's faces when they spilled a beer at a party and we'd reassuringly call, 'Just tread it into the carpet!' The boiler in the ceiling cavity burst and recreated *The Shining* all down the long hallway, thick rivulets of red from ceiling to skirting. We thought someone had hidden a body in the roof, and drew straws to climb up.

The lane down one side was lined with castor plants, which can spring up as tiny sprouts between the paving with their star-shaped leaves and fleshy red stems, but can keep growing to tree size with their stems becoming hollow woody branches. The fence was smothered in moth vine, with freakish alien pods that split open like *Little Shop of Horrors* to vomit a mess of silken seeds. The backyard was waist-deep in grass. My wrecked silver 1983 Volvo sedan sat amongst it for years, a second living room for people who needed to escape a party. When it was finally hauled to Valhalla the axles had rusted solid and it took 20 passing drunk cyclists to bounce it out to the street.

Among the trash was a kind of magic. It was a place where people dropped in unannounced and left three days later; the staging point to start a night and the fallback when it ended. With no neighbours, noise didn't matter. The endless hallway channelled pockets of people into lagoons that glowed from doorways, muffled music and voices and a dozen cheap pizzas from the Iraqi place. The front porch was lined with couches and looked out through the twined shadows of the gum trees next door. The back porch was a tiny timber square lost in the grass, like a deck at sail on a billowing sea.

There would be afternoons when the grass was gold and you would crawl through its jungle like tigers. On quiet nights you would climb via the collapsing garage onto the peaked slate roof as the soft night sky burned that dull orange and deep blue that belong to certain cities, the scent of jasmine on the air, the clink of brown glass rolling down into the gutters, until dawn coursed up over the treetops and the lights in the milk bar clicked on. One morning a guy whose name no-one can remember fell off that roof, losing his balance in a lazy graceful pirouette, vanishing to thump flat on his back before standing unscathed thanks to the grass below.

It was the kind of place where a guy slept on our couch for a week and everyone assumed he was friends with someone else. The spare shower didn't work, so the room got filled with inflated goon bags. One housemate was a classical pianist, and around 3 am at every party he would stumble into the front room and hammer out Bohemian Rhapsody, drawing everyone in for a singalong, before he did Rachmaninoff's Third without missing a note.

Three of us stayed from start to finish, while the other rooms saw a rotation of at best estimate 44 housemates. PhD students, bike mechanics, crypto traders, psychedelic lobbyists, young lovers, accidental dads, a musician named Dr Shush and his bipolar Italian girlfriend who hallucinated fire and angels and held my hand all night when my wisdom tooth cracked, two simultaneous residents named Hope and Sunshine, three Welsh backpackers who shared a bed, a New Zealand master bong-maker, and a guy universally known as Shit Rick.

All of this is in aid of saying that when it was time to set up a studio for unofficial cricket commentary on the internet that had no prospects of making money and might attract the ire of people with a lot of it, the natural location was Davies Street. It didn't matter whether I was home: fellow commentators knew which windows to climb through. The living room became the beating heart of White Line Wireless, the solution when Australia's Test team toured and no radio stations went along.

The idea arrived in 2013. Michael Clarke's lot were heading to India, and the rights holders decided to jack up the radio price by a factor of half a dozen. The ABC declined and lead commentator Jim Maxwell had his accreditation blocked. I was furious. I lived for cricket on the radio, the intimacy of the voice right in your ear. I'd flirted with cricket for years but really fell in love care of India in 2001, when Jim and company brought that epic series back through my Walkman while I was pretending to pay attention in uni tutorials. Now the ABC wouldn't go to India? No radio at all?

I'd been talking for a while with my friend Andy Lane about commentating games for fun. Now there was a reason. Sports site *The Roar* agreed to host a stream if we could make it run. Andy had been in a band called Good Buddha, so he knew audio engineering. It was budget as – a tiny mixer and two SM58 stage mics running into a laptop. No effects, no music, no stings. In the infancy of audio streaming we had to run it through Google Hangouts, which went live onto YouTube. The sessions had a three-hour time limit before needing a new link. We'd lose half our audience every time it dropped. We were celebrating when we hit 50 simultaneous listeners. But it worked.

We gathered half a dozen friends with an interest, then a blessing arrived. The broadcaster Glenn Mitchell was writing for *The Roar,* and the editor suggested I call him for tips. Glenn had been one of the voices on that 2001 tour that I remembered so well. We ended up talking for an hour as he gave me every detail on rosters, timing, tone, match-ups, terminology. Before he hung up he said, 'If you need an extra voice when you're running, let me know.' Seriously? He followed through, and we patched him in through Skype to do a few stints with us every day.

Half a dozen idiots with no idea what they were doing got to learn from one of the best. Glenn was so in control, describing the action, offering an entry point to the other caller, resuming the description seamlessly if they didn't take it up. He gave each of us tips off the air. Glenn had spoken publicly about the mental health breakdown that made him leave his job at the ABC and attempt suicide in 2011. Having recovered, he missed commentating. It was a joy that when he was on air with us you could hear his love of calling the cricket coming down the line.

We were on a high, for the fun of this new adventure and for the love of radio. Then we started to get the emails. Several during that first series from blind or vision-impaired people thanking us for putting on the game. There were all these people out there who couldn't get the detail they needed from TV commentary. Not to mention the people who couldn't afford pay TV. That sealed it.

White Line Wireless settled in. The centrepiece commentary station was a pair of faux-retro couches with quilted backs of white vinyl and cushions of red velour. Around the room were giant blocks of foam that I'd picked up for free from Gumtree for reasons lost in the mists of time. We marked our Twitter location as 'international waters' so as not to give any help to snooping lawyers. By the next series we had a streaming platform and listeners in the hundreds.

We got sponsored by Moon Dog brewery, a loose arrangement where one of us would back up a car at their Richmond plant and have it filled with slabs, then we'd talk about those slabs on air as we emptied them. We got all their experiments fresh off the tap, leading to a couple of interesting nights when they forgot to mention a new batch was 9 per cent. Our equipment evolved: better mixers, compressors, equalisers, headset mics, sound effects. We got a theme song from Casey Bennetto, who wrote the prime-ministerial musical *Keating!* We did an Ashes series and some tours in friendlier time zones and the numbers were into the thousands. It was working.

While Clarke's team got pancaked by Pakistan in the UAE in 2014, Adam Collins hit me up online. He too had been dreaming of alternative commentary. He turned up on a Sunday night straight from cricket, still in his grubby whites. He sat down with Cat Jones and attacked the mic at a million miles an hour. We'd found a natural.

That series caused another realisation. There were a dozen or more people involved now, notionally supporting Australia, but we all fell for Pakistan. Yasir Shah debuted, with his bounding Warne-replica action. Zulfiqar Babar, the left-arm spinner, 'looks like he's fought in a few wars', said Adam. Younis Khan tucked off his pads into oblivion. We received an email that was factually accurate: 'Every time I've turned on my television for the last four days, Younis Khan has been batting.'

The crowning moment was when Misbah-ul-Haq started demolishing a young leg-spinner by the name of Steve Smith. Pakistan supporters gave Misbah the derogatory nickname of 'tuk-tuk' for the speed of his batting, so it was special when he went to lunch in Abu Dhabi on 52 from 21 balls, the fastest fifty in Test cricket. Adam resumed after lunch with Tom Cowie in a moment that showed the power of commentary. One had to play the roster like an orchestra conductor, giving extra time to finish a tangent, arranging a double change across two overs. The current pair were speculating about the fastest ton, so I left them to see if it happened. Their 20-minute spot went for an hour and it was worth it. The session was a long crescendo. The commentary got sharper and better and more urgent.

'Here's Mitchell Starc,' said Adam as Pakistan's captain kept blazing. 'This is going to be trash, short, over Misbah's left shoulder and getting the treatment. Here he comes. It's short! Trash! Over his left shoulder, hooked for four!' Tight bowling from Peter Siddle hampered the chance. Misbah needed eight runs in two balls to equal Viv Richards with a hundred from 56 balls. When he got them our studio exploded in cheers. The distortion through the mics would have sounded terrible, but it proved to us that *this* was the thing: the love of the game rather than the love of a team.

I had already been on a few tours to write about cricket. By 2015 Adam and I joined forces. We also started commentating overseas: in India, Sri Lanka, South Africa, New Zealand, the Caribbean, the UK. Commentators call this 'air miles'. They paid off. Less than three years after sitting together on the vinyl and velour of Davies Street, we were producing and leading the ABC's commentary of the Women's World Cup. Adam kept saying that we should buy the rights to a tour ourselves, do a kind of White Line Wireless in person. Then came 2018. Australia was back in the UAE. The first Test since the sandpaper bans. A month beforehand, the ABC and SEN pulled out. There would be no radio coverage.

'I can do it,' Adam was saying on the phone from his place in London. 'I'm talking to the Pakistan board on Monday. We've gotta grab the chance while it's there.'

I was passing through Albury, on my way for a long weekend of camping. 'Don't rush into anything,' I said. 'We don't even have a sponsor yet. We've got to line some things up first. Just wait.'

I was out of mobile range for a few days. When I got back, my phone pinged with a dozen messages. Chief among them, 'I got the rights. Put them on my credit card.'

Fark.

Three weeks later, after Adam in a frenzy cold-called every business across two countries, we had advertisers, borrowed equipment, a lease on massive servers that could handle traffic, an agreement with Wisden to host the coverage online, with Cricket Australia to run it on their app, and with Brendon Julian, Bazid Khan and Peter Lalor to commentate. Our White Line colleague Andrew Donnison asked if we needed a producer. Actually, we did. How much notice would he need to join us? 'Flights look like they'll take fourteen to eighteen hours. Three hours to pack and get to the airport in time. Two days, then,' Donno replied.

Dubai the city clings to a narrow strip of coast, with the gold sand desert of the Arabian Peninsula stretching out on one side and the blue salt desert of the Persian Gulf on the other. Dubai the emirate links up with six more, rich and tiny like mouse kings, to form the United Arab Emirates.

The UAE is a shocking joint, run by the kinds of governments that make me nervous to go back there having written this sentence. Arbitrary grudges from obscure relatives of important people land you in jail. The sparkling modern spires are built by a system of indentured labour that has no claim to be called anything but slavery. People from poor countries get enticed over by shady operators on the promise of certain wages, only to have their passports confiscated, get a fraction of the pay, and get whacked with extortionate costs for their recruitment, travel and accommodation.

Women mostly from the Philippines do domestic labour and are mistreated or sexually abused with no recourse in a religious fundamentalist state that would punish them for reporting it. Men from Pakistan, Nepal, Bangladesh and the like do construction work. There are camps an hour into the desert so the city doesn't have to see them, where workers are packed into metal sheds with rows of timeshare bunks split into 12-hour shifts. The night shifts at least are out of the sun. The dull ring of hammers and drills never stops. Even when it's 50 degrees with the wind blasting, workers are up on the scaffolds' burning steel. If they're lucky, after some years they get their passports back and get home, usually still owed a stack of money. The unlucky ones don't need either anymore.

Each new tower means apartments and offices for expats from corporations drawn by the zero tax rate. When Dubai's rulers wanted to diversify their income from oil they set up as a financial hub. For the rich, Dubai is one giant freeway spidering off into malls and marinas and indoor skiing slopes, sport facilities and entertainment complexes. Smiling people in exercise gear talk up how great it is for their kids. The Eloi and the Morlocks come to mind, except the underclass here takes no toll on the upper. It could change fast if the inspiration strikes.

Fifty years ago, none of this was here. A few fishing towns, quietly sweltering. Dubai didn't export its first oil shipment until 1969. Ever since, pavement has been laid onto desert like make-up in a mortuary. It's a city a mile wide and an inch deep. The desert pushes up through every crack and vacant lot to remind you that it will soon enough take all this back.

The desert is no place for cricket, born on fabled green. But the UAE is full of such idiosyncrasies. The need of the rich to spend their fortunes on anything aside from the poor means that the tiny Emirates are replete with cricket grounds. The location is handy for Pakistan, who needed a home away from home after terrorists attacked the visiting Sri Lankan team in 2009. The Emirates get the profile-building and sportswashing that they chase at a grander scale through professional football clubs and horse racing.

And here we were in Dubai, walking into the desert heat in Melbourne flannels and black jeans hauling hard-shell suitcases full of mixers and powerboards. Setting up an entire broadcast from scratch isn't simple. Especially when nobody knows audio engineering. We would be streaming rather than using the conventional radio ISDN line to an analogue broadcast centre. So we had a complicated split of the audio into a dozen different streams for different destinations with different requirements. A commentary box needs power, internet, sound effect lines, video, monitors.

Jurisdiction was handballed between the Pakistan board, the stadium and the TV broadcaster, spanning various language barriers to keep things interesting. Security guards kept inventing new accreditation levels to go through doors that you'd gone through for four days prior. At the same time we were assembling research notes, going to press conferences, doing interviews, taking photos, writing articles, promoting the coverage, and fielding calls from people with a stake who were worried about whether we'd pull it off.

Getting the internet connected took us rectum-clenchingly close to the first ball of the match despite several days trying to avoid exactly that, then the effects mic from the middle of the ground started blowing out in unlistenable spikes. I spent the first day doing 20 minutes of commentary above the desk, then 20 crawling around under it trying combinations of cables and sockets. We fixed it by the second day and things started to flow. Australia got pasted but there were moments to savour. We did pitch-side interviews, transcribed and distributed them for press, wrote match-day articles and recorded a nightly podcast. We were wrecked at the end of every day but it felt glorious. Four years before we had met watching the UAE series on the telly; four years later we were legit.

That final day at Dubai was a gift. There is a rhythm to the impossible becoming possible in Test cricket. You start out knowing that it can't happen, the outcome appearing in your mind as a consequence of you discounting it. Way too early, it starts to nag. A plucking at a taut thread. Patient, waiting to be proved wrong. But as the possibility gets closer there's a lurch from one side of the ledger to the other. It's hard to define when this happens, it just does, as the result gets close enough that it could defy impossibility. Not should, or will, but could. This changes everything. The tension dials up. Some teams are inspired, some fall apart. Now, the likely result would disappoint you. Only the unlikely will do.

In this case, even with no wicket by lunch, we thought the end of the match was close. The first wicket would trigger the rest. Travis Head and Marnus Labuschagne duly got out and the last rites were prepared. But Khawaja just kept batting, and Tim Paine settled in. The lurch came sometime in the hour before tea. As they pressed on after the break the nerves started to tingle. The session dwindled, the overs eroded, close calls were survived. The whole time we knew one wicket would change it all. It came with an hour to go. But Khawaja had got them close enough that the tail had a chance. Every over became a clawing stanza of anxiety, a volley from the bowler, a victory for the batsmen. More overs ticked by. Another wicket was prised out, another. Every ball was an event. We sat on high and tried to capture the feeling, to carry people along on that ride that only the live culmination of five days of effort can bring.

The end was a mix of elation, admiration, anticlimax. One side had been outclassed but avoided defeat. The other had been unable to cash in. We had witnessed a finish that would be long remembered and the individual performance that had made it possible. The idea of greatness for an innings can mean different things. It might be prevailing against outstanding bowling. It might be surviving hostile conditions. It might be the scope of a defensive masterclass. It might be pushing back valiantly against a team outclassing yours.

Khawaja's effort was all of these. There wasn't a trophy on the line but there was a Test match, and an expectant public wanting pride in its team. There were his struggles away from home and against spin. There was the physical strain of Dubai's heat. Khawaja batted through most of both Australian innings for a total of twelve and a quarter hours, and fielded at gully in between. Across the five days he was off the field for 21 overs, less than a session. Once or twice in a career, those who aren't necessarily great players can have a great moment, a match when everything just works.

As we said farewell and came off air, the enormity hit us – both of the match and the fact that we'd done it justice, that our plan had worked. Adam sank to his knees, speechless after five days of talk. I gave him a hug. Then we got up and set about the night's work.

One difficult task in the Emirates is to get a drink. Alcohol is limited to bars at big hotels where you'll get rinsed like a washed dog. On our budget, extravagance had not been an option. But with a match dusted something had to give. 'I'm going to buy a round,' said Donno, 'because I want to know what the experience of buying a round of $25 beers feels like.' By the grace of someone's god we found a bar with a temporally broad happy hour. Later still someone wandered in with a cucumber, claiming there was a Hendrick's promotion where they could swap it for a gin and tonic. The bartender was on board, so we found a supermarket and got a sack of cucumbers. The barter economy.

When the dust had settled it was off down the highway to the adjoining emirate of Abu Dhabi. Peter Lalor had headed home – his dad Mick had died after a long illness. It was sombre after the recent highs, and we missed Pete's rambling humour and geniality. Louis Cameron from CA's website and former Test bat Mike Hussey stepped in.

Abu Dhabi has less glitz than Dubai, with more modest retro buildings like the rolling concrete waves of the central bus station all painted in Islamic aquamarine. The palace precinct has an old-fashioned grandeur. It still has its share of shiny wonders, like the giant disc that makes up the Aldar HQ building, but it felt like there was a town underneath.

We were confident now that we knew how to get things going. So there was real alarm when our test streams kept cutting out. The equipment was set up, encoding the audio, splitting it for its destinations. But each stream lasted only a few seconds. We tried everything, spent hours on the phone with our tech whiz John-Paul in the UK, who stripped every part of the software back and built it up again, looking for the flaw. He knew everything in this field but was mystified. We could only get a signal out using a hotspot from Donno's phone. I started to work something out. Abu Dhabi's security services jam internet voice calls like Skype. Ostensibly this is to protect revenue for the royal phone company Etisalat, and quietly also because the security services don't want anyone using encrypted communications. That same firewall was interpreting our audio as an outgoing call. Donno's phone had a Dubai sim card, so it didn't hit the firewall.

This was, to put it mildly, a problem. We couldn't run a five-day Test match off a mobile phone without burning it to a crisp, and mobile data wasn't reliable. There was the irony that we weren't doing anything secret – it was a public broadcast that the security services could have listened to on the Wisden site while arranging an affordable deal on eyewear from Specsavers. But we couldn't arrange a government exemption in a strange country with one day to spare. If we couldn't get on air, our agreements with every advertiser and purchaser of the stream would be void.

We asked around, tested waters, visited corners of the internet. No-one wanted to speak directly, but we learned that in theory, a person with a problem like ours could consider using a virtual private network – a server that fakes your computer's location. The problem was that VPNs were illegal in Abu Dhabi, punishable by prison. You had to download the software, and all VPN websites were blocked. So yes, to get a VPN you needed to have a VPN.

On the night before showtime, out in the Abu Dhabi dark, feeling like we were getting trucks of contraband over the border, we managed to connect with a data tunnel under the firewall. I won't specify how. With our devices tooled up, we got into the ground on the morning of the Test and plugged in. Held our breath. Watched the numbers tick, the lights flash. Five seconds. Ten. Twenty. Twenty-eight seconds, the previous record. A minute. Donno's shout of triumph echoed through the cinderblock halls. From there we just had to use extremely vague answers to all the well-meaning questions about how we'd fixed the problem.

And we had to get our heads together to call a Test match, from what must be the most distant commentary position in the world. In Port Elizabeth, South Africa, the comm box is literally on top of the sight screen. You feel like you can reach down and tap a bowler on the shoulder at the top of their mark. The media boxes at Sheikh Zayed are at the back of the second level, behind long deep banks of seats. The figures on the pitch are hints of cricketers. You either commentate off the monitor or through binoculars.

It was another corker, with Pakistan's huge comeback. In the strange manner of a sport that goes for days, it was over in a flash. We packed up to leave, keeping an eye out for anyone who looked like secret police, and got out intact.

The house at Davies Street was a hole in the ground now, bulldozed at last for the advancing townhouses that it had gamely held at bay for so long, Khawaja in Dubai. The people who would soon live between new unblemished walls would never know the stories that preceded them, shadows flickering in the foundations. From among those shadows, born of white vinyl and red velour, one dream had come to pass.

Chapter 6

Reluctantly Crouched at the Starting Line

WITH THE INEVITABILITY of hindsight, it can seem strange that there was ever conjecture about whether Steve Smith or David Warner would be back to play for Australia at the earliest possible moment. At the time of their suspension they had 66 international centuries between them. By a rough yardstick, Smith and Warner were each worth 50 runs per appearance. The batsmen while they were gone were worth 33.

In March and April 2018 though, the view was obscured. There was no way to know whether either could slot back into top-level cricket, or how they would handle the pressure and scrutiny. After Cape Town there had been real tension with some teammates who had been implicated in the tampering plot by the botched attempt to protect Warner. The relationship between the two former leaders was in question too – it had even inspired a play at the Sydney Fringe Festival. Smith might have reached Zen forgiveness, or he might forever resent Warner as the source of his troubles. Conversely, those who get blamed often end up resenting the people they've supposedly wronged.

There was no way to ease the exiles back in. The next dates were the World Cup and the Ashes. The cup squad was to be named a fortnight after their ban expired. If picked, they'd be handed a ticket to the biggest tour in a player's life having done nothing lately to command it. They would take spots from players who had been contributing to the cause. But while the high stakes made that situation look bad, the same stakes made it urgent to get the parolees back. At their best, they were still the two top bats in the country by the leap of a seven-league boot.

Cricket aside, there was no way to know if the time away had helped Smith and Warner personally. Had it brought the change and growth and circumspection that was already being claimed? The powers at CA were content with their Soviet-badged 'reintegration' process: a single day visiting the one-day squad, most of whom hadn't been on the sandpaper tour to begin with, sitting awkwardly in a meeting room for a supposed baring of souls. 'Cape Town. It's a dark time. What do we do about it?' asked Justin Langer. 'We learn from it, and we keep getting better. We're going to make Australian cricket awesome again.' That had a familiar tinny ring to it. Teammates fronted the media to say how glad they were to have the prodigals back. It was never likely to go differently – this wasn't exactly a Truth and Reconciliation Commission.

Whatever the feeling between Smith and Warner, they had spent enough time around one another in the T20 leagues to diminish immediate angst, and it was firmly against their interests to let it be an issue. As for everyone else, a year had softened discontent, and incentive breeds forgiveness. Having those two back made everyone more likely to win things, with the bonus that every win is good news for the collective pay packet.

The players who weren't getting good financial news were the ones who would be displaced. As well as the World Cup squad, April was the time for national contracts, with 20 spots worth close to a million Aussie dollars on average. There were match fees of $10,000 for one-dayers and $20,000 for Tests. Missing out on contracts were current Test players Marnus Labuschagne, Joe Burns and Kurtis Patterson. Peter Handscomb got a contract but not a World Cup spot. Ashton Turner, whose miracle in Mohali had sparked the drastic shift in mood, missed out on both. Usman Khawaja and Shaun Marsh both got contracts and plane tickets but were bumped to second-tier status in the squad.

The working method that the ODI team had put in place in 2018 started with Khawaja and Aaron Finch at the top. Since being recalled to the format Khawaja had made 50, 38, 104, 91, 100, 24, 88, 0, 62 and 98 on tour. Opening the batting worked for him as a strokeplayer with a conventional range of cuts, pulls and drives. He rarely attempted sixes and wasn't great at working singles. Facing a new ball meant pace off the bat, while fielders inside the circle meant shots along the ground could hit gaps for four. He could keep a decent strike rate even if he found the field four times out of five. He wasn't the fastest starter and this method gave him time to build. If he batted down the order there was pressure to turn over the strike immediately, and his best shots were likely to bring him one run via an outfielder rather than four to the fence. Khawaja partnered beautifully with the beefier style of Finch, whose return to form in the UAE spanned 116, 153 not out, 90, 39 and 53. Their list of partnerships in a couple of months included 83, 193, 76, 63, 209, 56 and 134, with two of Australia's eight highest opening stands in the history of the format.

At first drop Marsh had played as a pillar for others to build around. In England the previous year he had been one of the few success stories with two centuries, and by the Australian summer that streak was four tons in eight matches. He moved around as Langer experimented in India, but resumed his spot with a match-winning 91 not out against Pakistan. His white-ball cricket had a confidence and ease that he rarely had in Tests, where a slip cordon and a moving ball had lately made him a wreck. In the one-day game he could start in a similar vein to Khawaja but with aerial acceleration near the end.

Handscomb at four had the engine-room adaptability that a one-day innings needs. He had honed this skill in T20s for the Melbourne Stars, making the most efficient use of opportunities. He was excellent against spin, rapid between the wickets, and accumulated through the middle overs with barely a wasted delivery. As the end drew closer he could go up through a range of gears, with boundary options and six-hitting ability lifting him to an overall rate of a run a ball. He had made his breakthrough ODI century to power that crazy chase in Mohali, followed by 52, 30 not out and 47.

Marcus Stoinis at five was out of nick, but Glenn Maxwell and Alex Carey began to flourish while finishing things off. Maxwell showed his range against Pakistan with a devastating

71 and 70 either side of a sensible 98 the one time Australia had a collapse. He revived the innings and they won by six runs. The bowlers had never been a problem, and after a lot of anguish the batting was primed.

It would all be upended just the same. Warner had played 106 one-day matches and been listed to open 106 times. Once, at the 2015 World Cup, he shifted to five against Scotland when Michael Clarke needed a stroll and Australia had only 130 to chase. If he was to play in the next World Cup then it would be at the top of the order. Finch similarly had left the opening slot twice in 126 matches, in two failed experiments to let D'Arcy Short go bananas while chasing massive scores. Khawaja already batted three in Test cricket. Regardless of runs he would be the one to take that spot.

Pushing Usman down the order meant pushing Marsh out of it. He would tour England as a pine-rider. In the middle, a strike-rotating number four with speed between the wickets and shots in his locker described Smith and Handscomb equally. There was no room for both with two all-rounders filling the fifth bowling quota before the wicketkeeper and the tail. Maxwell and Stoinis were the only bankable options for late-innings sixes.

It ended up a strange sort of squad. Australia had finished major renovations against a hard deadline, then knocked out the foundations and started half of it over. Khawaja, Marsh, Warner and Finch – four batsmen suited only to play top three. Marsh the only spare, no option for versatility like Handscomb or power like Turner. No spare all-rounder meant Stoinis and Maxwell had to play every match regardless of results. Adam Zampa and Nathan Lyon were the spinners, with fast bowling from Mitchell Starc, Patrick Cummins, Jason Behrendorff, Nathan Coulter-Nile and Jhye Richardson.

Still, one can never write off Australia. That's certainly the perspective in England, a cricketing nation living in fear that Australians will lurch out of the shadows like it's the eighth instalment in a horror franchise. It didn't help English anxiety when after years of their team's 50-over dominance, the ragtag Australians showed up and beat them in a practice match.

That was in the county of Hampshire at what can charitably be called the least good place to watch cricket in England. The town on the schedule may say Southampton, but the ground is in the middle of nowhere. You can take a bus through an hour of *Midsomer Murders* country, or drive to the car park known as the M27 motorway, drawing up your last will and testament while you wait. The ground does have a proper oval with no idiosyncratic short boundaries, and seats for 15,000 people. The countryside is pretty once you've made it through the gates. The squat white blocks encircling the oval are less picturesque, but having a Hilton on-site seems appropriate when there's a stand named after Shane Warne.

The match was a circus. Australia left out Starc, Cummins and Maxwell. England captain Eoin Morgan had a fractured finger, meaning Chris Woakes had to fill in while unable to bowl with a sore knee. Leg-spinner Adil Rashid couldn't bowl with a sore shoulder but was drafted in to bat after off-spinner Liam Dawson cut his finger. Mark Wood limped off for an ankle scan, so Jofra Archer had to cancel a rest day to substitute. Then Archer hurt his shoulder diving on the boundary and was replaced by Joe Root, who had the day off after a death in his family. When seamer Liam Plunkett went off for treatment England were reduced to having fielding coach Paul Collingwood pull on Wood's shirt and stand at gully, one day shy of his 43rd birthday. The end of the run chase came when Archer, who wasn't listed to play for England, was run out by Maxwell, who wasn't listed to play for Australia.

The game was instructive for the response to and from the returning Australians. One spectator raced around the outer dressed as a giant inflatable cricket ball with a sandpaper hat. Warner was booed all the way to the crease and back after a controlled 43. The noise of his departure morphed into a bigger chorus of opprobrium for the incoming Smith. While Australian public opinion broadly saw Warner as the corruption behind the throne, the English response was harsher towards the former captain.

The booing recurred as Smith reached fifty, stronger again for his century. For those thinking only of the game, Smith did his job to perfection. A blameless 30 overs of accumulation gave way to carnival mode, slashing Stokes over backward point for six and ramping Plunkett over the wicketkeeper. He was dismissed by an umpiring mistake for 116 with one ball left in the innings.

The Australians gave the impression of sanguinity. When Bairstow completed a running boundary catch off Warner, the Englishman played to the crowd by saluting and whipping up a cheer. When Warner caught Bairstow in similar fashion there was no retaliation, just a trot towards the umpire to return the ball. Smith said after the match he'd 'heard a few things as I went out to bat' but that 'I'm trying to just keep my head down and do my job. It doesn't bother me.'

The line of questioning marked the start of several months of tedium. The reception of disgraced players was interesting, but it was interpreted reductively by the duration and decibel count of every jeer. Every Australian match of the season had a trailing tail of boo stories: reported, analysed, debated and moralised about. It's a lasting truth that the resentful are far louder than the content. Over the weeks to come, the loud would make themselves known. For Warner and Smith, there could be no doubt that they were back in the thick of it.

Chapter 7

The Redemption Myth

A MONG THE OVERBLOWN themes of sports writing, through all its stained and dog-eared lexica, the one that comes up most is surely redemption. Across the dirt of suburban outfields and the paint of city lanes, redemption and the seeking of it. Blessed is its pursuit. Something to be striven for, to be craved, to be grasped, to be squandered. Teams, athletes, entire nations take their turns to be redeemed. Someone somewhere is always hovering on its holy cusp. Some recidivists make it a cycle, a new fall before each corresponding lift, the trip through a spiritual carwash. Each time a crowd will assemble, dancing with the idea that now things could be different. The desire to see someone rise is unquenchable. We are a world of sporting sinners endlessly swimming towards the light.

The concept lives way beyond sport. Action heroes wrestle their pasts, the prodigal son makes his passage home. We saddle up the Xbox to ride the range in *Red Dead Redemption.*

Even our frequent flyer points get redeemed, becoming shitty appliances in a late rush before the airline goes bust. Hold on to this receipt, redeem this offer at any participating outlet. 'I know that my redeemer lives, and that in the end he will stand on the earth,' says the Book of Job, and duly on a mountain above Rio de Janeiro you'll find the firm footing of Christ the Redeemer, eternally signalling a wide.

Sometimes the formulation fits. A team that wins the year after fumbling a final? A footballer slotting a crucial penalty after blowing it last time? The headline reflects the feeling. More broadly though, it's applied to any success that follows any lack of success. In the churn of sport results this isn't a narrative, it's a sequence. But Lord, we love narrative. 'One common thread runs through almost every major sports moment so far this year, and that is redemption,' wrote *The Sport Digest* in 2017. It could have been any other year. After the US men's basketball team committed the sin of not winning gold at the 2004 Olympics, the narrative got so baked into their 2008 campaign that the Dream Team nickname became the Redeem Team.

The other kind of redemption story involves off-field failings. Between all the world's athletes, the money, the youth and the high-risk personalities, these form a substantial body of work. The basics are drink-driving, car crashes, messy nights on the town. These might aggregate into alcoholism or addictions to any of the substances ideal for those with a lot of ready cash and a need for a clean system in 12 hours. Transgression can get more boutique, like NFL player Michael Vick's dog-fighting ring. It can be as mundane as sexual infidelity, as serious as sexual assault. There are often greater consequences for the former than the latter. Money and legal clout ensure those implicated in crimes are rarely convicted, and a lack of conviction in both senses is used to stifle the question of whether violence should prohibit a return to the public arena.

There are unique redemption stories – Rubin Carter with a reputation as a fierce boxer, falsely convicted of murder, campaigning for his eventual release; South Africa after apartheid appearing in Rugby World Cups and cricket Tests and Olympic Games. Dopers, match-fixers and other cheats are their own genre, as their failings are personal but take place within the sport. Former match-fixers can come back to win without suspicion but never lose. Drug cheats who win are assumed to be still on the gear and when losing are derided as nothing without it. Any Australian bowler generating reverse swing will generate suspicion as long as David Warner is in the side.

The academic Alex Parrish parses the redemption cycle into six stages: loss, shame, punishment, repentance, triumph and forgiveness. The first three are largely enacted through media coverage; parts four and six can be engineered through the same. There's the newspaper double-spread with photos of domestic relatability, or the montage of sobs and synthesisers on a TV profile. Wholesome influences take the spotlight: childhood hockey coaches with wisdom carved into faces like Treebeard's, family priests whose urging brought on a Damascene moment of prayer, mothers or fathers or their surrogates before whom our subject is at last humbled into gratitude. Babies and marriages become catalysts for a moral before-and-after picture.

Any of these can apply to athletes current or retired. The retired need bigger arcs, like the autobiography addressing mental health or addiction. These are marketable where struggle contrasts with sporting success – as long as there's an upbeat ending. The subjects can go through Hell itself but must come out the other side. People who live with mental health conditions know that these are only ever managed rather than cured. But those sorts of stories aren't the ones that sell.

Thomas Patrick Oates writes in *Sport Documentary and the Politics of Redemption* about portrayals of athletes who didn't succeed at the top level. Despite that premise, each subject 'ultimately overcomes his athletic failures in some significant way. Given the conventions of the documentary profile, it is perhaps unsurprising that these stories would be framed in terms that emphasize redemption. Because profiles so often involve the subject as the central participant, narratives documenting their failure usually end on a positive note, or at least allow the central subject to share some important insight on the human condition.'

Those are a few of the ways through the six-part cycle. But for part five – triumph – current athletes have a direct option that the retired do not. They can get out and play. New success is an adrenaline syringe to the redemption veins.

On a Monday in 2010, Lynn Zinser looked back at the weekend in her Leading Off column for *The New York Times*. 'Having absorbed a day full of stories of redemption, the NFL has officially taken over the word. There was so much redeeming going on, it's amazing anyone remembered to play football … Vick became King of the Redeemed, while also redeeming Coach Andy Reid for making him the starter. In sports, this is how you re-write your reputation. Similarly, [Braylon] Edwards patched over that pesky little arrest for drunken driving and redeemed the Jets' decision to wallop him with that whole quarter-long suspension with a touchdown catch that helped beat the Dolphins ... The redemption of the Cowboys and the Vikings, two over-hyped teams avoiding 0–3 starts, saved them from being overtaken by waves of panic ... Still awaiting his redemption opportunity is the suspended Steelers quarterback Ben Roethlisberger.'

This redemption is lightweight, painted polystyrene. It just means that the most recent public memory is no longer the most embarrassing – your profile photo is a cheery thumbs-up instead of you stapling your foreskin to a table. It gives minor actions a disproportionate emotional heft, like that very British practice where a footballer observes some basic piece of civility online and an infantry of accounts with club logos line up with the single-word reply: 'Class'. Media expediency drives this stuff, but it works only with an audience. 'There is something in us, as storytellers and as listeners to stories, that demands the redemptive act, that demands that what falls at least be offered the chance to be restored,' wrote the novelist Flannery O'Connor, whose protagonist in *Wise Blood* forever sought the same.

Foundational to storytelling is progress. The cinema's three-act structure needs a character to be confronted with a challenge and emerge from it changed. Greek myth has the twin concepts of miasma and catharsis: a shadow or a stain on the soul, then the purge of it that only an act of valiance can bring on. The same impulse echoes through our monotheistic religions: our visits to confessionals, our knees bruised on flagstones, our prayers made with lips or with strands of knotted rope. The secular versions are in gym sessions, self-help sections, therapy couches. This is our inexhaustible need: the idea that we can be forgiven, that we may mimic divine example by transcending our form and existing anew.

The Jesus myth uses a different version: suffering without a preceding wrong, for the good of those who remain. 'In him we have redemption through his blood, the forgiveness of sins, in accordance with the riches of God's grace,' says the Book of Ephesians. Earlier religions used the same structure for millennia, a sacrifice of a sacred figure for harvest or protection or appeasement. The most potent sacrifices involve youth, innocent and blameless. Likewise the Greek miasma might follow accident or misfortune rather than wrongdoing – not so much a moral judgement as a burden imposed by fate. Heracles is made to slay his family while possessed by a god, but must still perform his Twelve Labours to be cleansed.

Those conventions remain with us: if an apocalypse movie plays in the forest but no-one dies to save the world, does it make a surround sound? Bruce Willis is Jesus on an asteroid, nailed by a nuke – a true muscular American Christianity. Other action movies with more localised scopes of damage still need the emotional ballast of a character saving the others, the 'Go on without me' moment: think Gorman and Vasquez in the air duct in *Aliens*, think Miles Dyson's ragged final breaths as he holds up a detonator long enough for John and Sarah Connor to escape Cyberdyne Systems.

It's tempting to peg this modern prevalence as a substitute, interpreting like religious scholar Joseph Price that 'contemporary secular rituals manifest fundamental religious proclivities of human beings and reflect the sacred rites and myths of previous, religiously oriented cultures'. This can be a chicken-and-egg argument, but the length of its history suggests that redemption symbolism had a power that attracted religious thought, rather than vice-versa. Secular redemption stories are as marketable under religious regimes as they are in the cliche of the godless modern city.

One crossover area is repentance. Any banned athlete can show dedication to make amends by their physical preparation. Reports will include liberal use of the word 'gruelling', quotes from teammates about training the house down, numbers on how much muscle was added or weight was dropped. Sweat is an offering. In religious tradition, an ascetic was a holy person who refused comfort and luxury, leaving society to live as a hermit and concentrate on God. The word came via Latin from the Ancient Greek áskēsis, meaning an athlete's training or exercise. Physical improvement was equated with the rigour of religious devotion. There turns out to be a short thread between John the Baptist chowing locusts and a Rocky Balboa montage.

These options aren't available to most of us. For a person of humble abilities, the only currency of repentance is time and effort, suffering and expiation. Normal wrongs are met with exclusion, prison, fines, shame, contrition. We need to hurt and be seen to have hurt. After the Freedom Summer murders in Philadelphia, Mississippi, the Reverend Martin Luther King Jr said, 'Somehow I still believe that American suffering is redemptive.' Pain is a path to something better. For an individual to win back social standing, the route lies through charity, doing notable acts for others the way Jesus hopped up on the woodwork. This might still take years. To be seen as reformed without major good deeds, just by living a quiet and honourable life, might need decades.

So the athlete takes their shortcut. Loss, shame, punishment, repentance, triumph, forgiveness – but triumph can be had in the arena even if the other five have nothing to do with it. Zinser put her finger on the obvious contradiction: 'By scoring touchdowns, did any of these guys actually make amends for what put them on people's Don't Like List? ... [It] was definitely a warped off-field message, but football success erases all doubts.' Swap football for your sport of choice.

On the day that Smith's ban was handed down, in March 2018, the radio broadcaster Declan Byrne put up a post online. 'I've saved everyone the time and created the front page of every paper in 15 months,' he wrote. Attached was a photo of Smith holding aloft his bat with a weary Stuart Broad in the background. 'REDEMPTION' read a huge banner headline, with the subheading 'Smith hits ton on Day 1 at Edgbaston to open 2019 Ashes'.

That prediction wasn't supernatural. The conventions and concepts were already set. If Smith played in the Ashes, that's exactly how any success would be presented. Personal improvement or otherwise in his time away would mean squat. In May the following year, with the World Cup about to start, Smith stood with Warner and Ben Stokes on the edge of exactly this promise. The big contests were about to start, and anyone who succeeded in them might get his slate polished clean. You had to avoid the pitfalls – the professional failures or personal failings that would double down the disapproval of the crowd. Succeed, though, and you would be folded into the endless redemption story, just one more comeback spun into a moral good.

Chapter 8

Off With a Bang

IT HAD TO start with Ben Stokes. Standing on the ramparts on the last day of May, looking out at the biggest summer that England cricket had ever attempted, with so many different strands of hope and expectation riding on it, the announcement of its commencement couldn't have come from anyone else.

The match itself had been petering out. The home team and South Africa for the World Cup opener was scheduled as one of the marquee confrontations, but aside from the second ball of the tournament, when the manic leg-spinner Imran Tahir ran a lap of The Oval gasometer in celebration, there hadn't been the desired fizz. England made a hefty 311 but it wasn't the sort of six-fest their own hype had promised. New sensation Jofra Archer bowled at thrilling pace to bounce out half the South African top order and concuss their lynchpin Hashim Amla, but his skill pretty much squashed the contest just past the innings break.

Andile Phehlukwayo the all-rounder was hitting and hoping at 180 for 6 when he got a leg-break on off stump from Adil Rashid. The left-hander knelt and swept hard with the spin. He got a proper piece of it, low and flat over midwicket. It was going to clear the boundary. Then Stokes appeared.

By his own admission it was an accident. From his spot on that boundary he had moved forward in anticipation of a top edge. Too late he realised the shot was out of the middle. He braked perhaps 15 yards from the perimeter and tried to get back, legs whirring for traction like Scrappy Doo. He was running towards the rope while looking back over his shoulder towards the pitch, tracking the path of the ball. He had to add a diagonal angle to meet it.

Still it looked like the ball would clear him. Stokes wasn't under it. At the last instant he had to dive towards the rope in the hope of gaining a few more yards, turning his head forward in the process and losing sight of the ball. He threw his right arm straight above his head with the wrist reversed, his cupped palm pointing towards the centre of the ground while his body flew towards its extremity. Somehow, in that last fraction of a second of blind flight, the battered white Kookaburra nestled into that solitary palm.

Stokes was mid-air at that point, almost in a cartwheel, four limbs skewed around a circle like a drunken clock. His catching arm was strained against its socket. His left arm was straight down ready to brace a fall. His legs trailed as scissored afterthoughts. He had leapt from the left foot, but hung so long in the air while trying not to rotate away from the ball that the left foot was also the first to land. His body made a T shape, completing a glorified hop that continued into a forward roll, left arm taking the fall, protecting the right to make sure the ball would not jar free. In the middle of everything he was only thinking about the catch. There was no need to worry. Stokes rolled over again, found his feet just inside the rope, and pointed the ball and an index finger into the crowd.

That crowd was alive. The photographs show hands locked on heads, mouths frozen open. The sound on the day was the opposite, instant and transient, a singular percussive shout of disbelief half a second behind the action like a sonic boom follows a jet. The single point of detonation spread and softened into the foam of cheers. Stokes stood with hands on hips for a long moment, looking back into the crowd as though seeking a witness. It was one of those rare catches so great that the other fielders come to the source. Rashid sprinted the full measure from the bowling crease, beaming. Stokes, no stranger to remarkable sporting moments, laughed in amazement.

There would be one clip on the news that night, one clip thickening the online feeds: a thousand flicker-quick repetitions of a streak across the turf, the baby blue of England's new uniform against green. The scores didn't matter, it was about sizzling the collective synapses. That's what England needed. It's what their tournament needed.

The lead-up had not been encouraging. No cities draped in banners, no welcoming choirs at airports. The signs of life were a few ads on the Tube, a smattering of team shirts and some sparsely attended fan zones on match days. Most of the taxi drivers didn't know it was on. When you follow cricket it's easy to forget how little it means to those who don't. In Australia's summer the game has a background omnipresence, but the United Kingdom version has retreated to the grounds of private schools and the living rooms of those with enough cash for pay TV. If you said 'the World Cup' that summer you had to clarify which one: there was netball, women's football, and not long until rugby.

It wasn't like cricket could afford an Olympic opening ceremony. The compromise was limp, wet and cold, the event version of boiled asparagus left out overnight. The promise was a free party in the park outside Buckingham Palace: suitably British and festive and public. The reality was a freezing May afternoon, so far from the Palace that any royals trying to walk there would have died of exposure, in a dystopian outdoor prison built of 16 miles of cyclone fencing and a hive of fluorescent security guards, each armed with exactly zero idea what was happening and the apparent suspicion that everyone trying to attend was smuggling a hacksaw baked inside a chocolate cake.

The dozen entrances were blocked except for one gate, which changed randomly depending on mood. Anyone approaching was sent on a circumnavigation of the entire bloated complex, channelled through races and chicanes until they got disillusioned or hypothermic and went away. One security guard would tell you that he cannot tell a lie while his brother cannot tell the truth, and that you could ask them each one question before choosing a path to your destination or certain death. The wire fences were covered with World Cup cladding to block the view on the off-chance that passers-by were lured by the decor of an impound yard. Strongly outnumbering members of the public was the world's least spontaneous flash mob, kitted out with replica vintage team shirts and plastic bats and waiting to dance in batting-adjacent fashion to the World Cup theme song. A camera drone that zoomed up into the sky laid bare the sparseness of attendance.

The only choice to host this event was Andrew Flintoff, the one cricketer in England who is still broadly recognised given his defining 2005 Ashes came just before the sport vanished behind a paywall. He teamed up with his *Top Gear* mate Paddy McGuinness and IPL anchor Shibani Dandekar, the three posters on any teenager's bedroom wall. The best part was McGuinness saying, 'Let's welcome the captain of the host country,' with an accent that sounded like, 'Let's welcome the captain of the horse country,' causing a brief but intense vision of Eoin Morgan descending on London in a rage-fuelled churn leading a thousand head of bays and chestnuts and greys.

The centre of proceedings was a game called 60 Second Cricket, where an increasingly loosely defined cricket legend and celebrity compatriot paired up in a street match against two dozen volunteers with rubber balls. Who would have thought Kevin Pietersen's triumphant return to an England shirt would come in a partnership with Chris from *Love Island*, a guy whose last name was so immediately lost to history that he is only ever addressed as Chris from *Love Island*? What yells Australia more than Brett Lee with a headbanded Pat Cash who gives the impression of having inhaled a source of enthusiasm in one of the portable toilets? Mirwais Ashraf could pass an evening talking you through his two World Cup wickets while Aryana Sayeed chats about being a judge on *Afghan Star*. Sri Lanka's batting maestro Mahela Jayawardene paired perfectly with South Asian

Games sprint medallist Damayanthi Dharsha. Who could count the hours that Anil Kumble has spent in the nets with Indian film director Farhan Akhtar? Sprinter Yohan Blake played junior cricket in Jamaica, making him the perfect counterpart for the greatest one-day batsman of all time, Viv Richards. What says cricket more than South African all-rounder Jacques Kallis and former Everton winger Steven Pienaar? Imagine the chats that Pienaar once had with Mikel Arteta at Goodison Park about the vagaries of left-arm spin on a wearing surface. And Pakistan naturally teamed up former Test captain Azhar Ali with the youngest winner of a Nobel Peace Prize, Malala Yousafzai.

In a faint gesture to the incongruity, Malala was asked a couple of earnest questions about cricket inspiring young women before the less-than-headline band Rudimental played for 11 minutes and everyone was sent home. The message all day was that a billion people around the world were watching. You bloody well hoped not.

The early stages on the field weren't much better. Pakistan and Sri Lanka got destroyed, giving run-rate boosts to West Indies and New Zealand. Any lustre to England's opening win diminished as South Africa became a shell of a side and the English turned around and lost to Pakistan. Then the rain swept in, two weeks watching the hectic colours of precipitation radars as purple splodges trudged from Ireland like the least enthused army of the Uruk-hai. Pitches slowed to sludge, days dragged into evenings, delay recalculations made scores unrecognisable, four matches were lost to rain. The reliable chorus rang out that England should never be allowed to host cricket, as though the game hadn't managed to get born in the country between showers.

It was easy to forget that there was a lot of tournament left to come. Ten teams, each playing each other once before the top four hit the knockouts. Australia enjoyed a rare sojourn below the radar. The five-time champions were between third and fifth for favouritism. But a combination of luck with rain and a back-ended campaign let them get on with banking wins. Afghanistan. West Indies. Pakistan. Sri Lanka. Bangladesh. India beat them comfortably, yet Australia had all but qualified for a semi-final by halfway.

Most significant was Warner making runs. First 89 not out chasing Afghanistan's small target, then 107 against Pakistan. The century meant his first media conference since his comeback, and his wranglers would have been delighted that it came in low-key Somerset with few English journalists present. He followed up with 166 against Bangladesh.

None of these were Warner's old bullocking self. Against Afghanistan in the 2015 World Cup he had battered what remain the most lucrative 100 balls of his career; against the same opponent four years later he faced his lowest-scoring 100 deliveries. He poked and played out maidens and edged past slip. Against India he made his slowest ODI fifty, finishing with 56 from 84 balls. He followed up against a modest Sri Lankan attack with 26 from 48. He had long since refined his game from hitting big to hitting gaps, but now was incapable of getting off strike.

Even during his hundreds he battled, miscued shots, got dropped. Yet there was something about this version of Warner: craggy and weathered, elbow cased in a thick black bandage, feral beard sprouting out the sides of his grille in an alarming shade of orange. Less The Reverend than *The Revenant*, out of the wilderness, mauled by a bear. There was satisfaction in seeing a player blessed with ability having to drag himself onward.

It had a cost though. The Afghan chase should have been a run-rate booster but Australia crawled. Warner blew the match against India, the target of 353 difficult when he started and impossible when he finished. It called to mind Stokes in 2018: performative responsibility, a dasher making his game penance. After his Bangladesh ton, Warner implied this was how he wanted to be seen. 'It's generally not my game to stick there, I usually try and go after it a little bit, come down the wicket or something. But must be a bit more maturity, I think.'

Documentary series *The Test* was more revealing. 'I feel like I've got no rhythm, I feel like I've got no timing,' he told his teammates. 'The only thing I can think of is I've got a fear of getting out. And that's not how I play. I play with a free mind, a clear mind, and back myself all the time. It just felt I had this, sort of, something was over me.'

Finch had always played differently to his destructive T20 batting: three-quarters of his ODI innings were slower than a run a ball. Khawaja was the same. Smith was a faster accumulator but could lose shape when asked to drop the hammer. At times he pushed up to number three, leaving Khawaja at five or six doing jobs he'd never done even in domestic cricket. Having Khawaja swing for the pickets in the 45th over was like asking a chef to use a Santoku knife on firewood. Stoinis remained in a rut. Time and again acceleration was left to Maxwell, who turned in strike rates of 200, 200, 184, 320, 150, but couldn't last at that throttle. The team was flattered by Alex Carey, who turned in a streak of 45, 55 not out, 20, 4, 11 not out, 38 not out, 71, 85 and 46 at better than six an over.

Regardless, Australia kept winning. The West Indies game was saved by Nathan Coulter-Nile, a longtime reserve bowler with more soft-tissue problems than the Sorbent puppy, who walked in at number eight that day and bashed his highest score in any cricket for 92 from 60 balls. The target for Pakistan wasn't big enough but Starc saved it at the death. India exposed a lack of power, but that was on the truest batting pitch all tournament. The surfaces got tacky, and on those surfaces Australia's bowling was so good.

It helped to have Starc. In a format where batting teams had to attack, he had an often unstoppable combination of attributes: a left-arm action that curved the new ball at the start, bent the old ball at the death, and pushed 150 kilometres an hour. His bouncer kept them wary, then time and again he bowled a full length and slithered past a groping bat onto the stumps. Nearly half his ODI wickets were bowled, more than half were bowled and lbw. He had carved through the 2015 World Cup for 22 wickets at 10 runs apiece, one every 2.5 overs. The greatest left-armer, Wasim Akram, took five wickets or more on six occasions in 356 ODIs. Starc did it seven times by match number 83.

In the 2019 World Cup, Starc was at it again. Top wicket-taker, 27 this time at a cost of 18. His hooping obscenity of a yorker to bowl Stokes within reach of a century was the ball of the tournament. Pat Cummins was a metronomic offsider in every match, conceding less than five per over. Maxwell and Stoinis did enough to control the middle. A rotation of spare quicks and spinners came in depending on conditions. Jason

Behrendorff made the most dramatic entrance, picked to exploit an English weakness against left-arm pace. He delivered, using the slope at Lord's perfectly for five wickets. In this match and against New Zealand a middling 200s score was defended easily. Maybe this was all Australia needed: five an over batting, then bowl.

Warner's confidence was recovering. Against England he made 53 in quick time. Searching for a lost ball against New Zealand he leant against the fence for a chat and casually munched a spectator's bag of chips. The next day Candice Warner gave birth to their third daughter. They had a few days with the new arrival before David smashed another ton against South Africa.

Smith moved between three, four and six, depending on the day. His 73 was vital when West Indies had Australia five down, and it took the catch of the tournament to stop him – Sheldon Cottrell outdid Stokes with a Fred Astaire along a boundary tightrope. But without Coulter-Nile's blitz, Smith wouldn't have been enough. His 69 against India went smoothly at six an over but by the time he was out Australia needed 11.5. When he came in to hit from a good base – against Pakistan, Afghanistan, England – it didn't work. Through the tournament he was agitated even by his standards, shouting at himself and dramatically gesturing at gaps in the field when he failed to find them. His big shots were awkward, heaving at the ball rather than striking it, intention compromising something pure.

But if Australia had worries, England had concerns. The national sporting fear of screwing it up – whatever *it* may be – is rooted so deep that dwarves have stumbled across it while mining gems. England may have invented cricket and the one-day subgenre, but the men's team had never been champions, though the women had four times. Three of the first five men's World Cup finals featured England losses of varying frustration, then for a quarter century the team genteelly withdrew from contention.

Through that time the English fear of screwing up was based on the overwhelming likelihood that England would screw up. But in 2019 a different fear was bubbling away, the fear that England might screw up when by rights England shouldn't. England had abruptly got good at one-day cricket. This was a team that had stumbled towards the 2015 World Cup thinking it was a good idea to have Alastair Cook and Ian Bell pottering about at the top of the order, and got punted from the group stage by Bangladesh. At least the result galvanised them. Trevor Bayliss and Paul Farbrace took over as coaches with a new tack. With an emerging generation of all-rounders, England would pack hitters all the way down. They would be backed, told to play fearlessly until it became a habit. Misfires wouldn't risk places. They were told to feel the adrenaline and go with it.

The polite compilers became marauders. In the span between World Cups they set a target beyond 300 runs in 26 of 41 innings. Five of those targets got up to 400. Their trademark became the 300-plus score when chasing. From a dozen attempts they chased down nine successfully. Chasing less than 300 they won 24 out of 29. Their trick was that they didn't stop. Get an England batsman out and the next would swing as hard. Roy, Bairstow, Hales, Morgan, Stokes, Buttler, Moeen, all with the ability to hit the light towers. The bowlers biffed too: Rashid, Woakes, Willey, Plunkett. There were matches when England fielded 11 players with first-class centuries. The message for those bowlers was simple: whatever they get, we'll get one more.

Coming into the World Cup nobody was supposed to be able to keep up. This was home turf for the team with the firepower. As much as it made their supporters uneasy, England were clear favourites. Then Pakistan piled up 348. That was fine, it gave England a chance to do their party trick. There wasn't one of the occasional implosions that were the price of all-out attack. Joe Root got a brisk ton as the anchor, Buttler got a faster one down the order, and ... England still lost. Short by 15 runs. Tremors began to tickle the seismograph. Surely England hadn't made all this progress to stuff it up?

The machine looked in order through the next three outings: 386 against Bangladesh, 397 against Afghanistan, and a rollicking completion of a small chase against West Indies. Those were all wins that England expected. So was Sri Lanka. But the Teardrop Isle was having its own gloriously erratic 2019. Straight after a Test thrashing in Australia in February, an extremely green squad became the first Asian side to win a Test series in South Africa. It was an extraordinary result, overcoming difficulties with fast bowling on fast pitches.

Ahead of that series, understated opener Dimuth Karunaratne had been made captain. After it, Sri Lanka's selectors didn't want to mess with that kind of luck. Despite him not having played an ODI since 2015 he was handed the World Cup team. Sri Lanka got demolished by New Zealand's seamers, struggled past Afghanistan and had two rain-offs before a feisty attempt to chase Australia's 334. They didn't so much have a form line to follow as a trail of breadcrumbs. They were fiery though, boycotting their press duties after the Australia game amid a suite of complaints that their pitches had been too green, their bus too small, and their hotels to date hadn't had swimming pools. Getting into the water, they said, was a key part of their success.

Well. You could call the Headingley game Karunaratne's Pool Party. On moving to Leeds the Sri Lankans found facilities to their liking. Back in the pool, back in the competition. An England team fresh off hitting 25 sixes against Afghanistan suddenly got apprehensive chasing 232. Lasith Malinga took wickets early, Morgan and Root soaked up overs through the middle. Dhananjaya de Silva's off-breaks and Nuwan Pradeep's seam made use of the slow surface with accuracy, and Malinga returned to pick up Root and Buttler through the middle. Stokes did all he could but the rest fell around him. Sri Lanka by 20 runs.

The competition was alive. The top four had looked preordained, but England had dropped two likely wins. They were hunting for fourth with Pakistan, Bangladesh, West Indies and Sri Lanka. A few days later England lost to Australia, again done on a slow deck in a modest chase. All guns blazing had become damp powder. A team that had lost three out of six now had to beat India, New Zealand, and two knockouts against either those teams or Australia. There was a real chance England could miss an invitation to their own party.

It was here that the Summer of Stokes began to take shape. Unnoticed at the time, inexorable in retrospect. He had already been the main man against South Africa with his 89. But when his team was down he was the one digging them out. After the ninth wicket against Sri Lanka, Stokes belted 25 of 46 runs required, ending on 82 not out with three overs left. He looked set to win it had Mark Wood not nicked behind. Against Australia he was similarly alone, 89 runs shifting from rebuild to bloom while no-one else got through the 20s. He bowled important spells in both.

With the competition tightening, pressure created diamonds. Kane Williamson's century against South Africa was one, taking New Zealand home at the death when his colleagues were proposing to lose. South Africa were out of contention and had nothing left to do but get on de Beers. But the next Kiwi outing against West Indies will shine the longest. First it was Williamson with 148, after his team lost two wickets in the first over, then the giant Carlos Brathwaite roaring down the beanstalk. West Indies were 128 short at the seventh wicket, 81 at the eighth, 47 at the ninth, but Brathwaite just kept hitting sixes. He made 101 before Trent Boult took a stunner on the fence.

Honestly, Brathwaite blew it: he was ahead of the game, needing 8 from 12 balls, but was preoccupied by his imminent century and scored 2 from the next five. He put his energy into celebrating, then tried to finish the game with one glory hit although he had an over to come. Still, the lasting image will be the loved and lovable Brathwaite blowing a kiss off the blade of his bat, and the excitement he had generated raced through the tournament like wind through the wheat.

Afghanistan had a spirited end to their adventure, agonising neutrals with how close they came to knocking over India, then Bangladesh, then Pakistan. Each time they bowled and fielded like demons but were undone by brittle batting, along with too much of a tendency from bodybuilding captain Gulbadin Naib to believe that he was the solution in whatever moment presented itself. An off-field shambles hadn't helped: Asghar Afghan sacked as captain in a political dispute just before the tournament, wicketkeeper Mohammad Shahzad sent home as 'unfit' despite having been equally unfit every day of his career, and bowler Aftab Alam sent home after allegedly sexually harassing a guest at his hotel.

Bangladesh stayed well in the mix thanks to earlier wins over South Africa and West Indies, and there was a buzz in the way they cruised past 300 both times. Historically Bangladesh had scrapped upsets but these were the wins of an equal. Shakib Al Hasan was imperious with 606 runs and 11 wickets in eight matches. Losses to India and Pakistan were missed opportunities, as was an early wafer-thin loss to New Zealand and a washout against Sri Lanka. It was tempting to view the campaign as a coming of age but really this was the peak for an experienced core of players. You couldn't assume that Bangladesh would have a better chance four years down the line.

Then there was Pakistan, the team that refused to let you avoid its stereotype. Erratic. Mercurial. Bowled out for 105 by a team that scraped into the tournament as the last-placed qualifier, days before smashing 348 against the best in the world. Nearly beating Australia, meekly folding against India, towelling up South Africa and New Zealand to open the finals race. Crawling past Afghanistan, blasting past Bangladesh. They finished level fourth on points, that flogging by West Indies denying them a semi-final by net run rate. England would leap to third. New Zealand, who had spent most of the comp on top, squeaked in fourth.

The final shift in the arrangement came via Australia and South Africa, a dead game against an evicted team. It would prove decisive. The top team's semi-final would be in Manchester against New Zealand, a side with a rich history of choking against Australia. The South Africa game was also in Manchester, meaning that the Australians could have the advantage of staying put for a few extra days to prepare. Except they lost, blindsided by a ton from outgoing Proteas captain Faf du Plessis and unable to handle a big chase despite Warner's fast hundred and Carey's personal best of 85. Instead of kicking back to wait for the Kiwis, the Australians had to pack for a drive down the motorway to Birmingham, facing a partisan crowd at the ground England called a fortress. What's more, this was an England with some mojo back.

Stokes will be remembered as the face of their campaign, but the brave new world they had built since 2015 started with Jason Roy. He always faced the first ball. He was the one who needed the confidence to go full blast even when it had failed the time before and the time before that. He set the tune for the others to dance to. From his debut until the West Indies group match when he pulled his hamstring, Roy had batted 77 times for more than 3000 runs at 6.4 an over. He also got the best out of his partner Jonny Bairstow. In the three games Roy missed, his replacement James Vince played like someone under a vicious hex and England began to lose.

For a couple of weeks there was a lot riding on one hamstring. Roy got back for what was in effect a knockout against India. He bombed 66 from 57 balls, while a happy Bairstow made 111 alongside. The opening partnership was 160, England soared to 337, won comfortably, and got their buzz back. The win was at Edgbaston, giving good vibes about a semi-final there, so they went and steamrolled New Zealand to make sure they got one.

Australia had the opposite turn of fate. In the nets before their last group match, the fast bowlers were going full tilt. Maxwell left the net hurt when Starc hit him on the hand, so Marsh stepped in as the replacement. Cummins was supposed to have finished for the day but gave himself one more ball. It broke Marsh's arm. In the match that followed, Khawaja tore his hamstring. Both were disconsolate, leaving the remaining players shaken. Handscomb had to be drafted straight into the semi-final with no preparation. When they showed up in Birmingham, they found England very much at home, sprawled out on the furniture, advising that the visitors were welcome to stay a few hours but then should probably be on their way.

Warner drew within a run of Rohit Sharma on the tournament tally, but fell for 9. Finch was blasted out by Archer for a first-baller. Smith was more in his element in this sort of fight, battling for 85 to get Australia to 223. But where that might have made England nervous a fortnight earlier, this England was led by Roy snotting 85. Australia's best moment on the field came when he bounced a six off the fourth tier of the grandstand and Maxwell caught it one-handed at long-on. The favourite, the fated, the destined, finally looked like it. In the other semi with India the day before, New Zealand had pulled off what they thought would be the most remarkable result of their tournament.

Chapter 9

The Final Word on Tour

IF YOU'VE WATCHED a tour of England from afar, you know it as a strange, enchanted place. You sit up late through hours that have nothing to do with cricket, lost in the flicker of the screen or the flow of radio, rich with unfamiliar accents and intonations. You see the light shift from a particular grey to a particular gold. You say the names of grounds like a rosary: Trent Bridge, Old Trafford, Edgbaston, Headingley, Rose Bowl, Sophia Gardens, Chester-le-Street. None of it is real. Incantations, not places. You know the comical Enid Blyton sounds of Worcestershire, Leicestershire, Warwickshire, you know the urban heft of Manchester, Derby, Nottingham, but chances are you can't remember which ground is in which city, or which city in which county, and even if you can line up Old Trafford, Manchester, Lancashire, you still don't have a sense of what a place actually *is*.

A name with no face. You don't know if there's a bridge through town with a good view, or the way the cirrus clouds make herringbones high in the late evening light. You don't know how the main street on a Saturday feels after dark, which nearby city they hate, how lonely the station is off the last train. You don't know the cobbles or the concrete or if there are blackberries to pick by the towpath. You don't know what the walk to the ground is like or what you can see from the top of the stand. You don't know where to pin any of those locations on the crooked spud-sack of Great Britain.

Arriving in England for the first time is a bit enchanted too. You watch as the airport train blurs by rows of terrace brick in ditchwater brown like scenery shots from *The Bill*. You hear the voiceover lady's etiquette-school crispness enunciate 'Cockfosters' about 43 times and nobody cracks a smile. You are very aware to please mind the gap between the train and the platform. You read the Tube map for the panoply of ridiculous, surely imaginary, names: Piccadilly Circus, Leicester Square, King's Cross St Pancras, Angel St Islington, Covent Garden, Elephant & Castle.

That's London, then there's the rest. A whole different palette of greens. The leaves and grasses prime themselves through wetter months so that the tardy sun of summer makes them glow, a fat luscious gorgeousness of green like some Willy Wonka fantasy. And that sun, it comes down just as lush on you and on stone and glass and condensation. When you've grown up in Australia, where the hole in the ozone layer hangs above the country like a spiteful halo, and in the first minute past your doorstep you can feel the ultraviolet crisping your skin, you know the difference. In England a pale visitor can walk around for an hour at midday and come in little worse for wear.

England became real for me in the 2013 Ashes. *The Roar* jagged a sponsorship with British Airways, which got me and my uni mate slash cameraman Cam Fink two flights and £2000 cash. That was to cover two people for five Tests over eight weeks. We landed knowing that this was the most frayed shoestring operation possible. From Heathrow at 6 am straight to the Walkabout by the Thames to shoot a video with a crowd drinking morning pints and watching the British Lions smash the Wallabies in rugby. We sank a chunk of our money into car rental and hit the internet to find floors to sleep on.

The first Test was at Trent Bridge, and our first crash spot was a mansion on a slope above the city of Nottingham, a highly unlikely Couchsurfing address. Carvings in a huge stone dated the housing estate to 1820-something, older than the colonisation of our home city of Melbourne. Our host was a genial Englishman in his fifties with a flawless recall of the savings available on meals and drinks at Wetherspoon pubs by the hour or day. All the kitchen cupboards were padlocked to safeguard the wines from his boyfriend, who paced through the house all day sighing to himself and carrying baskets on his hip to and from the laundry. I worked out why when I heard him gulping at a bottle before stashing it back among the detergents.

There were spiral staircases and turrets and modernist canvases and a grand piano and carpet inches thick. Piles of stuffed toys on bright armchairs with six-foot backs. An older bloke was living in a campervan in the driveway, the doors covered in UKIP stickers, and he would come into the house to use the bathroom and tell us the European Union was a conspiracy to ruin Britain. One evening we got back to find an

18-piece string ensemble giving a recital in the backyard, while over a hundred well-heeled townsfolk applauded from folding timber chairs. The boyfriend stumbled across the front of stage in his singlet, heading for the laundry.

Our task was to shoot one video per day, and our plan was to make it the stupidest thing we could think of. We weren't allowed to film inside grounds on match days, so we set up pretend news desks outside on road barriers. We shot time-travel videos that had me outside the ground during a match interviewing me inside the ground from before it started. We vox-popped drunks and toffs and a guy dressed as Steve Smith. We went to Iceland between Tests and shot videos on glaciers and under waterfalls and on an abandoned fishing boat in the middle of a field. Our best moment came after England won at Durham, when a slew of England supporters adapted their 'Guantanamera' theme to sing, 'We're on a shit Aussie sport site. Shit Aussie sport site. Shit Aussie spoooort site.'

No-one had any idea who we were or why we were there. The press conferences were so boring that I started asking joke questions, probably annoying the proper journalists. We were scruffy and didn't appear to do anything during the day, though we were always the last to leave, past midnight, when no-one could see us steaming towards deadlines in Australian time zones. We worked like dogs. I would nap in corners of the press box in the afternoons. We left the lunch tables loaded with three meals because we couldn't afford breakfast or dinner. Sometimes companies would leave promo gifts on the desks and we would collect the unclaimed, presenting them to whichever household was providing a floor. Here, have three dozen wedges of cheese.

Cam and I had a ball. Our second day was watching Ashton Agar's 98 as the last man in, with his nonchalant strokeplay and his adorable shrug-smile when he fell short. The overflow press box was a big old structure on stilts with sliding windows that opened to let in the warm breeze and the sound of Trent Bridge cheering a teenage Australian. Our press passes felt like magic tickets; we couldn't believe that we got to roll up every day of an Ashes series and they had to let us in. We went to Manchester and London and Durham via tiny country inns and the trails of the Lake District and the Edinburgh Fringe and Reykjavik and Sauchiehall Street and the stone walls of Oxford. We found the pub where Bob Hawke set his yard-glass record and tried to match it and I threw up on camera at 11 am. By the end of the tour some of the press types had decided they liked us.

Skip forward six years and I was back in England. Cam had largely gone back to normal life. Now Adam Collins and I were a double act. We had proved ourselves, we could make a living. But the freelance grind still had shades of that first trip. There are no expense claims or rooms in the team hotel like the happy few at the newspapers. You pay your own freight upfront and hunt ways to make it back.

At the World Cup, that meant being at every possible game in a tournament crisscrossing the country. England's size and rail network make this a chance. But tickets are crazy expensive unless you book one exact service. Cue a lot of rushes to stations to avoid getting bilked 150 quid. We had to get back to London almost every night because long-term accommodation in one place is cheaper. Home late from Nottingham, crash for a few hours, up early to travel to Bristol in time for the first ball. Work all day, late train home, on you go.

But you have to be there. It's a bigger risk not going. Plus you're there for the experience. Maybe no-one ends up paying you to work at Pakistan–India, but why wouldn't you want to go to Pakistan–India? Why wouldn't you want to go to West Indies–Sri Lanka? Why wouldn't you want the chance to be there when something memorable happens, or even when it doesn't, to keep gathering information about the game or the ground or the people on the way there, always learning a little more about this strange small part of the world?

But even Adam and I thought we might have taken on too much this time. We were doing our *Final Word* podcast daily, 20 minutes on every match. These were played on Melbourne breakfast radio, meaning they had to be sent by 7.30 pm in London. Matches finished around 6.30. Doable. But I was also writing for the next day's *Guardian*, meaning a deadline that same hour, plus a piece for the ABC, and we shot daily videos for a couple of websites, which the TV rights deal again banned us from filming within the grounds of a venue.

Any given day might be: *The Guardian* live blog for 50 overs, fingers blurring to describe the action and answer correspondence. Gauge the game by halfway through the second innings to start an article. At the last ball, rush out of the ground carrying the kit to find a shoot location on a street corner and nearly get into a punch-up with three blokes named Kevin wearing polo shirts who are committed to immortalising their wanking gestures on tape. Back into the ground to send the video, 15 minutes hammering the article together while emails from the desk patter like rain on the windscreen, record a single-take podcast in 17 minutes with 20 minutes to do it in, send the audio to Melbourne. Out the door as the final per centage point of the upload ticks over, start the sprint to a train station. Finish the second article on the train surrounded by rowdy drunks. File it as you pull into Paddington. Ride the last Tube home staring into space. Rinse. Repeat.

Then there were the Mondays. Yahoo Sport, bless them, had decided on a TV-style panel show to add to our daily dispatches. For reasons best known to them this would be streamed live at 8.30 am London time, meaning script readthroughs from 7 am, meaning an alarm sometime before 6. Granted these are civilised hours for people in blacksmithing or hot-air ballooning, but they're daunting when you've worked 15 hours the day before, got home after midnight, and then have to smile on camera and form sentences. In the early darkness in the moments after that Monday alarm, I was bathed in a particular pain so refined that it was impossible to tell whether it was physical or existential.

Our other job was radio commentary. For the first half of the tournament I was filling in for Jim Maxwell as the ABC representative on the BBC – no pressure. But calling cricket is the best fun in the world. You're the conduit between action and audience, and getting your job right influences how much they can enjoy the game. You get going, you build a rapport with the person in the next chair, and you love it. The work is the preparation. Before any game I wanted to revise everything. Stats and history, achievements and failings, trends on how players contribute, lines from interviews and, crucially, identifying everyone from a hundred metres away without a shirt number. In a two-team series this recognition is easier to build than when the teams change every day. The night before each match was a mess of spreadsheets and browser tabs, knowing 90 per cent of it wouldn't be needed, but that I wouldn't know which 10 per cent would.

In the middle of the tournament, Adam had to build a new broadcast from scratch. The radio rights for ICC tournaments were owned by an organisation called Channel 2 Group Corporation, and those rights obliged it to produce a feed that could be taken by any station worldwide. The only other radio broadcaster was the BBC. But Channel 2 though was a cardboard cutout, a middleman rather than a broadcaster. It was listed in the Panama Papers as registered in the British Virgin Islands under the aegis of the scandal-ruined law firm Mossack Fonseca, with an intermediary in the UAE. At the time of writing it retains the website equivalent of an abandoned house near the train line, a mess of 2000s HTML containing little information except for praise of the company chairman.

'Sometimes you are lucky to come across a rare breed of people who reach for the stars with their feet firmly planted on the ground. Mr Ajay Sethi, is an inspirational individual who wears many hats as a entrepreneur, visionary and business genius,' it gushes. You've probably never seen a website squeeze its legs together until now. 'At an early stage of his already illustrious career, he recognised the importance of digitisation and has used it cleverly ... to intertwine the vivacity of sports along with the glamour of entertainment that is backed by superior technological solutions offering top quality news broadcast content.'

Channel 2 outsourced the production of the world feed to a company named Sports Flashes. But when the World Cup started the contractors were not in attendance. Their radio box at each ground was empty. Evidently they had decided not to bother incurring the costs of travel and hiring broadcasters, and instead had a bunch of excitable India partisans commentating off the TV out of a basement in Bangalore. I could respect the hustle, but their method wasn't likely to satisfy the custodians of the game's finances.

With ICC protestations ringing down the line, Channel 2 scrambled some on-site coverage. BBC producer Shilpa Patel came out of retirement for one last job, which always ends well, and paired with Nigel Walker, the tech-head originally behind *Test Match Sofa*. Adam joined Clive Lloyd, Neil Manthorp and others to commentate. It was built on fresh air and promises. Patel and Walker loaded up a car and their credit cards, driving hundreds of miles each night to set up for the next day. The commentators went unpaid to the point that they were about to strike. The ICC beat them to it when apparently a rights payment in the million-dollar region from Channel 2 got lost in the mail. The crew arrived at India versus Afghanistan to find their accreditation blocked.

Melbourne radio station SEN was one of many that now had no feed. But they did have Adam. He had a crew in Manthorp, Jarrod Kimber, Derek Pringle, Jeremy Coney and Damien Fleming. He made the phone calls, got the approval, got the ICC on board, got the dues paid, borrowed the equipment, and by the time Australia and New Zealand walked out to play at Lord's a few days later, he was on the air.

Such was the shape of seven weeks as relentless as a future robot sent to change the past. I got locked inside Trent Bridge and had to climb out over the perilously spiked railings. An

End Times nut outside The Oval kept wandering into our shot yelling about the Rapture. Adam and I recorded the daily show anywhere – by the boundary at Lord's, on park benches, on a walk through Nottingham, on a bin outside a Clerkenwell bar, on the motorway with Adam holding two microphones. We recorded the India–Pakistan episode with a live audience of a train full of supporters.

We caught blessed rides that saved us using 3 am bus tickets. Picture the BBC's Simon Mann swearing crisply and fluently at an increasingly long string of backcountry Hampshire villages after missing the turn-off to London. Fellow reporters Gaurav Joshi and Bharat Sundaresan in their *World Cup on Wheels* campervan, sitting at the folding table writing articles as we ploughed through the rain from Bristol to the Midlands. In the final weeks we hired a car for otherwise impossible trips. The Women's Ashes had started and we wanted to cover both. After Australia and South Africa finished the World Cup group stage with a night fixture at Old Trafford, we got out of Manchester via a hamburger stop by midnight, taking turns driving and writing through the night, arriving at a rental in Canterbury at 6 am, sleeping three hours, then off to the Spitfire ground to watch Ellyse Perry take seven wickets against England in an ODI before we drove back to Manchester for the semi-final.

That drive summed up the tournament: just stock up on glucose and keep going, knowing the only way through was momentum. *The Final Word* was working. Audiences in Australia wanted to follow the tournament, but not at 4 am. They could wake up to a recap while they made coffee or drove to work. They got the detail, more of the emotional sense of a match than they would from reading reports. The hard deadline meant we couldn't overthink. We were spontaneous and sounded like it. People all over the world started listening.

On the evening that Mitchell Starc bowled out West Indies a few runs short at Trent Bridge, we got onto the train from Nottingham and heard three guys call our names. We had to ask them to wait while we finished writing. They had been following the show. Laurence garrulously led the conversation after a very long day on the cans. He was a left-arm wrist spinner who had played county seconds, and went on a tangent about a dream of starting a left-arm academy with India's Kuldeep Yadav. As we left the train in London we noticed a slight figure in a flat cap – former Australian left-arm wrist spinner Brad Hogg. We made the introductions, and for an hour he and Laurence stood outside the ticket barriers in animated conversation.

None of it was easy. Not all of it was fun. But there were times when it shouldn't have been fun and still was. There were times when it was all energy, burning every reserve we had. A big help was the collegiality of those who know the road. Rival outlets don't mean rival journalists. When someone visits your home town, you look after them, and when you're in need then mostly someone helps you back. The circle goes around.

Remember Rudimental? I heard their theme tune 40 times a day for seven weeks. Before every ad break, over every montage, for the walk-on and the celebration. It was a fascinating song because it had all the ingredients of a banger – emotive register, upbeat synths, a big peak before a drop – while being completely unmemorable. A wallpaper anthem. After those hundreds of listens, after feeling it in my bones, I still can't tell you how it *goes*.

Not a hummed melody, let alone lyrics. I finished the tournament with an appreciation that Rudimental were hustling too.

Other things would stay with us more strongly. The night before the Birmingham semi-final, Merv Hughes bought me a beer. I was on a booze break. But there was my favourite player from when I was a kid, holding court in the corner of a pub in exactly the way you would imagine. My one drink in six months was that beer.

There was life. The night we left Laurence and Brad Hogg in conversation after that Windies game, Adam's partner Rachel told him she was pregnant. A welcome rain-off the next day let them have an evening together, and as they passed by a chemist she thought she might as well double-check. The Second Test, as we later called it, was played in the cinema toilets at Muswell Hill. It was a win.

There was death. The ABC aired a radio documentary by Mike Williams, who had interviewed us months earlier about Dubai. It was perfect, capturing what we'd tried to explain for years about why radio commentary was special. Towards the end, it had Pete Lalor speaking about leaving that tour when his dad had died. Mick Lalor had introduced his son to cricket. He'd been sick a long time, and they both knew that any of Pete's overseas trips might be their goodbye. During Mick's last couple of days he had the radio by his bed, able to listen to his son talking cricket from across the world. The thing they had shared brought them close at the end, a story that Adam and I didn't yet know. I listened to it on a country train and bawled.

I thought again of Davies Street: six years from the couch to the World Cup. The absurdity had hit me at The Oval when

Australia played India. One of the most storied grounds, the biggest teams, the prestige tournament, the iconic broadcaster. Michael Vaughan, Phil Tufnell, Mel Jones, Jason Gillespie, telling the story of the match to who knows how many people, the ground packed on either side of the commentary box. A couple of years earlier I hadn't considered that this might be possible. What really struck me when I put on the headphones that day was that I didn't feel nervous. Didn't feel nervous at all.

The morning after the World Cup final, I took a train to Canterbury to help the BBC cover Australia A versus the England Lions. Adam spent the day at home vomiting green bile, his body pulling a full *Exorcist* as punishment for the punishment he had given it. I got away with a retreat to tranquillity. All day that field seemed an unfathomable stillness, like the previous weeks had been a dream. The final itself, in all its mad intensity, had no right to belong to the waking world.

Chapter 10

Black and Powder Blue

IF YOU'VE SOMEHOW never heard the story of the 2019 World Cup final, you're in for a treat. If you know the story, you know it's worth hearing again. Cricket is a game of sequences, building gradually on one another. The same thing happens for a period of time before one difference shifts the meaning of all that has gone before. The end result is the cumulative effect of the anomalies. As this match moved towards its ending, everything happened. Every anomaly, every variation, one after another. The most unlikely, the unforeseeable madness, came together to make a whole. But it wasn't what a scorecard might suggest: a dull match until a tight finish. The final stanza and the highest stakes are what elevate its standing to the best one-day match ever played, but the skill and tension through 95 previous overs already made it worthy of the top echelon.

A big part of the story was that New Zealand weren't meant to be there. India versus England was the final everyone expected, before the tournament and before the semi-finals. The team that finished top of the group stage had Rohit Sharma with his penchant for double-tons and Virat Kohli with his 41 centuries, leading the batting riches of KL Rahul, Rishabh Pant, Dinesh Karthik, MS Dhoni, Hardik Pandya and Ravindra Jadeja, with the fast bowling of Jasprit Bumrah and Bhuvi Kumar, and the leg-spin of Yuzvendra Chahal.

New Zealand, meanwhile, had stumbled into the semis, with three blue-chip names leading a modest group drawn from a population a quarter of Mumbai's. They had started the tournament well but ended it wheezing. They lost to Pakistan, Australia and England, while captain Kane Williamson carried them against South Africa and West Indies. Bars in New Zealand couldn't show the final in full because a late liquor licence takes a week to process and before the semi-final nobody had bothered applying. And fair enough: when New Zealand were held to 238, the game was India's.

But this was no normal one-dayer. Rain pushed the second half of the match into the reserve day, and the ball swung on a juiced-up surface. Matt Henry and Trent Boult knocked over Rohit, Kohli and Rahul for one run apiece and Karthik for 6. It was 24 for 4. Jadeja nearly stole it with the innings of his life, 77 from 59, but Dhoni's slow batting meant Jadeja had to go too hard near the end, giving up a catch. New Zealand had scrapped to a score, then to a final.

As for England, the country was in a state. Those who follow the game had lived with decades of cricket comedy and had no confidence about seeing anything better. Being favourites only made it worse, because all the good work could go to waste. On the morning of the match, with London steaming beneath dense grey cloud that sapped the tones of all the foliage to a dark pine green, you could taste the English fear of losing. It was as thick as the humidity.

The players were probably in better nick than the supporters. A group psychologist session came at the right time for some. Sharing their anxieties helped. The captain Eoin Morgan was a picture of calm. If London's green was dark, England's blue was light – powder blue, baby blue, cornflower blue. The new uniform was vibrant, optimistic. It lifted the figures wearing it. Those heavy designs of decades past, navy and dark red in thick folds, had dragged down the shoulders of Vaughan and Trescothick, Stewart and Hussain, Gough and Bopara. The new shade with its shoulder stripes echoed 1992, perhaps the last breath of clean air before the great era of angst. The modern team could leave that past behind.

New Zealand's semi-final amplified their characterisation as underdogs, despite having played the semis of almost every World Cup and made the last two finals in a row. Their other cliche was being the nice guys of world cricket, because they managed to avoid being noxious pricks on the field. The praise couldn't avoid condescension, and some of the Kiwis hated it even as they smiled politely.

As far as competitiveness went, there were no nice guys around. They were there to win and had a plan for how. 'Wet-weather rugby' was former captain Brendon McCullum's cross-code metaphor for how they had played in the semis, and they fancied bringing down another firepower favourite the same way. A tournament supposed to feature freewheeling chases of

350 had gone very differently. Lord's had been tough for batting, with slow sticky pitches rewarding graft.

What New Zealand had was the ability to field as a unit of 11. To suffocate batsmen with positioning and saves. Their bowling could tackle anyone, especially in helpful conditions. Even in the damp and gloom on the morning of the final, Williamson won the toss and batted. Make a score, any score. Bowl tight, field like demons. Don't try to outgun them; raise the difficulty and let the situation do the work. Put the pressure on England and squeeze.

Martin Guptill had endured a miserable tournament. Four years earlier he had topped the World Cup runs list. This time around he totalled 167 before the final. He had blitzed 73 in the first match before a streak including 0, 0, 5, 8 and 1, with a top of 35 that was so slow and tortured that it was a benison when he stepped on his own stumps. On his last chance he started with a bit of everything: charging and missing, covering up, slogging from the crease, timing the pants off a back-foot steer for four, all in the first over from Chris Woakes. Jofra Archer got perfect seam movement and was doing the aeroplane celebration after hearing a nick, only to look back at the motionless Marais Erasmus. It was umpiring brilliance, the ball nicking the stiff corner of Guptill's pocket.

Umpire Kumar Dharmasena's finger was soon up for Woakes hitting Henry Nicholls on the back leg, but Guptill convinced him to review and the prediction said it would have gone over the stumps. Perhaps this little victory was the spark Guptill needed. He was trying everything, moving up and down the wicket to Woakes, trying to vary the lengths to nullify the swing.

He uppercut Archer for six over third man, then two balls later utterly baked four back over the bowler's head. At the first shot Archer tilted his head in a half shrug. He and Woakes stayed tight on the stumps, a constricting line, and when Guptill was the furthest back he had been all day, Woakes hit him in front.

He was prepared to walk but Nicholls gestured that it might have been going down leg. It wasn't. The team's review was burned with a start of 29. Enter Williamson. For seven weeks he'd been the man: two centuries, two half-centuries, averaging over 91, to be named player of the tournament when it was over. As the most important wicket, he had the entire leg side left open to encourage him across the line, and three slips with Ben Stokes standing very close at third to account for Williamson's delicate touch.

Archer started him off with a sharp bouncer and a test of his outside edge. Woakes had the ball swinging. Archer tenderised Nicholls' thigh pad, but with too much bounce for Erasmus to do anything but shake his head. The batsmen couldn't get away: 33 runs off the first ten overs. But only one wicket down. Woakes kept it up for seven overs, only once bowling full enough to let Williamson drive, but leaning down in his follow-through to pluck it on the bounce and save four. A cut shot was nailed straight at point. Williamson had two runs from 22 balls.

Having fortified the ramparts, the batsmen expanded. Nicholls timed the odd boundary, playing Liam Plunkett productively enough to have him removed after three overs cost 19. Williamson laced Mark Wood with a cut before starting after the leg-spin of Adil Rashid, skipping down the pitch, lofting over wide mid-on. Williamson's next 23 balls added 25. The fifty partnership ticked by, the team passed 100 in the 22nd over. It had become a serious base.

Plunkett's return was the decisive moment of the innings. Williamson nailed the first ball, but Jason Roy's dive at cover saved it. The next moved down the slope and away from a half lunge forward, a push rather than a drive. Dharmasena shook his head, Morgan went for the review, Williamson shrugged to Nicholls as they met in the middle. The waveform graph showed the slightest edge, and for 30 off 53 balls the key player was gone.

Suddenly Plunkett was bowling one-run overs, taking command as one of the most imposing sights on a cricket field: 6 foot 3 inches of ramrod posture, striding about with his chest out like he'd got lost on the way to the parade ground. Disconcertingly solid. Glutes so powerful that he could use them to snap the neck of a henchman. Even his run to the wicket was upright, tilting straight-legged into his delivery stride. It was like being bowled to by a tree.

He had been dropped after playing the 2007 World Cup as a young tearaway, then made his way back for England by 2015. The overs between the powerplays, the 11th to the 40th, were his domain. Since his comeback nobody had more wickets in those overs. Middle overs usually meant the best batsmen. His World Cup haul was Kohli, Pant, Pandya, Quinton de Kock, Hashim Amla, Mushfiqur Rahim, Chris Gayle and Tom Latham. His most-dismissed included Gayle, Dhoni, McCullum, Jason Holder, Kusal Mendis, Babar Azam, Yuvraj Singh and Faf du Plessis. Of 135 career wickets only 24 were tailenders.

His method was accuracy plus variation, especially holding the ball across the seam rather than along it, so it came out of his hand with a scrambled flight that made its bounce harder to predict. 'In terms of the cross-seam, I can hold it in the tips of my fingers, in the middle of my fingers and way back in my hand, and that's going to come out at three different paces,' he would later explain to Cricinfo. 'I got some more tools in my shed and when I got back in I was still consistent, I could still bowl a 90 mile-per-hour bouncer, but I had more subtlety, and I felt I made those middle overs my own.'

The scramble did for Williamson, landing on the cross-seam and moving ever so slightly away. The length was perfect. Where most of Plunkett's deliveries were on a good length or just back of one, the wicket ball had crept forward. Enough to hint at being full, drawing the drive, not enough to play without the risk of movement. A couple of overs later he bowled the exact same length to Nicholls, moving the same direction into the left-hander and taking the inside edge onto the stumps. The set player was gone for 55.

The infield came in tight for Latham and Ross Taylor. After 31 overs the score was 130. Hopes rested on Taylor, who had three fifties in the tournament and had spent the pre-Cup weeks playing 50-over games at Lord's for Middlesex. But Wood's first ball of a new spell was too fast, down the slope with perfect seam. Perhaps Taylor's groping bat obscured the contact, above the knee, because Erasmus thought a while and gave him out. New Zealand had no review, though the ball would have comfortably cleared the stumps.

Wood closed out a wicket maiden for the 34th over, and it was 141 for 3. New Zealand had to get moving. James Neesham came out denuded of the astonishing flight lieutenant moustache featured in his tournament headshot, and whacked a couple of boundaries off Stokes. He looked good, raising the 150, striking a pull off Wood that was saved by a diving Woakes on the fence. Latham joined in by getting up and under Plunkett, a flip-pull for four, before striding into a checked drive to send Wood through cover.

It was Plunkett again changing the course, working on Neesham for four balls that had him playing back, then easing the exception fuller, drawing a lofted drive with the batsman's weight backwards to miscue a catch to mid-on. A threat was gone for 19. Plunkett finished with 3 for 42 in what he didn't know would be his final appearance as an England bowler, a few weeks before he would be cut from the national contract list as too senior at age 34. He finished his work walking down to fine leg to a standing ovation from the Compton Stand.

With ten overs to go New Zealand were 179 for 5, in desperate need of a big last stanza. But Archer was back to bowl half of those overs, and he was in a mood. He shook up Colin de Grandhomme with a smash to the helmet, reducing him to a swiping mess. Half of Archer's deliveries in the spell were under 130 kilometres an hour, half were close to 150. Even his bouncers varied from slow to menacingly fast, and de Grandhomme couldn't lay bat on either. He was hit on the shoulder by Wood for four leg byes and hit by Archer for one. He nearly miscued to cover, got hit for another leg bye, and was hit again the next over. He smoked a rare full ball but couldn't beat the field, then nearly bobbled one off glove and body to the keeper via the back of his bat. His last three balls from Archer were dots, de Grandhomme throwing his head back as he missed the last slower bouncer. Frazzled, he was out to a simple leading edge from Woakes, having made 16 off 28 through the thick of the slog overs.

Latham also got the barrage but avoided the head knock. He got underneath one fuller ball from Wood to flick it over backward square for six, and was hit in the stomach next ball. Bouncers usually read low on the speed gun, so when Archer was bumping Latham at 149 kilometres an hour in the 48th over, he just had to duck and chew gum.

New Zealand couldn't take a trick. Their most profitable delivery came from Woakes dragging wide and Jos Buttler fumbling it for five extras. Latham chipped a catch next ball for 47. Woakes bowled a beamer but Mitchell Santner missed the free hit completely. Henry cleaned out the last ball from Woakes over midwicket for four, but was bowled by Archer in the last, the top of off stump at 148 clicks without bouncing. There were five singles in Archer's second-last over, two in his last. It finished with a moment inscribed in cricket memory: a team so frazzled by pace and indecipherability that Santner ducked the last ball of the match without attempting a shot, and neither he nor Boult tried to run a bye. The fateful 241 was set.

The vital thread through it all was that New Zealand never got away. Their best over was worth 13 with the five wides. Three others reached double figures. There had been so much focus on England's batting, but this was their best bowling performance of the tournament: Woakes and Wood shutting it down early, Plunkett and Rashid through the middle, Archer at the end. New Zealand had scored 62 in the final ten overs. Archer from the Pavilion End had conceded 22 from his final five.

But 241 could still be enough for New Zealand's plan. That sort of score had been enough for India. It just needed early damage. Which nearly came: first ball of the reply, Boult left-arm over the wicket swinging in to the right-handed Roy. Beating him, thumping his pad as Boult erupted. Erasmus considered and said no, worried about it swinging too far, when the live vision suggested much more of a yes. The inevitable review ruled umpire's call on an image of a ball that was pretty well smashing the leg stump. After a brilliant over, the usually calm Boult was cursing.

Near-misses kept coming. Henry, with immaculate seam to complement Boult, nipped one back up the slope and nearly cleaned up Roy's off stump. He jagged a shorter one down the hill past the shoulder of the bat. But the batsman stayed ready. After five dangerous dot balls Henry erred full and met a straight drive for four. Boult swung a ball through Roy's legs and past leg stump, only to have Roy advance to slap through point. Punch and counter-punch: Henry decking it, Roy charging and miscuing two over midwicket. Boult straight through Jonny Bairstow off the thigh pad to slip, then a half volley and a full toss disappearing through cover.

This was Roy and Bairstow, the demolition duo. In 32 opening stands they averaged 69.46 at more than seven per over, going into triple figures 11 times and past 150 on five of those. Each of them had nine career centuries, and each had made seven of those in matches with the other. No hesitation, no regrets, that was their style. Even against such tough bowling they were still finding ways to go at nearly a run a ball. Henry was driven on the up through cover, then seamed one away from Roy's edge. A loss, a win. That was when Henry was able to repeat the dose, seaming away down the slope as Roy pushed forward, a nick dying through to Latham who tumbled across. Gone for 17.

Out came Joe Root, tasked in this side as the non-boshing player, the sensible one who was supposed to distribute the strike and bat through the day. He couldn't get anything off Henry, blocking and beaten and cracking to the field as he faced out a maiden. Then it was time for the thing that New Zealand cricket loves above all else. Some middle-overs drudgery. Some nothing-ball. Some right-arm-over, lucky-to-be-medium, slower-than-a-secondhand-car, seam-up drudge. Wobbling to a good length, suggesting that an invitation is imminent but arriving at the doorstep mute. Unerringly accurate, dangerously innocuous, innocuously dangerous.

The practitioner was de Grandhomme, bowling the antithesis of what had caused him such trouble with the bat. A creased and crumpled gent who might have just emerged from between the couch cushions, with big friendly features and a hint of an equally friendly paunch. He started with a leave from Bairstow, then a push too early at the gentle pace that nearly lobbed to mid-off. Three dots, four dots, to an aggression merchant with a waspish backlift, ready to scythe through the ball. Five dots, then another mistimed drive, another chip, hitting the heels of de Grandhomme's hands to rebound off his sternum to the ground. The other opener should have been gone for 18.

Henry kept dotting up Root, so tight on off stump that Root resorted to walking at him but couldn't get past mid-on. A whoosh met fresh air. Three scoreless overs in a row. Henry bowled 17 dot balls before he slipped too straight and Bairstow whipped four. Root was helped to the other end but remained stuck against de Grandhomme. Even a wide pie was slammed into the ground for nothing. Root was hit on the pad, but missing leg stump. Charged, slogged, with no shape at all. Completely in his target's head, de Grandhomme offered the tempter, wide and swinging and seaming away even up the hill, reducing the drive to a gentle nick.

England's captain had the repair job, but Eoin Morgan was as loose as a night on the tiles. He cuffed in the air, charged de Grandhomme but missed. Soon Bairstow chopped on for 36, reaching and done by Lockie Ferguson's pace. At 73 for 3 after 20 overs, the team famed for scoring 7.5 an over was barely hitting 3.5. Now it was Stokes fruitlessly charging de Grandhomme, before reverting to blocking a bowler whose six overs had given up 14 runs.

Ferguson was the opposite style. He sconed Morgan with a bouncer reading well into the 140s, leaving a white scuff on the headgear, then in his excitement pinged five wides over the keeper. When Neesham came on, the taller medium pacer making up the fifth bowler's allotment with Santner's left-arm spin, Morgan prejudged that it was time to go. The first ball was wide, and Morgan's cut was a meaty slap with both feet off the ground. Watching from the stands, his top edge had the doomed trajectory of the true miscue, off the bat with a discordant thunk, limping into the air, hanging like rotting fruit about to drop. It looked safe until Ferguson came sprinting in from the point boundary, diving full length to claim it just above the turf.

Abruptly, at 86 for 4, England looked done. Making another 156 on a nice clean batting pitch would have been different, but the struggle had been evident all day. Root had made 7 from

30 balls, Morgan 9 from 22, sucking the air out of 18 overs of the chase in what by rights should have been a couple of World Cup–losing innings.

This is the context in which Jos Buttler should be appreciated. Stokes was battling. Everyone had battled. Buttler walked out and flicked his first ball for two, then patted a single. Stokes got choked up for three dot balls. Buttler got a single from his third ball, and his fourth, then drove his fifth for a couple. Stokes fumbled out an entire maiden and had 10 off 31. Buttler had scored off each of his first seven balls.

'Whilst I was out there I had to massively change how I was playing because it didn't feel very fluent,' Stokes later explained. 'Jos came out and was probably the only player who actually looked comfortable from ball one ... I remember him coming out and straight away hitting a few drives on the up, and I was like, I couldn't even dream about doing that right now. I'd be too worried about nicking it.'

The threat of de Grandhomme hadn't dissipated: in his final over he went through Buttler's gate and missed off stump by an inch, then got an edge short of third man. He finished with an astonishing 1 for 25 off ten overs. The batting seemed to get easier when the main man Boult returned, like it cleared the batsmen's minds. Buttler was suddenly 21 off 22. Henry also became hittable: sometimes a bit short, sometimes wide to the left-hand stance of Stokes where he'd been monstering right-handers. With Stokes scoring a sequence of twos, the equation was 109 required from the last hundred balls. The 50 partnership arrived. After 34 overs, New Zealand had been 141 for 4; England were 137 for 4.

That was when New Zealand had Stokes cold. Buttler worked Santner to square leg. Neesham was right there. You know when a fielder is on the scene so quickly that the runners are in trouble. He had to come around the ball to pick up but still had time if he was quick. Off-balance, his throw scrubbed wide of the keeper. Stokes came safely through.

Henry got back on his game, beating Buttler's inside edge and nearly bowling him, before reviewing for an lbw appeal that was just missing leg stump. The next ball, Buttler tried to take a second run that would have torched Stokes again, but this time got sent back. In between times Buttler was doing things like crouching and stretching way out beyond the return crease to smoke a boundary from what would have been a Ferguson wide, or waiting for the last ball of Henry's day, predicting that it would be a good length outside off stump looking for one more nick, and instead ramping it over the keeper for four.

The ramp shot is the ultimate Buttler move: the absurdly difficult made to look easy by demeanour alone. With conventional boundary riders in place, he wants the untenanted regions behind the wicketkeeper. Yorkers or deliveries back of a length can be hard to hit powerfully in front of the wicket. So he steps way outside his off stump, casual as a Sunday stroll. He leaves his wicket unguarded. While he moves he turns to face the bowler front on, both feet pointing back down the pitch like French cricket. He holds the bat in front of himself like a shovel, facing upwards while angled towards the ground, and lets the ball trampoline off the face over his shoulder, all while continuing his movement sideways out of the ball's path so that his own face doesn't wear the damage. The bowler's pace is enough to reach or clear the fence, in a triumph of efficiency, ingenuity and provocation.

It was the 38th over when the Sky television producer first suggested a tie, asking commentators to tell the audience that a Super Over would be the result. 'Our producer's got a sense of humour,' was Michael Atherton's preface. Stokes was still sputtering along with smoke coming from the exhaust, forcing a couple of boundaries but more often mistiming, including chopping Neesham past his leg stump for another near miss.

With ten overs remaining England needed 72. It took the first five balls for Stokes to get off strike. Ferguson sent down a scorching bouncer that had Buttler bailing out. Only two runs and a wide, and only four runs from Neesham's next over, including a yorker that landed Stokes flat on his face, digging his bat down under his feet just before it could bowl him. The next thundered into his pad for no run.

When Buttler reached 44 from 48, Stokes had 44 from 73. You knew that England needed a big over but you wondered where it could come from. The entire innings hadn't seen an over worth double figures. Ferguson gave up nothing but singles with seven to go, mixing pace with slower-ball yorkers that were unhittable, and a perfect bouncer just over leg stump that Stokes ducked – and then teapotted the umpire when it was rightly not called as a wide. Twice the frustration came close to creating run-outs. Buttler tried another ramp but had to wait for the slower ball and play off middle stump along the ground, another ridiculous shot where only middling it could save him. It was worth four but earned two, Neesham gliding around the boundary into its path, up and releasing in one motion. New Zealand were humming.

The ramp created opportunities for England though. With a fielder back for it, long-off had to come up to mid-off. Buttler aimed that way against Boult, slicing but clearing extra cover for his fifty. Stokes got his with a full toss that he could only dig for one. He didn't celebrate. Buttler had given a bare flip of the bat. 'No-one will remember these fifties if they lose. They will be heroes if they win,' said Nasser Hussain on the broadcast. Boult nailed a yorker and England needed 53 from six overs.

When a full toss slipped from Ferguson's hand, slapped over cover for four, Buttler thought it was the tipping point. Stokes felt the same. 'I remember being out there thinking, Jos is going to win this for us in the next fifteen to twenty minutes,' he later said. Buttler sliced two more to third man as Boult put in a scarcely believable save: sliding alongside the rope with one leg held aloft over so there would be no contact as he flicked the ball back, a matter of millimetres.

Buttler, brimming, had a fresh-air hoick outside off stump at a ball with too much bounce. The next was fuller on the same line but he was already clearing his front leg while moving away, and had to stretch for a huge drive while off balance. The skew soared high over cover point and Tim Southee, the substitute fielder, slid in from the deep. Buttler had made a win possible with 59 from 60 balls, exceptional on a day when no-one else could time a stroke. But as Stokes dabbed and missed at the last ball of the over and couldn't keep the strike, England's lower order had to bat needing 46 from 30 balls.

The required run rate through the last ten overs kept going up. From 7.2, to 7.7, to 8.1, to 8.4, to 8.8. After Buttler's dismissal it was 9.2. It would climb to 9.75, then 11.33, then 12, then 15. Each ball became an agony for England supporters. A dot as Woakes dabbed Neesham to point. Hope with a single to give Stokes strike, but a dot ball into the pad, then what would have been a wide except Stokes chased it for a single. Another run for Woakes to third man, then Stokes partly salvaging the over with a helicopter whip through midwicket that just beat Nicholls in the deep.

The press box at Lord's is usually quiet. The giant spaceship that hovers so incongruously over the Nursery End of the ground feels hermetically sealed from the ground outside. The only window that opens was installed in the *Test Match Special* box after much insistence, and the rest of the place is pretty well soundproof. There is a speaker system that can occasionally pipe in crowd noise. If not, you can be looking at your laptop in the shining Vogon vault and not notice when a wicket falls.

The other reason you might not notice is because the inhabitants are more or less a species of moss: alive but unresponsive. They attach to their preferred surface and slowly spread out across it. They absorb vast quantities of cakes and scones and cream, but otherwise don't interact with the world around them, especially the cricket. There's no barracking in the press box, no applause for milestones, perhaps now and then a mutter of praise for a century or an 'Oooh!' for a near miss. It is part professional jadedness, part preoccupation with the myriad tasks of the day, part studied indifference, adopting the dispassionate distance of the connoisseur.

On the day of the final in July 2019, all of that went out the non-existent window. The bulk of those present were English, and as the likelihood appeared that England would not in fact manage to win a World Cup, the anguish of 44 years started to bubble through. As the chance of a win revived, emotion came to life. As the absurd theatre of the final few overs played out, the long benches seethed and swayed with swearing, gasping, thumping, with strange non-verbal sounds of astonishment, and even with words of encouragement or desire or supplication directed to nothing in particular in the ancient human way that gave rise to prayer.

The best seat in the house is downstairs. Beneath the press box is a narrow metal gantry where the television cameras set up. There are equipment boxes to sit on, and for a long time there was a small wooden park bench right behind the bowler's arm. A handful of people come and go. Suspended over the crowd, you can hear their responses swell and roll up to you, with the perfect elevation and line of sight, the backdrop of the Pavilion, enough solitude to concentrate, and enough company that it's not isolation.

At this moment it was more populated than usual, a dozen assorted spectators squeezed into gaps and corners. It was Ferguson's last over; the equation 39 to win from 24. The late sun was strong across the pitch. Woakes swiped across the line at a length ball. It was basically a sacrifice fly: either hit a boundary or get enough hangtime to get Stokes back on strike. Latham took the catch. Plunkett marched Entishly to the middle. He could change things: his bowling aside, he was the hitter of some of the least complicated sixes in the game. There was a dot ball as he was beaten, another straight to midwicket. The equation was 38 from 20. Then his pet shot: a dip of the knees and a bludgeon through the same region, using all the strength of his chest and his arms and probably his beard, square of the fielder and airborne for four.

Three overs left, 34 runs to get. For so long Boult had led New Zealand's attack, their most skilful operator, their death-bowling specialist, their calm head under pressure. Now was the point when he started missing his yorkers. Too short first, a half volley that Stokes whipped for four. Too full next, a full toss sent the same way for one. A half-volley to Plunkett, adding two to midwicket. A perfect short ball angled across at Plunkett's front shoulder drew a miss, but another full toss gave up a loft down the ground for two. Only the last yorker landed, keeping Plunkett to an excavated single.

Stokes was on his haunches. He needed 24 from 12. England was losing from here. They hadn't scored more than nine from an over all day. Freddie Mercury and David Bowie were on the PA singing Under Pressure. The only chance was to go at Neesham, who had to do a job after Henry and Ferguson had used their overs. But Plunkett could only swipe a single, Stokes another after falling on his face again hitting a yorker. There was no time. Plunkett cleared his front leg to boom but Neesham had gone outside off, a little cutter coming through at 114 kilometres an hour, lofted long and high to Boult at mid-off. Stokes had the strike, Plunkett had done what he must, but it was 22 from nine balls now. My companions on the gantry groaned, hid their eyes, choked out words that the game was gone.

Stokes had to go too. Neesham had to pay. It was the very next ball. Around the wicket this time, very wide of off stump, another slower ball. Stokes was down on one knee for power, but trying to drag it to the leg side from that contrary line. A year after the final, Morgan spoke to Cricinfo about watching from the balcony. 'I remember the ball being in the air and you can see the trajectory of the ball – and you full well know when you hit it up the hill you have to absolutely smoke it to hit it for six. And it's gone high and not quite as long as he'd have liked, and for a minute I just thought, that's it. It's over, Ben's out, we still need fifteen an over. That's when I thought for a split second we were dead and buried.'

Boult was again the one circling under it. A couple of weeks earlier his catch of Carlos Brathwaite had been so celebrated: the way he waited under such a high ball at long-on, the way he arched his back with arms up to take it over his head, turning with the momentum and carefully treading inside the boundary, holding it safe to win the game. This time looked similar, calm under the ball, arching his back and taking it over his head. The only difference was that the ball was coming at him rather than across him, so his momentum took him backwards instead of in a half circle. He landed on his right foot and had time to balance, flamingo style, and look down to see his boot a couple of inches inside the boundary rope. Safe. Then his left foot stepped back.

As simple as that. Disoriented, the rope on the side of his body that he couldn't see was not exactly where he expected it. His heel landed on the cushioning, tripping him backwards as he threw the ball up to Guptill standing nearby. He might have been considering that throw anyway, and if he'd done so a moment earlier then the catch would have stood. Instead Guptill took the ball and turned to signal six to the umpire. Plunkett pushed through onto the balcony to see the aftermath as the mostly English crowd inside Lord's lost its collective mind.

Neesham could have been bowling for a hat-trick to win a World Cup. Instead he was bowling to stay in one. The requirement was still 16 from eight balls, though, and it still looked like too much. Stokes could only follow his six with one run down the ground. Archer was batting now, with effectively a free hit from the last ball of the over. Anything but a single. He just had to swing. Neesham bowled another cutter, rolling out the side of his fingers at the stumps, straight through off the pad to bowl him. A golden duck for Archer. Stokes sat on his heels again, breathing deep.

So it was 15 from the final over. Six chances to get there. Five chances, when Stokes dug a yorker to cover and didn't want to give Rashid the strike. England were losing this. Four chances, as a wider yorker from Boult went straight to cover. They had dominated for four years but had blown it. The stands were gnashing. Stokes had to change the angles. A left-armer to a left-hander was only going wide, to stay out of the leg-side arc. Stokes shuffled across a pace before the ball had left Boult's hand, then took a further stride. The wide line was now within his reach. A slog-sweep, fully down on one knee, getting underneath to lift it into the crowd. At cover Williamson allowed himself a rueful smile.

Three balls, nine runs. One good yorker would all but close it out. This is where Boult slipped again. A full toss, hip high. It still did the job – Stokes with his stance open couldn't get power at that height as he baseballed it. Guptill had a straight line from deep midwicket. Stokes had been slow to start running after losing balance in the shot, so a throw to beat him back was worth a try. Surely you know this part of the story. Stokes dived full length without looking towards Guptill. The throw hit his outstretched bat, ricocheted away from the keeper, and as Stokes lay spreadeagled, face down in the dirt for the umpteenth time that day, it rolled away from poor de Grandhomme at short third man, like one of those dreams where you try to run but you can't, slogging through sand as he urged his weary legs after it to the line.

Six runs. The gantry gasped, thrashed like stranded fish. All of England, alive. Three sixes in three different ways across seven balls, using every strand of the unorthodox. New Zealand had managed two sixes all day. Stokes knelt with his hands raised as a show of innocence and apology, indicating that he would have followed the convention not to take runs from a deflection he had caused. But when the ball hits the rope there's no longer a choice. Two runs plus four overthrows.

The forensics later showed that Stokes and Rashid hadn't yet crossed when the throw left Guptill's hand, therefore their second run shouldn't have counted. That would have left Rashid on strike needing four to win from two balls. New Zealand could have clinched that game. Or Rashid could have added to his tally of 141 boundaries in international cricket and won a World Cup. England coach Trevor Bayliss later spoke up for the umpires. 'It was unfortunate for New Zealand. But 99 per cent of people thought it would be an extra four runs and so definitely six in total. Ask any cricketer who says they think it should have been five, they're almost lying. How many times have we seen someone go back for a second run and then there's an overthrow? It's three. Who goes back to check when the ball was released? First-class cricket, they just say two plus one and on we go.'

Three runs needed from two balls, then. A moment ago Boult had a comfortable buffer; now he was the one at a disadvantage. Almost any ball would be a run – the non-striker could sprint regardless with another wicket in reserve, while Stokes could make his choice if there was a chance to get there and back. Hitting down the ground all but guaranteed that the throw would come to the non-striker's end. If there were one and a half runs in the shot, he would take them.

When the ball came it was short of a yorker length again. Stokes was backing away, looking for leverage, and somehow hit it off the line of his stumps with his back foot skidding from under him, ending up on one knee and falling forward onto his hands as it rolled to long-off. The throw back from Santner was wide of the stumps but Boult had ample time to collect and get across to beat Rashid home. The run-out kept the scoring to one, although Stokes' fall had caused him such a slow start that Santner could have dismissed him by throwing to the striker's end – by the time Boult took the bails on the replay Stokes had only just left the frame.

Again, it might not have mattered. That would have meant Mark Wood facing the last ball needing one run to tie, and with Rashid backing up they could well have got that single. Instead it was Stokes on strike with Wood at the non-striker's end. Walking out for the last ball of a match, with no chance of facing a delivery, needing only to sprint between wickets, Wood had put on his full pads, gloves, arm guard, helmet, the whole box and possibly dice, when his bat was the only thing the Laws mandated he carry.

Stokes had already decided that he wanted two runs. If he swung for a boundary, he worried that he might miss entirely or get caught on the fence. Getting one run was his insurance policy: with gaps everywhere they were sure to get a single and tie as long as he got bat on ball. Then if he worked the ball sufficiently wide of somebody, there would be time to get back for the winning second run. It was the per centage play.

With that in his head, Stokes couldn't adjust. In normal circumstances he could have put Boult's knee-high full toss on the moon. Had they needed more to win then he would have tried. Instead he patted it straight to Neesham at long-off. A throw to save the World Cup. The pick-up and launch were immaculate. Flat to where Boult stood leaning over the stumps, his hands in front of them to save a split second, taking the impact superbly before taking the bails to find Wood short.

The gantry howled, danced, twirled. We couldn't stand still, the energy torrential. An hour later I would notice that my face was sore from maintaining the same open-mouthed expression. A *tie*. In a World Cup final. Stokes kicked his bat away but he was the only one unhappy. This was the most ridiculous thing anyone there had ever seen. England had a golden duck and two diamond ducks to end the innings. They had been bowled out in a run chase. And they still hadn't lost. Hours ago – years ago – when they had been three wickets down, the TV broadcast had shown a long shot of London. New Zealand commentator Ian Smith had said, 'This is the greatest city in the world. It'll be even better in seven wickets' time.' Turned out he was right.

A Super Over, then. A T20 innovation in a one-day game. All the craft and the build through a 50-over innings, boiled down to a six-ball hit and hope. There was no question that Stokes and Buttler would be the two to bat for England, with one of them the standout striker of the day and the other bearing the kind of outrageous fortune that his career twinned with his ability. There was equally no doubt, at least in Archer's mind, that he would bowl – he was in the dressing room lacing up his boots before Morgan spoke to him. He also had a painkilling injection in his side. Stokes had a cigarette in the shower. Anything to take the edge off.

As for New Zealand, you could ask why they decided to go with Boult again. He was their star, certainly, their best bowler across a career. But he hadn't looked quite right in his last two overs, and Stokes had just faced a lot of him. Ferguson could have brought the Archer-like contrast between slower balls and pace, with the ability to rip through a fast bouncer that could be as useful as a yorker. Or de Grandhomme offered no pace for the batsmen to work with and the ability to make them overhit. If the thought was that an expensive over had got Boult ready to bowl a frugal one, it was astray.

The first yorker he missed on the short side, sliced by Stokes for three over backward point, leaving the batsman gasping at the safer end. The second he got lucky when Buttler found a boundary rider. The third was only six inches off, but Stokes had his one-knee sweep working again, so powerfully to midwicket that a diving Guptill parried it onto the rope. The fourth yorker missed in the other direction, another big full toss, not punished by Stokes, a single to cover. Boult nailed the fifth but Buttler still dug two runs square of deep cover. The last was a full toss again, Buttler easily dinking it for four in front of deep square. What would have been a manageable 11 runs became a difficult 15.

New Zealand knew it would be Archer. He was marking his run-up at the Pavilion End before being told that he had to go from the Nursery. Archer had got through most of his death overs bowling short, varying the pace and the grip. So Williamson sent out Neesham. He wanted a player who could play a pull shot with power, someone who could line up the leg side. At the other end was Guptill, not in form but the fastest between the wickets and with the biggest stride and wingspan. Williamson was the player in reserve. England formed a huddle before taking their places. They had rescued their fumble in the most improbable way. For the first time since Morgan's dismissal, they had a better than even chance to reach their summit.

Neesham. Never lauded as one of his country's best, often called upon for different jobs. This task was miles above any. It helped a little when Archer started outside the tram tracks, around the wicket to the left-hander, called for a wide. Ian Smith had already noted on the coverage that New Zealand needed 16, because England would win a tied over on boundary countback. The players had been briefed by the umpires. From there Archer got it right, and sprung a surprise with a yorker. Perfect length, nothing to hit, and the quality of the delivery created a second run for Neesham as it rolled so slowly towards long-off. Guptill's speed got him back to the non-striker's end.

The next ball was the moment. Outside off but a bit of angle in, full but not full enough, and Neesham had started deep in his crease, had shifted back even further, and had shuffled across just a touch to allow a full clear swing over square leg. It soared cleaner than anything that day, as clean as the crack of the bat, and nearly hit the scoreboard in the Mound Stand underneath Old Father Time. Even the England supporters partially cheered it, cheering the absurdity of this match, not knowing what else to do. Suddenly the ask was seven runs from four balls, and it was New Zealand's game again. It didn't matter how neutral you were at the ground that day, it felt like your insides were all seething to get out. They wanted to watch the game too.

One more boundary would pretty well do it. The next ball was almost the same, and could almost have gone the same way, but Archer had pushed it a bit wider and Neesham dragged it flat. Roy at deep midwicket fumbled his pick-up, and Guptill had already charged up and down for two. Archer, having done so well bowling short, was now doing it full. The fourth of the over he nailed the yorker, Neesham coming across from outside his leg stump and only able to arrow it at Roy, who this time threw to the wrong end where Guptill was already back. Buttler had his arms outspread at the striker's end shouting for the ball to no avail.

Three needed from two balls now, the same as England had faced at the end of the regulation innings. Archer had a long chat with Morgan. Four men in the circle on the off side. Didn't change his yorker field. And bowled a bouncer.

If ever you can find a better planned, better executed, more audacious delivery than that, bring it to me. The short ball really was Archer's thing. It was fast, angling in at Neesham's shoulder. Perfect in height and bounce. Neesham was all ready to step forward and found himself stuck in between. Had he held his stance and opened the bat in his backlift he might have uppercut it to vacant fields for four. Instead he pulled, a flinch response to get something, anything on the ball. It was a thick bottom edge, into the ground at his feet. It could have gone back onto his stumps. It could have gone away behind square for two. It hit his boot and rolled to short cover. Archer was on it. There was only ever a chance to score one. Two runs to win. One ball to get them. Martin Guptill was on strike.

The professional runner had done his part. He had got his team their twos, four times in the over. Perhaps they should have run for another on the fifth ball anyway, with Guptill calling from the striker's end to draw Archer's attention there. They might have spooked an overthrow in the heat of the moment, but even if he'd kept his head and run to the stumps, that would have meant a change of batsman. If you ever wanted a player to get you two runs from one ball with no second chances, surely that player was Williamson.

But no. It was the final verse in The Ballad of Marty Guptill. His sloped shoulders and tall-man hunch, his hangdog expression and jutting jaw. On the field Guptill always looks like a depressed PE teacher; he doesn't know what to say to his wife at dinner anymore, and his tackling has got a bit too aggressive with the kids in the football warm-ups. At the World Cup the gloom of months had followed him. There had been the odd sunray – his blinding catch of Steve Smith, his run-out of Dhoni – but the rest was storm cloud. First-ball duck against Afghanistan, first-ball duck against West Indies, kicking his stumps while taking off for a run against South Africa.

Early in the final there was that hint that his fate might have turned – a couple out of the middle, the umpiring reprieve – but he was done in all the same. He was the one who burned the review, then had to watch Taylor's wicket. For the Boult boundary snafu he was the one looking hopelessly on, calling for the relay, Cassandra ignored. It was his throw ricocheting off Stokes, taking the right option and punished for it. His was the diving save in the Super Over that failed, feeling that ball slip off his palm rather than stick. And now this. All that waiting, all that running, and after being the first player to stop batting that day, he had to be the very last to face a ball. One chance to change everything.

He stood, heaving breaths in a search for calm. Archer and Morgan had another conference, this time changing the field. 'He's gonna bowl short. He's gonna bowl short!' rasped Ian Smith on the broadcast.

'The field says short,' agreed Hussain.

'He's gonna take the pace off it, and Guptill's gonna wait for it. Now, is he gonna take the pace off it? This is the moment, folks. Archer to Guptill. Two to win!'

It wasn't short.

Archer arrowed in at Guptill's heel. Right-arm over to the right-hander. If the batsman had moved his foot it would have been a wide. He put his bat there instead. If the contact had been softer he might have bought more time. It wasn't. The ball rolled fast at Roy, third time lucky for him to pick up and throw to the right end. It came on the bounce, making Buttler come out to the batting crease. He collected and went for the stumps in one motion. In the replay or the freeze-frame he lives forever, body outstretched in profile, glowing in the late golden light, a powder-blue angel. His front knee pointing to the stumps, his one gloved hand reaches out to spark their lights with star-crossed Marty eternally mid-dive and nowhere near.

Buttler is the one who knew first, the one who told the rest of us, up and running in the same movement, sprinting as though trying to outrun this happiness, this delirium, just for the pleasure of having it catch him again. He knocked over two of the stumps as he went, throwing the ball up, then one glove, then another, twinkling away in little flashes of light from the tumult of his teammates pursuing him. From high in the stands they were a flock of birds wheeling, a detonation of joy.

Having made it to backward point for reasons only he knows, Archer lay alone, swinging his arms and thumping the turf. There is a shot from an overhead camera where he's the only one in the frame, an emptiness in all that crowded space. For a moment he is a freestyle swimmer across a deep green sea. Then he is standing and turning and throwing his arms wide as nine teammates swoop towards him in a Flying V. Four others are consumed in paired embraces. Seven clatter into him, engulfing him amoebically, while Root and Bairstow gallop past to the stands to end up in their own clinch. Wood pulls away to chase them, then turns and runs back, wanting everything at once.

Stokes was flat on the ground, his natural state. An earth sign. He had been out patrolling the boundary around from Roy. 'I just broke down. I slipped, fell over, and just starfished on the floor,' he said later. 'I had Mark Wood's glasses on, and I broke them. Didn't quite know how to react. Then as I got up off the floor, everyone was over the furthest corner at Lord's. I had to sprint a hundred yards over to them. It was pandemonium. I can't really remember what everyone was doing.'

He found them at last, winding up in another of those mashing hug-puddles with everyone available. The footage and the photos catch one more perfect image. Archer is alone again, on his knees, looking down between them at the patch of grass that has changed his life. Rashid runs up to hold him, leaning down, and Archer is laughing, laughing, his smile simply beaming and his eyes closed in rapture. Rashid pats his face and leaves as Stokes walks up behind, leaning down with a huge hug around Archer's shoulders: the two who really made this happen, twinned forever.

Bayliss spoke later about looking back at video from inside the rooms, with his players and staff 'jumping around like schoolkids. That said a lot to me about how much it meant, not just to the players out in the middle but to those who went before them. But then after only five or ten seconds I walk back inside. I just needed to be alone, to get away from it. Relief – that was the feeling. It was just such a relief.'

Cricket is a game of sequences. If you look back over all the filaments of cause and effect that had to build together for that final result, there are a million ways that would have averted it. Coming down to a margin of zero runs, the difference between two different worlds hinges on each of those million intersections, all the way down the line. Stokes with his 84 not out was celebrated as the man who won England the World Cup. Really, he was feted because he was a conduit, the bearer of outrageous fortune. There was the six he hit and the two bestowed upon him, and in human societies the fortunate can do great deeds. We prize them more highly than any.

Buttler's role has been a little overlooked. He kept the chase alive. But this match wasn't about the best player, it was every contribution. Roy's 17 was vital. Ferguson's wickets. Without those who chewed up overs, the finish wouldn't have won Stokes the plaudits. The outcome materially changed the content too. One run the other way, and Root and Morgan would have had a lifetime to agonise. Instead someone else gets to. Archer could have been the bowler who lost a World Cup with a wide on his seventh ball. Or the one who took a wicket from his eighth for an even better finish.

Spare a thought for Jimmy Neesham. The player who looked like he was going to drive a bigger total with the bat, but was undone. Missed the run-out that could have ended Stokes. Bowled that second-last over when the specialists had been run dry, got the wicket they needed, then was cost the wicket they needed even more. Sent in the throw that saved the game the first time around, and was the batsman who did almost everything required at the last. 'That hurts,' he wrote after the game. 'Hopefully there's a day or two over the next decade where I don't think about that last half hour.' You could imagine him years later replaying his pull shot, visualising the contact, miming through the air as he walked down the hall for a glass of water as the clock ticked late. The next day he posted one more line. 'Kids, don't take up sport. Take up baking or something. Die at 60 really fat and happy.'

New Zealand were a special form of unlucky in the final, but were lucky to be there. Their draw built perfectly from easy to hard, they had plenty of fortune in their three close wins, their washout with India gave them a point without risking a loss. They got walloped by the other finalists but finished fourth by the wafer of two enormous net-run-rate anomalies. The rain in their semi-final played into their hands. Losing the final on boundaries was nonsense: runs and wickets are cricket's currencies, not the manner in which runs are scored. Hitting two sixes is no more skilful than hitting six twos. Awarding the team with more wickets would have been fairer, a shared result would have been fairer, another Super Over would have been fairer. But the regulation had sat there for a long time without anybody noticing, much less asking to amend it.

After the way that the press box had rocked and heaved, it slumped into a state of blissed relief. Professionals who didn't know that they cared anymore had found that they definitely did. People who had never believed it would happen were digesting the opioid truth that it had. Derek Pringle in the 1992 final took 3 for 22 off ten overs and was stranded on 18 when his team fell around him. Now he was wearing a new England shirt with his name on the back, beaming. Watching the players do a lap with the trophy, waving, the radio broadcaster John Norman leaned up against a window frame and stared out mute, occasionally sort of pawing the air like a sleepy cat. After a day of speaking he was completely out of words.

Adam and I recorded our podcast on the camera gantry, empty now, as the post-match formalities and festivities unfolded below. We spoke though we had no idea how to describe it. We felt like our brains had been scoured. Even after a lifetime of watching the game, how could we have seen what we had seen?

It would be remembered for the strangeness: a 100-over game that took 102 overs, preceded by a one-day game played over two days. It would be remembered for the way New Zealand accepted a raw deal. For the thick gold light smothering the final eruption, those flitting figures in powder blue, baby blue, cornflower blue. A year later while I was writing these memories, a man I've never met named Matthew Share messaged me. 'I think I left a piece of my heart and brain out on that pitch, even though I've never been on the grass at Lord's. But I look at it now and it's like part of me is constantly still there. It makes feelings I am not entirely familiar with course through my body.' That was the magic, the feeling worth holding: when every possible thing that could have happened did happen, and nobody had the faintest clue what was about to happen next.

Chapter 11

Ungreased Wheels

O N THE MORNING after the World Cup final, two cricket teams trotted onto a field. It was a Monday, and it felt like one. A decent sun shone on nobody, a bare scattering of old stagers in the stands. Across England, cricket people were sleeping off the celebrations or lying back to process the euphoria, perhaps sparking a post-action cigarette. After the chaos in London, Canterbury was another world.

Players wore traditional whites with untraditional numbers on their backs. Australia A and the England Lions were the reserve teams of red-ball players who had been nowhere close to a World Cup squad. Most of them wouldn't get any closer to the Ashes. We were broadcasting it on the BBC in the absence of anything else to do, but nobody, nobody was paying attention.

Two months of World Cup was followed by a whole nine days without men's international cricket before England would return to Lord's for a Test against Ireland. The schedulers had used the gap to stage this, a worthy sort of match for which an audience was immaterial. It didn't feel coincidental, then, that the Lions would be followed by four days of the Women's Ashes Test in the distant and hardly bustling town of Taunton. The women's multi-format series was underway, with its ODI component having run in competition with the World Cup. Three T20s would overlap the Ireland Test and finish before the men's Ashes. In between, the women's Test centrepiece could only be described as having been slotted in.

The women's one-dayers had been staged with a shrug of the shoulders. No-one trying to sell a series would start it with two midweek day games in Leicester, a city so far below the radar that it's in danger of being collected by a power line. Attendances were paltry, atmosphere flat. They felt like practice sessions and England played like it, shovelling sacks of wickets Australia's way and being flattered by scorebooks that made the chases look closer than they were.

The third and last one-dayer was England's crowning embarrassment: sending in Australia under cloudy skies to concede 269, then collapsing in sunshine for 75. Ellyse Perry started her day with seven overs aimed at off stump, swinging the ball into the pads and seaming it away from the outside edge. She finished with 7 for 22, the best by an Australian woman in the format. Few compatriots were there to see it. The men had finished a World Cup group match after 10 pm in Manchester the night before. The women started at 10 am in Canterbury. Opposite corners of England, 260 miles apart, no way between them but driving through the night.

Playing a single Test was a recent peculiarity. England first played Australia in a women's Test series in 1934, and had done so at least once a decade since. Until 1998 these were in series of three Tests or more. From 1998 to 2005 the tours dropped to two Tests but increased in frequency. When the International Women's Cricket Council was absorbed by the men's ICC, with member boards absorbing their local women's boards, Ashes Tests dropped to one per tour. A brief burst did see India play five Tests, South Africa two, and Netherlands one, all one-offs, but no-one outside the Ashes has played one since 2014.

That was the year when England brought in women's professional contracts, and boards started to be nudged and shamed into better funding. Some even recognised the financial case – that broadening a sport's appeal means more spectators, more participants, more airtime, and another team for income. Making the investment was easier for the rich boards in India, England and Australia, but even they still don't want women playing multi-day cricket, domestically or internationally. The matches take longer, cost more to stage, and T20 is easier to market and sell. So the same administrations that routinely refer to Test cricket as the pinnacle of the game, the true test of a player, the original and the best, will happily confine women to formats that by their own definition are lesser.

That restriction then creates a circular logic. Playing a series of Ashes Tests wouldn't make sense when women don't play red-ball cricket at any other time. The premier formats of their game are 50-over and 20-over cricket, by design. Hence the multi-format series, where the forms of the game in which these players are expert decide the trophy. One Test remains because boards want the marketing power of the Ashes name, which would falter without a link to its Test history, and because the players want their rare chance to play the format that they've been told for a lifetime is the best. So they're judged on skills that they never get the chance to develop, with their performances inscribed as a Test record that will stay with them forever, from matches that the luckiest get to play twice every four years.

The one upside is that every Test has a lot of debuts. Amy Jones and Kirstie Gordon got their caps for England, Sophie Molineux, Ashleigh Gardner and Tayla Vlaeminck for Australia, with Gardner becoming the country's third Indigenous Test player after Faith Thomas and Jason Gillespie. Their reward in Taunton was a dour sky and a turgid pitch, another of the issues that dogs the game. Pace and bounce are conducive to good cricket anywhere, but they're especially important in the women's game given the bowling speeds are lower. Instead, with women's matches bumped down the priority list, they most often get used surfaces that are too slow for either bowling or shot-making to flourish.

Australia had an equal to the challenge in Perry. Her recent bowling triumphs had pulled focus from the fact that at this point she had turned herself into the most reliable and consistent bat in the world. She didn't have the attacking consistency of strokeplayers like Alyssa Healy or Beth Mooney, though she had gears and had been a clean six-hitter since the start of her career. What she had over anyone else was technique, calm, and apparently endless patience. In limited-overs games she would simply bat through the available overs, lifting her boundary rate as she went. In her rare Test appearances she could bat on without limits, so she did.

Healy initially forced the pace with a fifty, but after her the day was Perry's. The all-rounder batted through to stumps with Rachael Haynes, then on to 116 the next morning, at the majestic crawl of a cruise ship coming in to dock. For hour after hour she soaked up the bowling, knocking singles, dinking the odd full toss to the fence, occasionally stirring to greater ambition with a characteristically crisp pull or steer or square drive from pace. She and Haynes, with an even slower 87, were out before rain came at lunch on day two, but Australia batted on to 420 just before lunch on day three. The chance of sparking up the joint was now remote.

The problem from a spectator's perspective was Australia being ahead in the series. Batting out half the match at 2.7 per over didn't hurt the visiting team. Under the system of the time, each white-ball game was worth two points, as was a Test draw. A Test win was four points. The Australians were leading six points to nil, meaning a draw would see them retain the trophy. Giving England a chance to win was the only way of putting the Ashes in play. Right from the start the visitors had every incentive to avoid risk.

More bewildering was that England played with the same lack of urgency. For them the situation was even simpler: win. After that first innings they had one path, however remote, to victory. With five sessions to complete three innings, England had to race to the follow-on of 270 and declare 150 runs behind, putting the onus on Australia to bat and set a chase with enough time left over to bowl England out. The visitors would have the advantage but it would leave England a chance. Instead England crawled to the follow-on. Two of their best hitters, Natalie Sciver and Katherine

Brunt, combined to blot out 27 overs for 57 runs, then claimed the Australian bowling had been too good. They declared just before lunch on the last day, too late and beyond prayer.

That left Australia to write a final anticlimax. They could have come out swinging, piled up the lead, and at least had a shot at bowling out England in the final session. Instead Perry and Meg Lanning went as placidly as ever. The captain had adopted the steely joyless approach of the 1950s, telling her team that dominance in the one-dayers had earned them the right to secure the trophy without giving England a chance. Even with about 45 overs to go and nearly 250 in front, Lanning didn't want to send England back in.

Of course rolling them wasn't likely on that placid pitch but the start of a collapse is only ever a ball away. Fear of losing can do strange things. In a final dearth of imagination, the draw was agreed with Perry on 76 not out. A chance at twin Test centuries is exceedingly rare, even in a non-contest. But Perry batted through that innings as sedately as the first, and wasn't even sent word to line up a few boundaries in the overs leading up to the handshake.

Both sides had talked a good game about positive and entertaining cricket, and both had abandoned it as soon as the umpire said, 'Play.' You could only put it down to this sporadic Test outing groaning under its weight of significance. With so few opportunities in Test cricket nobody wanted to risk her wicket. No captain wanted to be embarrassed. It became a collective drawing into shells, even the side with everything to lose preferring the steady path to a safe result. Everything showed up the disadvantage that organisers have baked in.

The T20s were far more joyous, the format where these players are most firmly backed. The Australians were stung by the negative response from those of us covering the Test, with Lanning especially displeased that her post-match press conference had that focus. It wasn't the triumphant moment that a team retaining the trophy might have anticipated. There was also the factor that a clean sweep of the T20s could still see England tie the series on points. This had happened in 2017, when the Aussies secured the trophy at North Sydney Oval, celebrated like they meant it, then travelled to Canberra and lost the last two games. They had been furious, and vowed not to slip up again.

The culmination was Lanning taking out everything on England across 19.1 furious overs. Her previous knock in the Test had been 21 from 58 balls; this one was 133 from 63. The ground was Chelmsford in Essex, a venue that had come to be known as a fortress for England's women. Lanning ransacked it. She matched on-side aerial launches with off-side rasps along the ground, mixed up with a straight hit that nearly took out a gantry cameraman. Her shot for the hundred was an outrage, walking outside off stump to Anya Shrubsole's wide line, crouching in wait, and using a double-wristed flick with a horizontal bat to deposit a length ball over square leg for six. She finished with the record score in women's T20s.

England didn't get close, nor at Hove where Lanning was 43 not out in a simple chase. They managed a consolation win at Bristol, where Perry's unbeaten 60 got no support in a gettable chase. When spinner Sophie Ecclestone won a leg-before decision, it became the first time an English bowler had dismissed Lanning in a T20 since 2015. But the slip-up cost nothing but annoyance. Australia were handed the trophy that night and got to soak one another in champagne. The straitlaced Lanning didn't enjoy that part, and spent her post-play interviews wrapped in a towel to ward off the chill. Not every summer night in England is created equal.

It wasn't really a gala moment. There was a podium and some shiny streamers but it felt like what it was: a Wednesday night in Bristol. There was that lack of care in scheduling again, with the men's Test starting the next morning a couple of hours away in Birmingham, limiting to a handful the people who would or could make the effort to be at both. You wondered whether the women's Ashes would be better off splitting from the men's, held in alternate summers. Since 2013 the boards had combined them so that the hype from one would boost the other, but this time men's cricket had only been a hindrance.

It was notable as ever how distinct Australia's women were from the men. They were never the team whose behaviour was described as a national embarrassment. Women cricketers had never been caught on camera cheating. They weren't the ones who had used homophobic slurs, been punched out at nightclubs, shown up to games pissed off their heads, failed their drug tests, hung out with bookies, or toured apartheid South Africa for blood money. They had been models of professionalism long before being paid for it. They had won ten World Cups across two formats and would soon add an eleventh, and the contemporary team had won two Ashes in a row in England where the men had lost the last four.

The women had achieved all of this without the supposedly essential aid of abusing opponents on the field. They had been decent, respectful, and high achievers. They had done the right things for decades and were still a distant second in consideration. The squeaky wheel gets the grease. And so the Australian women's cricket team rolled soundlessly on into another cold quiet winning night.

Chapter 12

The Drawing of the Three

A FTER THE WOMEN'S Test and before their T20 finale, an entire herd of Australian men's players migrated across the plains of Hampshire to gather for a final selection rodeo. We were back at Southampton, the previously discussed weirdo ground dumped out in the middle of the country like some failed amusement park. At one end sits the club pavilion within a sort of castle made of corporate boxes, while spanning the other end from wide long-on to deep extra cover is the Hilton.

Because the hoteliers didn't want to waste space with a media centre that wouldn't be used for much of the year, the method instead is to briefly encamp media in the hotel. Instead of stepping into a commentary box you call the action from a King Deluxe Room with Pitch View Balcony, often with the bed still there in a corner, which is helpful for a restorative nap during a long innings. A conference room converts for the press, scaffolding unpacked from behind a huge curtain into tiered rows. At sparsely attended outings no-one bothers with the scaffold, just a dozen desks pulled up to the front. Sealed floor-to-ceiling windows magnify the light to roasting intensity and the westering sun creeps into the room as the day wears on, forcing journalists to edge backwards like caged vampires in a *Buffy* episode.

Assembling this Costco-sized squad of Australian players was a new idea that had been put in place by high-performance manager Pat Howard before he was punted from his job the previous November. It involved every likely Ashes candidate from the World Cup, the reserves tour that had been running alongside it, and from English county teams. Normally an Ashes squad of about 15 was announced weeks in advance. This time the 25 would play off for a squad picked less than a week before the first Test.

Initially this raised the tasty prospect for nostalgia fiends of Australia playing Australia A, echoing the mid-90s when the national second XI became a popular underdog in a couple of ODI quadrangular tournaments. As a forthright Toyota-themed banner at the MCG phrased it, 'Australia plays with itself. Oh what a feeling.' The A Team then had players of the quality of Merv Hughes, Michael Bevan and Damien Martyn, and the theory goes that national captain Mark Taylor was so irritated by home crowds barracking against his side that he sabotaged Australia A for the tournament final by 'promoting' their best bowler Paul Reiffel to run the drinks for Australia.

Reprising this structure in 2019 would have given a sense of the likely preferred XI and given the others a chance to impress against them. Instead we ended up with a more boring formulation. Usman Khawaja was out with injury so the other 24 were split into two fairly even teams. It was hard to read the Hick Twelve as anything but a group of felons in a murder cult, but they turned out to be cricketers led by Tim Paine with Steve Smith's batting, James Pattinson's pace and Nathan Lyon's spin. The other side had David Warner and Australia's premier pace grouping of Mitchell Starc, Josh Hazlewood, Pat Cummins and Peter Siddle.

This move to all-Australian preparation wasn't because only Australians would do. It was the lack of a viable alternative. Once upon a time a tour used to take in all 18 county sides to maximise its profit. Gradually the number of matches dwindled, though there were still some strong contests which helped with acclimatisation and Test selection. But on the Ashes tours leading up to 2019 the Australian and English boards had been involved in a reverse arms race, each host arranging ever-weaker opposition to deny its rival useful preparation.

England would offer whichever county teams were inspecting the footings underneath the second division; Australia would counter with a two-day trip to tackle an invitational XI in Alice Springs. Even the struggling counties would save their decent bowlers for domestic matches while preparing flat tracks and asking Australia to bat to ensure four days of gate receipts. In 2015 Essex opened the bowling with the seamers of New Zealand batsman Jesse Ryder, while minor counties seamer Richard Gleeson debuted for Northants with no shirt number, a pair of black trainers, and a captain who had to ask him what he bowled. By 2019 it made sense to control the quality of your opposition. The match still ended up feeling like a weird intra-club hit. The venue didn't think it was worth the bother of their ground staff, allocating a practice pitch on the south-eastern edge of the square. Any chip off the pads to that side would carry the fence for six, while shots to the other side had to cover an Olympic sprinting event to roll for four.

There were no hotel rooms for the broadcast either: a game of this calibre saw the radio crew banished up a fire escape onto the hotel roof with a couple of stools and a case of water, where we rigged and adjusted umbrellas and shades like sailors in an unending fight against the declining sun. In the interests of financial realism I was in the Holiday Inn next door, but on arriving near midnight to find they had lost the booking while everything was full, I had to return to the nicer joint and sleep on Jim Maxwell's floor. Luckily the Hilton has plush carpet.

The surface in the middle was influential too. A strange mess of a pitch, looking from a distance to be made of reddish dirt, stippled with dark thatch that sprouted with pubescent erraticness and enthusiasm. Team management had requested grass cover as a chance to face a moving ball, which had so often been Australia's undoing over the previous six or seven years. This surface made the ball move alright: 17 wickets went down in the first day. The whole show was over less than halfway through the third.

Marnus Labuschagne made 41 in the first innings, and the next best were Starc and Cummins with 14. Mitch Marsh's 29 was the best of the reply. The second go around saw Warner make 58, then Cameron Bancroft put together 93 not out to wrap up the small chase. All up 25 scores out of 40 were in single figures, and another eight were less than 20. The spinners barely bowled.

When chairman of selectors Trevor Hohns announced the squad there were few surprises. Cummins, Starc, Hazlewood, Siddle and Pattinson were the fast bowlers, Michael Neser the sixth in support. Marsh's seamers looked superfluous in that company but he was there as an all-rounder. So was Labuschagne, whose 1114 runs with five centuries that season for Glamorgan were probably no more important than his ability to bowl leg-breaks to support Nathan Lyon. Jon Holland was not retained as a second spinner, while Chris Tremain and Jackson Bird were the quicks to miss out. Nor would there be a reserve wicketkeeper for Paine, despite Alex Carey's cool head in the World Cup.

The parts of the batting order locked in would be Warner to open, Khawaja at three, Smith at four, and Travis Head at five after his breakthrough 161 in his previous Test in Canberra. At six was the near-miracle of Matthew Wade. In November 2017 Wade had been an underperforming wicketkeeper averaging barely 20 from a year-long stint in the team. Once Paine replaced him nobody expected to see him again.

Except that Wade lived out the cliched instruction to dropped players: he went back to domestic cricket and scored a metric shit-tonne of runs in every format. Three centuries among 654 runs in that season's Sheffield Shield, 1021 runs averaging 60 in the next. Another hundred in his next domestic 50-over comp, 843 runs across two summers of Big Bash. That booked his ticket for the Australia A tour, where he opened the batting and ransacked 155 and 117 in a couple of one-dayers, followed by 114 batting at five in the England Lions first-class match. The 155 was the fastest hundred in Australian 50-over history, off

45 deliveries. The guy who couldn't make runs as a keeper had commanded a place as a batsman alone.

That left Peter Handscomb and Will Pucovski omitted as expected, while Kurtis Patterson and Joe Burns joined the select club of players to make a Test hundred and get punted for the next game. At the time of writing Patterson hasn't added to his two Test innings and retains the best average in history at 144. Their hundreds had come in the same innings as Head's in Canberra the previous February. They were marked down for having come against Sri Lanka, but Sri Lanka did fly straight on to South Africa to smash that team 2–0. Burns had dug Australia out of a hole at 28 for 3, going on to a hefty 180 and adding 376 with Head. Patterson's unbeaten 114 was the far easier task after that stand.

Warner's return had created a log-jam at the top. Three openers were vying for two positions, one to partner him and one reserve. Each had a claim. Burns was the incumbent and had also made a hundred a couple of weeks earlier for Australia A. So had Marcus Harris, who had topped a thousand runs in the last Shield season, made a century in the final, and was Australia's top scorer in the recent series loss to India. Bancroft had made two centuries among 726 runs for Durham in the county season before his near-hundred in the intra-club.

For Burns, being disposable was a familiar story. He had debuted in 2015 as an injury replacement and smashed a couple of fifties batting at six. He was full-time at the top of the order by the end of that year and made two hundreds in the home season before his 170 to set up a win in Christchurch after Brendon McCullum scored the fastest Test century. That only bought him the latitude of two poor Tests, dropped in Sri Lanka in 2016. He got back for one match later that year, which let him be a scapegoat after South Africa walloped Australia in Hobart. In 2018 he flew directly from a Shield final in Queensland to Johannesburg to replace Bancroft and was straight off the plane to be among Australia's few decent performers in the broken team that got flogged by 500 runs. He was still dropped for the next tour and most of the home summer. Two Tests against Sri Lanka to close out that season and now he was gone again.

You had to wonder why, especially looking at the basics of four Test hundreds in 16 matches while averaging 40, compared to Harris and Bancroft with zero hundreds between them averaging 31. Perception may have played a part. Burns the batsman could seem diffident, though he had made a success of opening the batting at the Gabba where early conditions can be challenging. He was casual in the field, slouching or strolling with long hair spilling from beneath his cap, face hidden by a beard. One of the more popular videos from the last Shield season was of Burns doing the floss dance in the Queensland slip cordon. People from his Middlesex county days told stories of bomb-site houses and perennially lost keys. He was loose, basically, in a system that lauded fanaticism.

Then there was his health break, when he had called off a stint with Lancashire in May after his medical check revealed he had post-viral fatigue syndrome, a legacy of glandular fever the year before. 'Once I saw a specialist it all made sense,' he said afterwards. 'The immune system was basically operating like it was sick and after a few months of operating at such a high level, your vital organs start to struggle.'

He was cleared to return for the Australia A tour in July, and the fact he was invited meant that his illness shouldn't have been a barrier to selection. Yet at the press conference Hohns said that it 'probably didn't help his cause, going home. It would have been ideal for good preparation to put the best case forward for himself to stay and play county cricket'.

Another factor, substantial but unacknowledged, was giving Bancroft a chance to play for Australia again. Smith and Warner had already gone through their re-entry and begun their rehabilitation in the public eye with their World Cup campaign, and they were walk-up starts for a Test return. Bancroft had never been in the frame for the World Cup, so there was an even stronger incentive to get him his chance at being cleansed in the Test side.

Coach and selector Justin Langer was irritated by that notion, saying it never came into consideration. But it's hard to believe that even unconsciously there wasn't an influence. Langer had coached Bancroft's entire pre-Test career at Western Australia and was the one to collect him from the airport on returning home distraught from South Africa. The general view within Australian cricket was that Bancroft was unlucky to have been dragged into the mess. Until he got a comeback chance, it left an unbroken link between the scandal and the present. At the moment of selection, Bancroft was giving just enough reason to pick him. What if selectors didn't take that chance and he never got close again?

That was the nightmare scenario. As long as Bancroft hadn't come back, the wound wasn't closed. Smith and Warner wouldn't shake the tag of having ruined a younger player who they were supposed to lead. They couldn't have the 'Last Test' field on his Cricinfo profile read 'Cape Town 2018'. The ghost of his career would haunt theirs. A second chance got everyone absolved. If he succeeded, happy days. If his career was going to end, they needed him to end it himself.

Bancroft had a less emphatic claim to an Ashes spot than Harris or Burns. His county runs had come in the second division. His 93 not out was impressive against Cummins, Starc and Hazlewood, though by the fourth innings of that collapse-a-thon the heat was out of the game, and he was facing bowlers who knew they would be picked. They mostly bowled at the body, letting Bancroft hang back to pick off runs rather than challenging him on the front foot the way English bowlers would do. Put it another way: had Bancroft been the player that selectors felt most inclined to leave out, his recent record would not have stopped them.

Contrarily, Bancroft was the first of those contenders to be inked in. Hohns didn't mean to be explicit about that but twice let it slip. 'Desperately unlucky,' he said of Burns and Patterson, 'but of course with the three we've just spoken about coming back in, there was always going to be a squeeze on.' So the three were a job lot, and the others had to take what was left. Harris, he went on to say, 'had a wonderful season back home … so he probably got the nod over Burns in that area.' Meaning the last spot was between Harris and Burns, not between Bancroft and anyone.

Whatever the motivation, the sandpaper three were a trio once more. Sixteen months since they had last pulled on Australian creams and walked out together under dark clouds and the gaze of Table Mountain, they were set to do it again in the industrial Midlands city of Birmingham. It had been a long interregnum full of private conflict. With conflict about to resume on the field, there was a chance of them finding personal peace.

Chapter 13

The Return of the King

M̲ORE THAN ANY sport, cricket is obsessed with form. Discussion of any player for any reason will begin with whether they're in form or out of it. Every selection or omission, where they should bat, how they should bowl, revolves around form. All success is attributed to it, all failure is apportioned to its lack. Form is magic, fey, a kiss on the arse from a pixie. It alights on you like sunlight through the foliage, a momentary blessing until the breeze stirs and it's on its way. The fortunate will feel its fleeting enchantment again. Cricketers must abide by its whim, trusting it like the dashboard Buddhas or Virgins that keep a million buses on narrow mountain roads.

Form does exist: with a finely tuned skill, there will be times when its exponents can't get it right or when they can't miss. But mostly when we talk about form we're talking about results. Anyone getting runs or wickets is said to be in form, anyone missing twice in a row is out of it. This doesn't add up in a game where failure is the norm. History's best with the bat fail two times out of three. Within the normal scope of probability this ratio will fall unevenly. You can succeed five times in a row or fail ten. You can be happy, healthy, playing well, and get low scores, because getting out is likely. We project form because cricket's individual results are so quantifiable, unlike sports where players can disappear into the work of a team. Human minds are geared to recognise patterns. When players pay those patterns too much attention the prophecy fulfills itself.

Because form is seen as so fragile, we worry about maintaining it. The spectator following this superstition puts their faith in preparation. Every practice match for a player is a tribute to the gods, the drip of sweat onto the altar. If someone hasn't played for two weeks we think they're rusty. If it's a month they must have forgotten the game entirely. We imagine them arriving at training as newborns, fresh with wonder. We're upset when players are picked after layoffs that in the normal world would represent a holiday. Any resumption is a comeback. We think a lifetime of practice will evaporate if it isn't constantly, tremulously maintained.

For Steve Smith, David Warner and Cameron Bancroft, though, the first day of August 2019 in Birmingham was a huge unknown. A few weeks is one thing, 16 months is another. They had been playing other forms, but Test cricket is different gravy. Most international team sport is a kind of family reunion, occasional and a bit awkward. In cricket it's the highest standard. For Test cricket, add the weight of significance, the extra attention, the examination guaranteed of you, alone, as a player. Preparation is more important than at other levels, to get the rhythm to succeed by the finest of margins.

On the external wall of the main stand at Edgbaston a huge banner was hung. Moeen Ali and Eoin Morgan left-handedly swatted at unseen deliveries like inmates at the Home for Broken Cricketers, with Moeen in the red T20 shirt on a red background and Morgan in the one-day kit on blue. Chris Woakes was in a white square in his Test attire, doing spirited jazz hands in a bowling appeal. The order of the tricolour had been arranged so as not to be the French flag, which was smart, though red-white-blue was the International Code of Signals shipping semaphore flag for the numeral 3. Mathematically apt. Each square bore a motto. 'We are summer. We are The Fortress. We are Edgbaston.'

English cricket does have an impulse from time to time to mimic Australia. After good players came through the ACB National Academy under Rod Marsh, the ECB set up a National Academy run by Rod Marsh. After Steve Waugh's era of winning everything, Australian coaches flooded the UK. England's bowling brilliance in the 2005 Ashes was planned under Troy Cooley; England's World Cup breakthrough was under Trevor Bayliss. So when their Test team started building a decent record at Edgbaston, the immediate comparison was with the Gabba. The Brisbane ground is sometimes off-handedly referred to as Australia's fortress, but the Birmingham ground was formally stylised as such. England players like Ian Bell made it explicit: 'It's a Gabba-style cauldron – Edgbaston is our equivalent.'

As the meme goes, 'Lord I see what you've done for others and I want it for myself.' But no visiting team had won at the Gabba in over 30 years – people were voting for Bob Hawke and Maggie Thatcher, and watching *Die Hard* at the movies. Edgbaston's streak topped out at ten years, and some of those years hadn't even had a Test. Since being whacked by South Africa in 2008, England had played there eight times for six wins. Four were against India and Pakistan, who struggle in the conditions. Australia and West Indies each had one loss and one rained-off draw where they had much the better of England.

After the long World Cup campaign led by Aaron Finch, Australia's Test captain Tim Paine entered the fray. A direct character, he had no patience for media frottage about Edgbaston as Thunderdome. Despite his playing history there consisting of two T20s against Pakistan in 2010, he was asked if there was a more intimidating ground in world cricket. 'Than this?' he asked, deadpan. 'I could name you fifteen.'

Locally this was taken as a grave insult to Edgbaston's virility. How dare he question the reputation that the place had decided for itself? True Painiacs, though, got the reference: he had played Tests at 15 grounds before starting to repeat venues in the previous home summer. (He had actually added a sixteenth with Canberra's debut, but forgetting that was excusable.) His meaning was that a Test was a Test, no matter the venue. As he left by the stairwell he shared his bewilderment with media manager Brian Murgatroyd. 'What's so intimidating about Edgbaston? We don't play against the ground, mate.'

For Australia, there was enough to be apprehensive about in their own camp. The returning batsmen couldn't be expected to hit their best straight off. Usman Khawaja had never imposed himself on an Ashes series in a decade of attempts. Travis Head was genetically loose outside off stump. Matthew Wade had been dropped as a wicketkeeper for want of runs. Paine had one first-class century in a career dating to 2005. The spares were Marcus Harris and Marnus Labuschagne, without a Test hundred between them, and Mitchell Marsh, whose two tons in 2017–18 were a passing flash in years of mediocrity.

The opposing batting was just as frail. England had spent six years since Andrew Strauss retired in 2012 searching for an opening partner for Alastair Cook, and were beaten to it by Cook's retirement. Number three had lacked a regular tenant since Jonathan Trott in 2013. A *Wheel of Fortune* of contenders had whirred through all three. For this series, Baby John Burgess had read out the names of Surrey grafter Rory Burns and World Cup buccaneer Jason Roy.

Joe Root as captain liked to bat at four but bowed to the Australian orthodoxy of Bayliss that the best player bats three. Joe Denly had got into the national frame as a T20 handyman and somehow ended up in Root's old spot. Ben Stokes was a lock but his best position wasn't clear; Moeen Ali tended to freeze in Australian headlights; Jonny Bairstow and Jos Buttler were wicketkeepers whose attacking batting made them luxury picks singularly, let alone together. Bairstow's Test form had gone off a cliff after a wonderful 2016, but he curled a lip territorially at suggestions he might give up the gloves to concentrate on one discipline.

Both sides were mismatched against the quality of bowling. Pat Cummins was the top-ranked bowler in the world. James Pattinson and Peter Siddle were the picks to join him for the first Test. Mitch Starc was the World Cup's top wicket-taker and wouldn't get a start until the fourth Test. England initially didn't pick their own World Cup champion Jofra Archer, whose red-ball county record was outstanding. Their old firm was established: James Anderson held history's fast-bowling record at 575 wickets, while Stuart Broad's 450 included an Ashes-winning burst in each of 2009, 2013 and 2015. Chris Woakes had 27 Tests to the other pair's 276, but had featured across six years as a skilled swing partner for one or both.

Australia getting knocked over on the first morning had been a theme of recent tours, so it would have been with a deep inhalation that Paine chose to bat. Warner and Bancroft walked out together as the crowd gave them a double serve. The first misfortune was Australia's, Warner not reviewing a hit on the ankle that would have missed leg stump. A bigger misfortune hit England after seven overs. Anderson had been through weeks of injury recovery, sitting out the Test against Ireland in order to be cherry ripe. He managed four impeccable overs before his calf gave way. Before half the seats were filled he was out of the series.

Initially, Broad and Woakes filled the breach. With Bancroft taken at slip, Smith was at the crease in the eighth over. Within an hour Khawaja nicked behind, then the far side of lunch saw a procession of Head, Wade, Paine, Pattinson and Cummins. At 122 for 8, with Smith on 42, Siddle and Lyon were all the company he had left.

The atmosphere was thrumming. Edgbaston does deliver on its promise of rowdiness. The Eric Hollies Stand, named after the man who denied Bradman his 100 average, is the engine room. A long raked terrace of seats bordering the western side, it packs from front to back with a mix of die-hard supporters, day-trippers in group fancy dress, and blokes who just fancy hammering 43 plastic pints and shouting a lot because it's several weeks since football season. 'It was so loud,' Paine said on *The Test* documentary. 'You get to a point with volume sometimes where it's like you can physically feel it.' You can – sound waves are physical. Songs, chants, the eruption at each wicket, all of those rolled down the slope of the Hollies to crash over the field.

Any day at Edgbaston could be like that, but with the tampering story having transformed the Australians into actual villains, the tenor was harsh. Bancroft was surprised by being surprised. 'I knew that I'd had millions of people round the world hating me. To walk out, even I underestimated myself how huge that was. I don't reckon I did block it out as well as I could have done.' People waved sandpaper and chanted 'Cheat, cheat, cheat!' at players coming down the race. They made masks from photos of Smith's tearful press conference, and used the tune of 'Guantanamera' with 'We saw you cry on the telly'. Abuse came over the fence all day, clearly audible in a lull.

During the World Cup, with the dial at about a quarter of the Ashes level, Langer had deplored the jeering as disrespectful. It was an interesting stance given the treatment his Australian teammates had dished out to visitors, let alone Australian crowds. Still, you could understand a coach feeling protective of those under his care, and he spoke of mistakes being universal and consequences uneven. There's a remarkable clip of him eyeballing a bloke over the fence with kung-fu-movie intensity after hearing a Brummie-accented shout of 'You cheating bastards!'

The person best equipped to handle all this was Smith. He had been prescient the previous December at his Vodafone press conference. 'I guess one thing that I've always done pretty well when I'm playing is just blocking out exterior noise and getting on with the job at hand.' Time and again over his career he had shown his powers of focus, narrowed to the cut strip. When he was in that zone he said he felt 'untouchable'.

In Birmingham he was ready. At the reintegration meeting in April he had told teammates about his headspace. 'I've had times throughout the year where I didn't even really want to come back and play, to be perfectly honest. It probably wasn't until I got my brace off my arm a few weeks ago where I said, shit, I'm ready to go. I want to play again.' At the intra-squad practice match in Southampton he and I found ourselves in a lift together one evening. I ventured that he had a big few weeks ahead. The expression on his face was intense, never breaking eye contact. 'I just can't wait to get out there,' was his reply. Playing in the World Cup – sure, that mattered. But it wasn't Smith's natural environment, his foremost domain. His was the Test arena, and now he'd rejoined it.

Getting the job done had long been Smith's specialty. During his temporary elevation to captaincy in 2014 he made a century in all four Tests of a series against India. Since getting the gig full time in late 2015 and losing six senior players to retirement, he'd had to carry the rest. In Sri Lanka in 2016 he was the lone hand. In Hobart when South Africa knocked them off for 85, he was the one unbeaten on 48. Through the 2017 trip to India he kept his side in the series until he could do no more, three centuries in four outings. He saved the first Ashes Test in Brisbane later that year, and dominated the sealer in Perth. Touring in 2018 it was only as South Africa started to get on top of his batting that his team started to lose.

Now after that long exile, from his first hour back, he was being asked to save the day again. It was lucky he had Siddle as a partner in the enterprise: perennially cheerful while up for any amount of work. Nine months earlier in Dubai I'd interviewed Siddle after the team spent a day in 40-degree heat for three wickets. His smile was unkillable. 'I loved getting back out there and getting stuck in,' he'd beamed. 'It was actually enjoyable out there today. You get the ball in your hand, you want to be the one to make something happen.' In Birmingham he was similarly can-do. 'The boys were feeling it,' he said of the moment he left the rooms. 'I was actually pretty relaxed. It was just about build a little partnership, get something going ... All I kept thinking about was just staying in there and get him to a hundred.'

At that stage Smith hadn't even got to his fifty. He did so with a few singles and a leg-glanced four, then stirred for a powerfully pulled boundary off Stokes before reaching the safety of tea. He had batted nearly three hours and played that one expansive shot. From the start it had been seriously hard work. Broad was threatening to go on another of his Ashes tears, seaming and bouncing the Dukes ball viciously. Woakes was bending inswingers off the straight. Smith had to deal with that and the parade of wickets. He had to hold on. While teammates were drawn into edges or beaten on the inside, Smith left everything that was too wide to threaten and smothered everything coming in.

The old Smith who had tormented England in the southern summer of 2017–18 had clicked straight back into place. His usual mannerisms were there before each ball: use his glove to tap his left pad, then right pad, then box. Tap the bat twice behind his foot, look up at the bowler, tap twice, look at the bowler, dip his knees, tap once between his feet, look up, dip his knees, then stand with bat high as the ball is delivered. By then his trigger movement across the stumps had started, letting him come forward or back, or continue across his crease to make the line of the ball whatever he liked.

Bowlers see a batsman move laterally and are drawn irresistibly to his stumps, wanting to target him leg-before. For anyone else it would work soon enough. Not Smith: his hand-eye coordination is supernatural. He just doesn't miss. In 101 Test dismissals to that point he had been leg-before to a seam bowler eight times, including after scores of 199 and 239. If the bowler stayed on off stump, then the ball that someone else might have edged was nullified by Smith's movement. If they went wider he knew it was no threat to his stumps. At Edgbaston he worked a run or two whenever he deemed it safe, and otherwise just waited, just watched.

The only calm part was the scoreboard, it must be said. Smith in person was a sight to behold. He had always been twitchy, but in his time away the tics had swarmed over his body. His leaves became lavish productions, swishing the bat high over the ball in an arc that had people photoshopping lightsabers into his hands. He would swat the bat down afterwards, adding a follow-through to the absence of a shot. He turned half-circles to watch the ball pass by, ending up with his back to the bowler as though emphasising his denial of their work. The moves were erratic, with no particular logic: one side or the other, stuttering down the pitch and turning, talking loudly to himself, waving his arms about, an endless kind of extempore jazz dance in the middle.

Smith was prepared to trust Siddle, who took the first two overs after tea in full. Five times after that Smith took a single from the first ball of an over. Each batsman already had an incorrect dismissal overturned on a bad day of umpiring for Joel Wilson and Aleem Dar. Siddle responded with a series of well chosen drives and sweeps for boundaries in between defending with soft hands and evading bouncers. He would have had confidence from a useful half season with the bat for Essex, with a top score of 60 and a couple of not outs in the 40s to go with his 35 wickets.

Smith kept going with singles, aside from nailing one more Stokes short ball. By the 64th over the pair had forced England to bring on Denly's leg-spin. Siddle took the score to 200. It was already an outstanding recovery. I ran into Smith's former batting coach Trent Woodhill in the stands and asked how his prodigy could be playing so well so soon. 'Sometimes we want to make it more complicated than it is,' he said. 'There might be others who love batting as much, but not more: Kane Williamson would be one, Virat Kohli. Most players can get result-oriented. You want to score an Ashes hundred or whatever it is. To those three guys in particular, the next ball is such a gift.'

After nearly two hours, Moeen had Siddle caught off the inside edge at bat-pad. Siddle's score of 44 was exactly half the partnership. With Lyon to the middle, Smith started going for broke. A pull, an uppercut and a flat-bat whack in three balls from Stokes, but one shot missed entirely, one found the infield, and the other offered a single that Smith declined. He took a deep breath and started to leave the ball again. Farmed the strike once, only went after Moeen when dished up a full toss, trusted Lyon for the following over.

He needn't have worried. Lyon saw out Stokes without worry and even square-drove him for four. Smith, newly composed, launched Moeen for an enormous six over wide long-on. Given so much of Smith's work had been leg-side, Stokes was taking care to bowl well outside off. Smith stepped across in his usual fashion, but instead of covering the line to bring the ball back across his body, he stayed leg-side of it. He twisted his bottom-handed claw grip around to turn his bat face out from his body, and stepped into the ball to cover-drive Stokes inside-out for four. From 99 to 103. He was restrained in the moment, closing his eyes, opening his arms, and waving briefly to all parts of the ground even if their allegiance lay against him. The trademark of his hundreds was there, his blue-grey headband soaked with sweat. He had taken fewer innings to reach a 24th Test ton than anyone bar Bradman. The third act was to come.

With the formalities done, fuel dwindling, and the knowledge that a last-wicket partnership can be a fleeting pleasure, Smith went from stealth cruise to ram-raid. He bobbed and weaved around the crease, no longer creating the line that he wanted to defend but the line he wanted to attack. Stokes and Moeen first, but accelerating when Broad and Woakes were brought back in tandem. Dipping at the knees to get under the ball, Smith would line it up and launch it over the leg side, the full range from long-on to fine leg. England threw everyone back and tried to get Lyon on strike; Smith ignored that and waited for the balls he wanted to smash to the fence or over. Every boundary stung England as the score soared past 250.

He had been in the nets with the tailenders a lot in recent weeks, doing extra sessions that meant he overlapped theirs, and helping them out as well. 'Everyone gets to bat, so you might as well try and improve it,' he said after play. 'The bottom four and the bowlers that are on the bench have worked incredibly hard the last couple of weeks to try and find a game plan that works in England.' The chemistry was evident: after the 88 with Siddle, he added 74 with Lyon at better than a run a ball. Lyon's share was 12.

The crowning moment came facing Broad, with four wickets on the day, who nonetheless had Smith shift his front leg out, get under the ball, and send it into orbit over the eastern side of the ground. Broad eventually produced a cross-seamer that cut in sharply, getting under Smith's shot to take off stump. By then the score was a competitive 284, and Smith turned on the spot and ran for the pavilion to prepare to field, last man out for 144. Booing resumed but there was a lot more applause to leaven it.

The entire spectacle was outrageous. Steve Smith had long been special, a batsman who plays like others don't, does what others can't. But to do *this* – to play like this, with such concentration and polish and eventual flourish, to immediately find the tempo, to dominate such bowling after seeing nothing like it for so long, to walk back out after being humiliated on a worldwide scale, to tune out a day of abuse, to do all this on the first day of the biggest series of them all, not just playing but putting out fires, to flip who was on top and then blaze the aggressors to all parts – that took this performance beyond the excellent, beyond the outliers of excellence. This was one of the greatest innings of all.

It didn't yet mean the match was saved. England hadn't batted. And if you love life's contrasts, you had to see the second day.

It's hard to describe Rory Burns in a way that adequately conveys either his physical series of actions or the deep unease they engender in the viewer. Burns is a left-hander who has developed the idea that his left eye is stronger than his right. Instead of standing sideways and turning his head down the pitch like a player who is not an abomination in the sight of God, he twists his whole head back almost over his shoulder so he can look at the approaching bowler with his left eye. His knees bend so that he forms a Z shape drawn in crayon by a child during turbulence. As the bowler lands he moves to the off side, head bobbing like he's trying to watch a movie over the headrest in front. Then he plunges into the ball, all arms and legs as he descends towards its line.

The whole combination would make a chiropractor's palms sweaty. He faces up like he's been squeezed through a mangle and then arranged on a coathanger. Everything dangles. There's a scene in *Death Becomes Her* where an immortal Goldie Hawn belts an immortal Meryl Streep in the face with a shovel, and Meryl's head ends up hanging down between her shoulder blades. Rory Burns is Meryl Streep. And look, Smith had been awkward too. But when he was done being awkward, he hit the ball. He hit it where he meant to. He may not have hit it where you expected, but he hit it where *he* expected. In this innings, when Burns did hit it, he had to look around to see where it went.

It was one of the most extraordinary streaks the game has known, the kind that got Dustin Hoffman banned from a casino. It wasn't just the standouts like Lyon's plumb lbw that wasn't reviewed, or the charge where Burns ended up doing the splits to knock away a stumping, or the missed off-break scooting a millimetre past off stump and through Paine's legs for four byes. It was a parade of plays and misses from the seamers, inside edge and outside. Periods of awkward defence then an inevitable heave for another boundary between the slips, over them, under them. This wasn't a case of playing straight to let the ball pass, or nicking to ground with soft hands. All the false shots were genuine, they just didn't get Burns out.

A *Guardian* reader named Phil Russell wrote to me: 'it seems for all the world as if he is a natural right-hander attempting to bat left-handed. The way he's holding the bat seems very awkward. However fair play to him for being so sporting and giving Australia a chance. If he can get to 50 batting like this imagine how good he'd be batting the right way around.' Even when Burns was in the 90s, Australia still had a third man and a stacked cordon. After he raised his hundred he nearly fell over for the umpteenth time. He continued the next day to 133 before Lyon ended the torment.

Like discussions of form, a lot of punditry looks no further than results. The assembled media had started with descriptors like 'gritty' and 'determined' that are code for the unwatchable, but once the innings became a century it became compulsory to call it 'magnificent' or 'amazing'. A much more notable quality went unremarked: that of being comically bad. It had been extraordinary in as far as being the batting equivalent of Frank Woodley getting stuck in a ladder for six and a half hours. It was extraordinary that someone could survive so long while never being in control.

This isn't purely opinion. The data analysts at CricViz have calculated across all Test innings an average of 12 false shots per wicket. That is to say, once you've shanked a dozen shots, you're past the normal span of luck. By the time Burns reached his century he'd played 54 uncontrolled shots. By the numbers he should have been out five times. His proportion of false shots across his innings was 24 per cent.

Thus the work of Smith and of Burns, some of the best and the worst you could see, were chalked up as Ashes centuries side by side, revealing both the fallibility of unvarnished statistics and the benign indifference of the universe. England's supporters had loved their man's work, cheering every let-off exactly as they should. 'He's sort of heroic,' muttered *Guardian* writer Barney Ronay, 'because he offers a degree of the possibility of emulation.'

There's a great resistance in sport to accept the role of luck. The implication is that you insult effort by acknowledging chance. But however you prepare, there will be times when luck is the difference. Burns would go on to play much better innings. His resilience to face fierce bowling all day was admirable. His persistence was impressive. The actual batting was not. It's alright to admit that.

Once the work from Burns was topped off by a tail-wag from Broad and Woakes, England had a lead of 90. In the context that was substantial, even more so when Warner and Bancroft departed quickly again. While Khawaja batted well for 40, he was out with Australia still 15 runs in deficit. If England could get through the next seven wickets for about 200, the Test was likely theirs. Australia had to go big, and again the demand was on SPD Smith. By the time bad light stopped play he was 46 not out batting with Head, and their lead was 34.

The barracking and mockery from the stands followed them into the street and onto the bus, where the drunkest spectators kept up the chanting and singing and sandpaper mime through the windows. It carried on through the streets on the way back to the hotel. Smith and his teammates found a way to turn it into comedy, laughing at the persistence of these punters. Most spectators only came for one day, and this was their one chance for the summer to have a pop at the Aussies. Every day there was a fresh shift ready to get stuck in.

Yet there was a kind of good nature to much of it. Doing pantomime performances of ball-tampering was also a way of saying that we know who you are. It's a bond, a means of connection. It's probably better than being ignored. There were definitely people who were actively unpleasant, but a larger proportion who really believed that what they were doing was somewhere in the vicinity of friendly.

That was the feeling down in the Hollies. Getting into the thick of it is overwhelming. The volume, the shifting sprawl of sound, the equally loud colours, the ceaseless traffic, the sense that you very much do not want to bump into anyone carrying eight pints. The horse costumes, Beefeaters, monks, an island chain of tropical shirts. When there's an Australian wicket or an England boundary the place erupts. Many things look deceptively peaceful from a distance, but the Hollies is the opposite. As hostile as it seems from the middle, it's friendly up close. Whenever I wandered down, everyone was up for a chat. There was no antagonism towards Australian spectators, and there were plenty of them. All those I spoke to were loving it and happy to return.

On the fourth morning Smith was preparing to get back in his zone. He sat alone in the dressing room, looking out over the ground while England's fans sang their co-opted cricket hymn Jerusalem. Oblivious of *The Test* camera on him, Smith cheerfully sang along. He's a strange cat. Langer had given one instruction: 'Just bat and bat and bat and bat and give them absolutely nothing.' The morning metric was simple: if Smith got out, England would win. If he batted until lunch, Australia would. He never stuttered. On day one his skill and willpower had to be cranked to 11; on day four he was supremely in control. With better support he could score faster. It was no counterattack, just a steady opening of distance. The first ton had been incredible; the second was the simplest thing in the world to believe.

Broad was tired. Moeen started the day with a ball over Smith's head, the first in a case of the yips that never settled. Denly's spin was overused and Woakes wasn't given the ball until after lunch. Smith took on the spinners, and against seam went more often through cover and down the ground as they changed their lines. Accompanying the team as a mentor, Langer's former captain Steve Waugh was effusive.

'His preparation is amazing, he's thorough, he hits more balls than I've ever seen anyone, and when he goes out to bat it's almost like he's in a trance-like state. He knows exactly what he's trying to do, exactly what the opposition are trying to do, how they are trying to get him out. He seems to have an answer for everything. He's an incredible player, don't think I've seen anything quite like him and his appetite for runs is second to none. His technique is amazing, it's unique, but he knows what he's doing and how to score runs. He analyses every ball and it's like a computer, he spits out the answer.'

Smith the person is extremely human, both strong and vulnerable. Smith the batsman does at times fit the computer analogy. At the time that helped create balance with the fallible Head and Wade. Like pairing left-handers with right-handers or leg-spinners with off-spinners, these were partnerships putting one part organism with one part mechanism. The stability and security of Smith's presence gave the others freedom. The runs they stacked up meant he never had to push.

No-one is more human at the batting crease than Travis Head. The minute he walks in you're waiting for him to get out. His strategy is to go at the ball: hit early, hit often. He attacks seamers with a diagonal bat, to force square on the off side. If there is width then he carves, but even close to his body he plays little back-cuts to the field on the bounce.

The batting coach Woodhill advocated this as Head's best method, saying that when his bat is straight his hands are further from his body, giving less control. It still looks ropey. Time and again the ball beats the edge. Head is the player who was caught at third man twice in a Test. But his method works, or works for long enough. Consistently, Head racks up runs before you've noticed. Between a duck on debut and Edgbaston, he had never failed to reach double figures in 16 innings. His 35 in the first had given Smith some breathing space. Second time around, Head went to 51. He was inevitably out top-edging close to his body, but the lead was 115.

Smith was on 88, and able to bring Wade with him. The former wicketkeeper favours drives through cover and midwicket when full and the hook when short. He was in no mood to wait, and with footholes outside the left-hander's off stump, had dicey moments against spin. It never stopped him attacking. He raised fifty with a bottom edge through the keeper's legs, a century with a reverse sweep against Root out of the rough. He left England demoralised.

By the time Smith edged, Wade had 69. By the time Wade was caught on the boundary for 110, taking the lead past 300, he too had scripted an audacious comeback. Smith's precision had taken Australia from danger; his colleagues had carried the advantage. As the Wizard of Oz taught us, even the machine needs a beating heart. Paine and Cummins made fast runs, Pattinson belted four sixes, and Australia declared at nearly 500. England were set 398 after twice having the match taken away from them, and on the fifth day they folded to Lyon and Cummins.

Smith had done the absurd. A double of 144 and 142. He was back to the lab again, yo, this whole rhapsody, to capture the moment and hope it don't pass him by. No more games: he'd changed what you'd call rage. Tore this non-existent roof off like two dogs caged. He was playing in the beginning, but the mood all changed. He'd been chewed up and spit out and booed off stage. But he'd kept striving, stepped right in at the next five-for. Best believe somebody's playing the nice drives, four. All the pain inside amplified by the fact that he couldn't provide the right type of runs for his country, and man, that goddamn year ban felt like life. He'd had to lose himself, in the abuse and the moment. He'd owned it, had never let it go. He'd only got two shots, but did not miss a chance to blow.

Across his last ten Ashes innings Smith had put together 1116 runs. Predictably the only better streak in ten attempts was Bradman, the eternal one-upper, with 1236. There had been other performers in the match, but really it was about Smith. Australia would have been gone without him, and from a first-up loss the series would almost certainly have followed. Instead he had taken them to a lead. 'It's extremely special,' he said in our boundary interview for *Test Match Special*. 'I've never scored a hundred in both innings in any form of cricket, ever in my life. To do it my first game back? In an Ashes Test, knowing how important the first Test is?'

Of course the media framing of his story only went one way. 'Redemption is complete,' Nasser Hussain said on commentary when Smith raised the second hundred. 'There was a beauty to these innings, the beauty and power of human reform,' wrote Mark Nicholas. Smith's triumph as a player, the work and effort he had put into a superlative sporting performance, was also held to be his triumph as a person, his return to the side of goodness and light.

Inside the ground, a few hundred exceedingly well marinated Hollies residents were clumped together in the middle of the terrace, singing over and over and over the 'Don't take me home' song about staying and drinking beer. Fluorescent stewards were going in like ants stripping a carcass, peeling off one souse at a time and steering him (always him) down the steps to an exit. Out on Edgbaston Road, departing crowds streamed down the footpath beneath the gaze of three figures on a tricolour billboard. Moeen had made 4 and a duck, took 3 for 172, and hasn't played a Test match since. Woakes bowled well in the first innings but barely got a go in the second. Morgan had been stuck at home watching on the telly. Nobody was running after Steve Smith on the bus today.

Chapter 14

London Blitz

THERE WAS NEVER any doubt, from when he first appeared on England's radar, that Jofra Archer was special. When he stepped out in the summer of 2019, first in some one-dayers, then the World Cup, he was compelling. There is a particular enjoyment to athletes who make the difficult look effortless: Martina Hingis with court placement, Leo Messi across his body on the left, Eddie Betts dancing the boundary line, Simone Biles landing the triple-double. We admire and appreciate toil, but we're differently captivated by ease.

Archer is tall, slender, the kind of mover who demands the word 'languid'. He seems to be part liquid. He barely runs, even; he flows to the crease, then releases a ball that is anything but gentle. Jeff Thomson shuffled in but had to produce an extreme contortion to make his body a catapult, front foot pointing to the stars, back arm draped to the ground. Archer cruises off a handful of paces and maintains perfect anatomical balance, no lean to strain for leverage. He has his front arm raised early. Steps into his delivery rather than jumps. His only flex is a subtle opening of his shoulders so that he gains power by closing them, carrying over a locked front leg to deliver. His bowling arm is straight up, release point as high as it can be, and he snaps his wrist forward for the last bit of extra bite.

Australians had seen him in two seasons of Big Bash, not just his bowling but his return catches, his run-outs doing his own fielding, his work on the boundary. He had the grace coupled with precision of the truly exceptional. He drew the stereotypes about Caribbean cricketers that stop pundits from seeing players for who they are. Archer isn't laid back, he just plays with a sense of calm. Quietness combined with confidence can be characteristics of something dangerous.

He was exciting enough for the ECB to reduce their qualification period from seven years to three to get him playing in time for the World Cup. With a British father and Barbadian mother, Archer had always been eligible to play for England, but representing West Indies at under-age level activated a waiting period. He spent it gathering attention and admirers and experience in the Big Bash and the IPL. His county bowling for Sussex in the long form gave equal confidence that he would fit into Test cricket, so much so that when announcing the pre-Ashes Ireland squad, England described Archer as 'rested' from the Test even though he'd never played one.

In first-class cricket his exceptional quality is being several bowlers in one. He's a proper new-ball operator with seam and accuracy. His top gear is high but he bowls within himself, on a fuller length. His highlight reels are long sequences of stumps departing the ground, with occasional jags to the cordon. If batsmen settle then he can bowl long spells with a more defensive length. If someone goes for broke then he has the variations to bring them undone. And if it's time to attack, he can crank up the pace to extreme with yorkers and short balls.

Archer had been on the money with his bouncer since the first day of the World Cup, when he had concussed South Africa's Hashim Amla and picked up three wickets on the hook. Matthew Wade had played alongside Archer for Hobart and now gave his Australian teammates a pre-match warning. 'He'll hunt for wickets a lot. His load-up is the same, it can come out 130, it can come out 145. You've just got to watch the ball and react, you can't pick anything.'

On *Test Match Special*, another bowler with the ability to scare batsmen tried to decode why Archer was so hard to evade. 'His bouncer I don't think is as short as most are, because he has that bit of extra whip,' said Mitchell Johnson. 'It's almost back of a length. So it's getting them into trouble because they can't get under it. It's almost like a ball that you'd like to play off the back foot. But it's got something extra.'

Ahead of the Lord's Test, Archer and Smith was the battle to anticipate. By now England supporters were in a state of slow agony. They had shrugged off Smith's 508 runs in 2015, given his match-winning 143 came at The Oval with the series already lost. But the inexorable way he stalked their bowlers on their next trip south had haunted English fans as much as players: his long slow century that flipped Brisbane, his double that ignited Perth, nearly twin tons on the Melbourne mudflats, almost another hundred in Sydney to close it out. He was a bad dream that got banished, Freddy Krueger dragged into the mortal realm to meet a pipe bomb, but at Birmingham he had popped out of the fridge to start a new spree. Now he was in every English head, with the BBC's Jonathan Agnew recording an announcement at St John's Wood Tube station asking for anyone who knew how to get Smith out to report to England's dressing room.

He had become impossible to bowl to, averaging 139 across his last seven Ashes Tests. That was a whole lot of stepping across the stumps to knock a single to square leg. England's best bowlers couldn't make a scratch. In a game that hinges on getting players out, what happens when you just can't get a player out?

There was some fizz before Lord's about a weakness against left-arm spin, but that was statistical noise based on a couple of Asian tours where Rangana Herath and Ravindra Jadeja did most of the bowling. England selecting left-armer Jack Leach was mostly because off-spinner Moeen Ali was cooked. Regardless, Smith spent days facing local lefties. I asked one of the net bowlers for his observations. 'No margin for error with your length, and you have to have your pace right up there,' he said. 'No false shots. Just to bowl a dot to Steve Smith is an achievement.'

Against a player they couldn't stop, England had kept on doing the same thing. Only Anderson's injury forced a change, creating the chance for Archer to be something different. A bolt from the blue, at the site of his triumph three weeks earlier. He cut a different visual this time, a sharp outline in gleaming whites, little dreadlocks bouncing free rather than the tightly bound braids he had worn in the one-day team. He had to wait through the first day for rain, then the second day for England's

258, only getting time for four evening overs: he pitched up for swing, clocked his bouncer at 145 kilometres an hour, and hooped a ball through Cameron Bancroft's defence to whisper sweetly at off stump and swing past the wicketkeeper. On the third day he rose again, and launched into his Test debut like he'd been doing this all his life.

Nine overs in a row he bowled before rain wiped out the day, going short at Bancroft's body. Bancroft is the type to tough it out, and Archer gave him that forum. Leg slip nearly took a catch, the pace too much. Bancroft escaped strike, but through each of the next three overs Archer pinned him like a butterfly to cork. A bumper drew a dodge. Slanting into the pads drew an appeal. Outside off drew a false shot. The next over hit him in the ribs, bounced off his hip over the keeper for extras, then pitched up for a nicked boundary. Two bouncers closed it out. Archer went full for an entire over to get his target tentatively coming forward, then the final over only needed five balls: two at the pad, two at the body, then cutting in down the Lord's slope, hitting the pad in front of off stump and just low enough for his first Test wicket.

Even watching this sequence was exhausting: the state of concentration, the highwire survival. Almost half of Archer's deliveries to Bancroft were short. Almost half drew false shots. The excitement, for spectators and the press, was palpable. Put simply, English cricket is not used to having pace. The proper stuff, uncut. Harold Larwood and John Snow got ostracised. Frank Tyson played a few Tests and became a Sydney schoolteacher. Steve Harmison and Andrew Flintoff had moments. Every couple of years some county kid would generate talk about being rapid, until his spine pretzeled before he'd voted more than once and he'd wind up as an HR manager. Meanwhile Australia, Pakistan, South Africa, sometimes New Zealand, even India now, kept producing the express delivery goods.

Archer knew Smith, who had been his captain in the IPL months earlier. Now they were opponents. Archer came wide on the crease, sharpening his angle into the batsman. Bowled the line at the body that had Bancroft hopping, the length that had him fending, the pace that had him mistiming past catchers. And here was the new man: walking across, absorbing the height, calculating the angle, on his toes to ride the bounce. Bat straight and elbow high, lifting and turning the face, playing without alarm into the ground, fine of leg gully for the safest and surest run.

When rain came before lunch, Usman Khawaja and Travis Head were gone and Smith was 13 from 40. The next morning with the sun out he kept doing the same thing he'd been doing all along, gathering without hindrance. He was more commanding than at Edgbaston, with some glorious punches off the back foot against Broad, driving dead straight on occasion, coming down to biff Leach. He was happy to duck and leave as Archer bowled eight overs straight aside from a change of ends. Yet it was only after lunch, having already bowled 21 overs for the innings, that Archer really got serious.

It's easy to get used to the idea of cricket as genteel. Especially in England, where all these people are wearing straw hats and blazers and carrying around plates of cakes, and others stayed up all the previous night cutting the crusts off sandwiches as though even a strip of slightly harder bread was too much to bear. The way matches burble on through an afternoon until they fade into a background for the catering. The intervals, the rain breaks. The odd surge or swell, but the lull always returning.

But then, a match that has done nothing but pulse damply for days can explode into visceral life, tearing through the caul to land on the floor fully formed. That was what happened when Archer took on Smith, and Smith took on Archer, on one dry day amid the deluge.

It started with dislodging Tim Paine, who had played out 70 deliveries over an hour and a half. There aren't many dismissals a fast bowler enjoys more than caught at bat pad, and perhaps that fired up Archer. Perhaps it was the sight of Pat Cummins, the first of his bowling rivals. Perhaps it was bowling short at 147 kilometres an hour and having Cummins flash it through gully for three. Or the mid-pace delivery steered by Cummins for four.

Archer's next two bouncers were faster than anything all day, and one went swerving past Jonny Bairstow for four byes. In the same couple of minutes a change came over the ground. Out of a sunny day a chill wind struck up. Heavy cloud dropped into place like a curtain falling. The colour leached away into darker shades. It felt ominous. The setting suddenly matched the action.

Speed radar in cricket is more a guide than a bible. The main shortcoming is that it measures best along a straight line, and measures the ball out of the hand. Short balls have a steep downward trajectory and less distance to travel before hitting the ground. Even though there's more force behind them given that bowlers hold the ball longer, they still register as slower than full deliveries because of their angle. In London money, a bowler whose yorker reads 95 miles an hour might have a bouncer read 88. In the metric, 150 and 138.

Archer's *bouncers* in this spell were registering at 94 or 95 miles an hour. This wasn't down to faulty tech. From the camera gantry behind the batsman, they were absolutely scorching through. Perhaps it was Smith's dismissive slap through cover when the speed clocked only 141 kilometres that was the final straw. Archer cranked back up past 150. He bombed them in short, some bouncers that Smith didn't have to play and a couple that were called wide. The last ball of the over had to be bowled again. From the bonus attempt, Archer's line was perfect. It speared in, lifting from not far back of a length. Smith wanted to duck, tried to duck, but there was no time. Only a flinch, a tensing of his whole body, before it crashed into his left forearm.

At first it seemed certain the arm was broken. He had yelped, clearly audible. Blows near the elbow can easily fracture. He was in pain, and his prolonged treatment included practising his grip without being able to fully use his top hand. His fingers were numb. It doesn't matter how tough you are – being hit shakes you. In a state of shock your bloodstream is pumped full of cortisol and adrenaline, and a drop in blood pressure reduces oxygen to the muscles and brain. Endorphins hit your system, triggered by the pain. All of it throws out the split-second reflexes that cricketers need. Time and again, a player who gets hit gets out soon afterwards.

Smith would later say that the effect was purely mechanical. After Cummins blocked an over of spin it was Smith to face Archer again. Both knew the mode of attack, and Smith felt the pitch was erratic, the bounce unreliable. His method was to take the duel right back to Archer. He had to manufacture shots, a sort of flip-hook to lift the ball away behind square, because he couldn't straighten his front arm for power. His eye enabled him to do it: a swooping stroke edged over the keeper for four, another hooked just as savagely for a bouncing single from a ball reading over 150.

The over was the fastest recorded by an English bowler, averaging 149.33 kilometres an hour. Archer's next, all to Cummins, was 148.04. Back in the rooms, Peter Siddle and Nathan Lyon were frightened, just as Johnson in 2013 had put fear into England's tailenders. Even professionals feel it when the deal gets real enough.

There are times watching cricket when you know that you're seeing something special, something that will be remembered beyond the scorebooks. You lean forward, grip the railing, soak it in. Archer's sixth over started with a bouncer at 147. With two catchers in the deep plus a backward square leg halfway back, Smith took it on. He scooped his bat on an upward diagonal to lift deliberately over the closer man for four. This was crazy-brave, like Stan McCabe hooking Larwood in the Bodyline series all those years ago, recognising the threat and countering with the most audacious shot in the game.

It couldn't go on forever. Through his three comeback innings Smith had created an error-free zone. He had built it to his specifications. He transcended mistakes, manic on the outside but at peace within. At last, someone had made a crack to wind a tendril through. It was brutal, it was basic, but it was working. Smith was rattled. He was batting wounded. A mistake, once impossible, was now a matter of whether Archer could sustain the effort. Smith was on 80. The deficit was 55. Archer touched 148 on the radar. It wasn't as short but it climbed. It was outside off stump but Smith was moving across. Again he was stuck, wanting to duck but not knowing early enough, the ball not lifting. Knees bent, halfway through a lunge forward, he could only turn his head as it smashed into the left side of his neck under the ear.

He pitched face forward onto the ground. It was a couple of seconds until he moved his head, pushed his helmet off and rolled onto his back, but it felt much longer. Those seconds were a long moment of genuine dread. The visual, of course, mirrored Phillip Hughes, struck on the back of his neck during a Sheffield Shield match, falling forward in that way that so rarely happens on a cricket field. The ball had split an artery, and Hughes later died. As Smith fell, everyone in the Australian dressing room thought of the same thing.

The crowd too fell to a hush. Like so many sports, cricket has its underlying threat of violence. We love the risk, we thrill to it. Whenever suggestions to ban the bouncer come around, there is a strangely unified response in a risk-averse world: that this is vital to the game, not an extra; that feats of batting are heightened by danger. The ball missing the helmet gets the biggest response, long vowels of excitement. We love to see players *nearly* get hurt, as long as they're not. When Smith was hit in the arm the Lord's crowd had exulted, baying for blood. Now that the chance of blood had arrived, they had lost their taste for it. That howl died in the throat, like a wolf giving voice down a canyon who hears something more than an echo coming back.

After a minute, with England players making sure he was breathing, Smith was back on his feet. He wasn't wearing the neck guard that had become common since Hughes was hit, but the ball would have missed it anyway. Archer stood to the side with Jos Buttler reassuring him, then walked back to his mark. Clickbait Australian media criticised him for not offering aid, which was nonsense, as the best thing he could do was stay out of the way. The batsman was arguing to play on. For a strange minute it was comical, little Stevie in the sandpit begging for five more minutes. Dr Richard Saw wasn't having any of it. Siddle was due in next. 'I didn't want to see what was happening, so I went to a corner of the room and started preparing. I had to go out there and bat. It's pretty daunting, to be fair,' he said. It had been Siddle's birthday when Hughes had been hit, and every year brought that reminder.

It was no surprise though, after Smith retired for a concussion check, that Siddle bought the team 40 valuable minutes. It went little appreciated how brave that was. He and Cummins managed to see off two more overs from Archer that ended the spell at eight in a row. By that stage Archer had bowled 29 of England's 81 overs, well over a third of the work.

When Siddle was out, it was a shock to see Smith come back. Courageous, but it felt wrong. A concussion in basic terms is when the brain is shaken in the skull. The force of the blow through Smith's jaw meant he had to be concussed. He had passed the alertness and memory tests, but symptoms are often delayed. And concussions compound, meaning that taking another blow was a terrible risk. But Smith told Langer that he wanted another spot on the Lord's honours board, and the regulations couldn't stop him. Most in the ground applauded him back to the middle, though in the least edifying moment of the series, a loud few gave another round of booing.

He probably didn't notice one or the other. He clearly wasn't right. Once you've watched a player make 20 Test hundreds you get to know how they work. His decisions were off. Second ball back, he wound up and wiped Woakes over midwicket, a shot he would never play to a quality seamer before the dying overs of an innings. The very next ball he played a gem, punched off the back foot through cover. Later he would say that he was telling himself to defend but couldn't do it. Something had shaken loose in his head.

He missed a glance that he would normally devour, edged four through gully, then wonder of wonders, inexplicable of inexplicables, shouldered arms and watched the ball hit him in front of middle. The man who was never leg before wicket, the Mr Creosote of leg-side runs, had just let a ball go, eight runs short of a century. He was so plumb that he started walking as soon as he was hit. The umpire accepted Smith's decision. For a final flourish of the erratic, Smith signalled a DRS review, then left the ground before it was complete.

He hadn't got his third century in as many innings. He had got Australia close to parity in a match that was forgotten while its most compelling session played out. There was more to come. Four English wickets by the close. A whirlwind century on the last day from Ben Stokes. A declaration with 48 overs left to bowl Australia out. The pulse through the ground as it started to work. The first concussion substitute in Test cricket when Marnus Labuschagne replaced Smith, only for Archer to smash him in the head as well. Luckily his grille dissipated the impact. The way Archer looked at the batsman and walked back to bowl, even as Stokes at slip flinched with hands over his head, barely able to look. The substitute bounced up and stopped England's charge. Australia ended six wickets down, England baying for more in the failing light, the 1–0 scoreline intact.

But there are moments that you know will live beyond others, and here it was Smith and Archer. As thrilling and as brutal as anything the game has seen. On the fourth evening when we tried to capture it for our podcast, Adam was expansive. 'We got to see a guy on debut prove that he is going to be the most important bowler of his generation. Against a guy who is already the most important batsman in red-ball cricket of his generation. Seeing both of those things together from the Pavilion End at Lord's on a Saturday of an Ashes Test that is still in the balance – I mean, you can get a couple of those variables, but we got all of them today, in a spell of cricket that I'm convinced that we'll be talking about for however long we're on this planet.'

When I sat down to write that night, my fingers were still shaking on the keyboard. Stale adrenaline cutting laps around the circuit. This had been the kind of contest that shocks you to attention, leaves you feeling a bit sick. A reminder that the game can be frightening. As Smith later pointed out, Archer hadn't got him out. But this was a duel that thumped with a heartbeat. It emptied the bars. It left a champion face down in the dirt. It came on a day when the cold wind blew and the clouds loomed and the whole place choked with tension. It created a memory to rival any before it. There were three more Tests to come.

Chapter 15

Four Pacemen of the Apocalypse

Fʀᴏᴍ ᴛʜᴇ sᴛᴀʀᴛ of the 2010s a promise was whispered to Australian cricket. The trace scent of gunpowder, the hairs on your forearm standing up. Little by little, through school ranks and age groups, grade cricket and second XIs and state regional teams, came fast bowlers: one, two, three, four, born between 1990 and 1993, each of them sworn to be the real deal, collectively an unprecedented bounty of pace.

Patrick Cummins was the youngest and at first the fastest. The others had all played one-day matches for Australia but he beat them to a Test debut. He looked his age of 18, rawboned limbs and features that his face hadn't caught up with, but he hurled the ball as fast as he could to tear through South Africa in Johannesburg with six wickets in an innings before closing out a big run chase with the winning partnership.

It was November 2011. Ten days later Cummins was recuperating from his exertions while James Pattinson and Mitchell Starc debuted together in Brisbane. Pattinson was right-arm, strong across the chest, muscling down furious outswingers at 150 kilometres an hour. In the second innings he knocked over New Zealand's top five for 27 runs. Starc's swing was left-arm and about as fast, with his pace generated from a long lean frame that allowed him to become a human trebuchet. Josh Hazlewood was the last to play a Test, at Brisbane in 2014. He used his height and high arm for bounce and movement off the seam. He was the most immediately consistent in performance and selection.

Starc took much longer to settle into Tests, but became the top one-day bowler in the world. He relished the simplicity of 50 overs, knowing his exact job in each spell. Test cricket's blank canvas left him less sure, though he could still be devastating, especially with reverse swing. Pattinson physically became a tank, maintaining the strength to red-line the speedometer without losing lateral movement. Cummins matured into the most dangerous bowler through a relentless work rate coupled with venomous seam.

Never, though, were all four available at once. As the years passed there were always a couple, if not the lot, stuck in the rehab room, on the exercise bike, the massage table. Stress fractures of vertebrae were a common theme, the grim price of pace. Around those long layoffs were the briefer range of muscle strains and bone hot spots and medical miscellanea. From 2011 to 2017 Cummins only managed a couple of first-class games and a few one-dayers. Pattinson was fit for 17 Tests out of 85 from debut, and had his back fused as a last resort. Starc managed to impale his leg on a metal set of stumps, needing 30 stitches. Hazlewood had a run of hamstrings and side strains.

All through those years, the promise became messianic. These four, the full quartet, would be visited upon us on some day in the future that was beyond our reckoning. 'Watch, therefore, for ye know neither the day nor the hour.' When they arrived together, when all were fit and firing and ready to unleash, it would be a sight to behold. Batsmen would quail. Spectators would flee. The milk would turn sour in the press box fridge. They would slot together like Voltron to form a force far greater than any part alone.

It took until the 2017–18 Ashes before even three of them were available at once – Starc, Cummins and Hazlewood demolished England 4–0. After another year and a half, for the return series in England, the final piece would be added, with Pattinson having come through a run of matches for Victoria unscathed and with wickets to boot. It had been the first year of the decade when the talk began, and the last year of the decade when it became real. All four were in the Ashes squad and ready to roll.

The one obstacle to unbridled cricketing joy was Australian conventionality. Nathan Lyon was about to go past Dennis Lillee's mark of 355 Test wickets, and his off-breaks had long been an excellent foil for quicks. Adventurous selectors might have picked the lot, given that Pattinson's very useful batting at seven wouldn't be any loss compared to recent anaemic contributions from the top six. But with standard operating procedure sure to win out, only three quicks would be picked at a time. As to which, there were lessons to be learned from the trip to England in 2015.

As Australia's coach at that time, Darren Lehmann had some inflexible ideas. One of them: everyone had to bowl fast. Not fast? Not good. Never mind Vernon Philander or Jimmy Anderson, Bhuvneshwar Kumar or Mohammad Abbas. Obviously their thousand-odd Test wickets were burgled because the ball arrived at closer to 120 kilometres an hour than 150.

Blasting out the English worked in Australia – Lehmann ended with nine wins from ten home Ashes Tests. In 2013–14 Mitchell Johnson led the demolition job in an unchanged pace trio with Ryan Harris and Peter Siddle. Four years later Starc, Cummins and Hazlewood went almost unchanged, with Starc missing one match with injury. But exporting the plan to England in 2015 failed. By then Harris had no knees left and Siddle's speed had diminished. Starc had just bossed a World Cup. He was put into harness with Johnson, and three times out of four their pace was neutered on English surfaces and turned to the batsmen's advantage, while England's bowlers prospered with accuracy and movement at lower speeds.

Siddle was an excellent practitioner of those English arts. He had been included in the 2015 squad as a grudging nod to restraint, like tossing a head of broccoli into your shopping trolley alongside a dozen bags of M&Ms and a tub of wrestling lard. Similarly, he was the last item to be used. In the final Test of a lost series he took six wickets at 11 runs apiece while conceding 1.77 per over. He showed the kind of work that was necessary in that part of the world.

Having taken over Lehmann's job, Justin Langer remembered. Starc, Cummins and Hazlewood were the stud attack at home, but Langer looked at what his team needed overseas. He briefed his six Ashes bowlers about working as a unit, so that combinations could change depending on conditions and suitability. Ahead of the first Test in Birmingham, factors included Starc having tailed off towards the end of that year's World Cup, looking fatigued and with a sore knee to monitor, and Hazlewood remaining on the comeback trail from hamstring and back problems that had cost him six months.

Cummins was the only lock: number one in the world and able to shift modes between tracks that offer assistance and those that demand toil. Pattinson had been bowling beautifully for Nottinghamshire and the rare chance to have him play was irresistible. Then there was Siddle, back for another tour aged 34, coming off two fine seasons with Essex. Langer wanted a bowler who would make best use of the conditions while offering reliability and control to support the others going for broke.

It worked. Siddle contributed wickets, but an economy rate of two runs per over in the first Test was why he was picked. He allowed Cummins and Pattinson the aggression that got them wickets, especially in the first innings. Lyon was able to clean up the win with Cummins in the second. The plan for the following Test had already been to rest Pattinson, taking no risks with his body. His report of soreness guaranteed the decision. Starc and Hazlewood had used a tour match in Worcester to stay warm. Starc was an obvious option for Lord's with left-arm swing coming into right-handers down the slope from the Pavilion End, but Hazlewood was picked to bowl outswing from the Nursery End.

He would also offer consistency at a ground where pace merchants had lately struggled: Johnson in 2009, Pattinson in 2013, Starc in 2015. The move in 2019 worked a treat. Hazlewood got the anticipated movement to draw an edge from Jason Roy, got a ball to hold against the slope to trap Joe Root, then swung away again for Joe Denly's edge, the first three to fall. Denly's wicket demonstrated how a bowling partnership works, with his calmness undone after being hit by Cummins. Without Starc for aggression, Cummins provided an appropriate ration, bouncing out Rory Burns, Chris Woakes and Jofra Archer. Hazlewood worked closer to the stumps while Siddle continued the tight line that won him two dropped catches and the wicket of Jos Buttler.

After that draw, Pattinson was due back for the third Test and Hazlewood had impressed enough to stay. The coach shuffled his tiles again. Siddle made way. Langer gathered his selected trio at the Headingley nets. 'I've been waiting for this moment since I became coach,' he told them. 'You three boys together.' Cummins, Pattinson, Hazlewood, three of the anointed with the fourth raring to go, walked out at one of England's hallowed grounds to visit upon the home team a special humiliation.

Australia had already batted, and it had been hard work as Leeds often is. Steve Smith, their lifeline, was out with the inevitable delayed-onset concussion. After a rain delay Australia were sent in by Yorkshire local Joe Root under what was less a blanket of cloud than a stack of quilts. The ball swung like a sweet chariot. David Warner battled through two and a half hours for 61, Marnus Labuschagne was again Smith-lite with 74, and the other nine Australians made 31 between them. Archer had the smarts to put the rush of short bowling out of his head, pitching up all day at more like 130 kilometres an hour than 150, using the movement on offer to take 6 for 45. The visitors were done for 179.

This was how England had won in 2015, using first-innings conditions to repeatedly demolish Australia's batting. That year, the Ashes were alive when play commenced in the fourth Test at Trent Bridge, and half an hour later the Ashes were not. Mitchell Johnson at number eight was batting after six overs. Australia made 60; Stuart Broad took 8 for 15. But at Headingley in 2019, Australia would get a measure of payback.

The second day dawned bright and sunny, and Tim Paine looked out the window with an inward groan at the batting conditions. Hazlewood and others were more bullish. 'I remember Smithy saying it, and I was already thinking it a little bit,' said the bowler. 'A bit less movement today and they'll nick them all.' That's how it panned out. According to ball-tracking, the two Australian batting innings at Headingley had the most swing and seam movement in the series. England got the session in between. Burns and Denly each hung around a while. Everyone but Root got off the mark. Everyone but Root and Jack Leach hit a boundary. And still they marched through a procession of dismissals.

Australia's tactics were as considered as their selections. No-one was immune to the charisma of Archer's performance at Lord's. But where previous Australian attacks would have felt the need to retaliate to his London bombardment by setting off the air-raid sirens in Leeds, this group treated fast bowling as a more dispassionate art. Langer had already said that his team had no interest in a bouncer war. 'We're here to win the Test match, not see how many helmets we can hit. You can't get out with a bruise on your arm.' They employed the short ball sparingly but effectively, defaulting to a full length to make best use of the Dukes and the surface.

Opening the day, Hazlewood set up Jason Roy with seven in-duckers to threaten the pads. Roy pummelled a wide one to gain some sense of control. Two more balls were angled in, then a final wider one was pitched fuller and moved off the seam. The drive was inevitable, the edge a formality. Warner took the catch.

I was running *The Guardian*'s over-by-over coverage that morning, a text commentary of play whose largely English readers write in with observations. The messages told the story of a slow-motion sporting disaster.

NICK MANNION: 'Can I ask if the sunglasses Ed Smith and James Taylor always seem to be sporting at the cricket filter out Jason Roy?'

CLIVE DARWELL: 'Joe Root is undoubtedly a very good batsman but it seems to me that corporate necessity makes it an imperative to talk about him like a true great. Greats bend big games to their will and neither the World Cup, this, or the last Ashes suggest this is true.'

Root lasted two balls, receiving a corker to start Hazlewood's next over. It hit the perfect length, leaving the batsman marooned between going forward and back, then it moved away just enough. That edge was unavoidable. Warner, again.

JOHN STARBUCK: 'Here the critics mass at the gate, chanting a dirge in unison. / They may bewail poor Roy's fate, yet offer him no benison. / Coincidentally, Joe Root: out for a duck from a real beaut.'

Having identified Burns as weak against short stuff, Cummins used it for three overs, having him fend more than once near short leg. Denly gave Burns a reprieve for six deliveries, but with the first ball of the next over Cummins nailed Burns in the chest, had him slice to point, then delivered a proper bouncer over his right shoulder. Burns averaged something like 13 in county cricket playing hooks and pulls. He duly gloved behind.

GEOFFREY BAYLDON: 'What a wonderful pace attack the Australians boast: skilful, complimentary, rapid, beautiful athleticism. How I adore watching them at work.'

Where discipline had worked for the first two bowlers, creating a lack of it worked for Pattinson. Pace was his advantage. His third ball was the 13th for Ben Stokes. It was full, wide, and fast, and Stokes went for it in the manner that he does. Warner took a third.

PHILLIP HARAN: 'Looks like it is back to unionised cricket for England – one out, all out.'

GEOFF WIGNALL: 'So, will Denly's innings be counted as (yet another) failure if he finishes as England's top scorer?'

Denly indeed top-scored with 12, the lowest ever for England. A brief tour of his 49 balls: outside edge, lbw dismissal overturned, play and miss, lbw appeal given not out, play and miss, play and miss, play and miss, off the mark, chopped past his stumps, play and miss, chopped past his stumps, play and miss, play and miss. Pattinson bowled two overs at the stumps or straying to leg, so when he next slipped in a full wide tempter Denly went at it just like Stokes. The only difference was that the wicketkeeper caught it instead of slip. Five down for 45.

BRIAN WITHINGTON: 'Good job for England that it's been easier for batting this morning in the sunshine. Someone ought to tell the Australian bowlers.'

GEOFF SAVAGE: 'All the discussions yesterday about the pros and cons of Joe Root choosing to bowl, but I'm beginning to wonder if it was just to delay England having to bat.'

Hazlewood was doing a power of work: four overs off the top, gave Lyon a single over at the left-handed Burns, then returned for another six overs before this wicket. A simple push from Jonny Bairstow in the channel outside off stump, pointless for scoring or defence, and a fourth catch to first slip.

EAMONN MALONEY: 'I thought Warner was dumped from the cordon? Or has a scratchy 61 been deemed confidence boosting enough for a recall? Clearly nothing wrong with the mitts at the moment.'

KARLA TAYLOR: 'According to many Pommy supporters yesterday, Australia was England in disguise, so does that mean today England is in disguise as Australia in disguise as England? This match is turning into an Escher painting.'

There had been so much traipsing back and forth that only 24 overs were bowled before lunch. Woakes lasted one ball after it, another short-ball target for Cummins, giving up a glove down the leg side. England's collapse had not been terminal with Woakes and Jos Buttler at the crease, but now it was. Seven down for 54.

DAMIAN BURNS: 'Currently stuck in Johannesburg airport on an eight-hour layover. Just as I thought my day couldn't get any worse I've had a promotional email from Eoin Morgan. "And there's a new cricket competition coming, The Hundred, starting in July 2020."'

SIMON CHERRY: 'I see from a correspondent that Eoin Morgan has been promoting the new 100 ball innings. Bit optimistic, isn't it?'

Buttler was known for doing things that other players couldn't, and here produced the least explicable dismissal of the innings. Hazlewood spent some time and theatre bringing in Usman Khawaja to short cover a few yards in front of the batsman, probably to mess with his rhythm getting onto the front foot. Buttler stared at Khawaja and drove a catch straight to him.

For a minute it looked like England might fall short of the Trent Bridge 60. Fittingly it was Broad who equalled it by glancing a boundary off Hazlewood, before Archer climbed into a pull shot against Cummins. The next ball Archer ducked while leaving the periscope up, nicking to the keeper.

CHRIS LINGWOOD: 'I miss the days when I could visit the gentlemen's conveniences and come back to the same two batsmen, and if it was going really well the same score. Test cricket used to take a really long time.'

In one more over it was done, with Leach dropped at short leg before wandering so far across that Hazlewood bowled him behind his legs. The bowler had 5 for 30.

GAVIN ROBERTSON: 'Catching up on the preamble I notice an earlier correspondent was basking in the confidence of knowing that England had already avoided the follow-on.'

MARK CARRINGTON: 'The positive note: I dropped my Aussie mate Travis at the airport this morning. Regretfully he has reached his destination and from the numerous texts he seems to have full access to the score.'

Cummins had 3 for 23, Pattinson had 2 for 9. Lyon had provided six deliveries. The innings had lasted 23 balls after the sandwiches, shy of 28 overs. Shellshock didn't begin to cover it.

DAVID WIGAN: 'That my friends is the match and the series. Brexit next. What a country.'

The Trent Bridge demolition in 2015 had felt like a force of nature. Every ball was nicked, every nick was caught, every fielder joined the cordon. Broad and company visited the humiliation of being done over not by ferocity or intimidation but a pure, perfect display of skill. Australia's riposte four years later was less dramatic, in that it took longer for the scope of the disaster to become clear. But it was no less compelling. One back page had an image of Root's shirt number, 66, next to his team's score, 67. Leaving out Warner and Labuschagne, 20 batsmen from the teams combined had made 95 runs at an average contribution of 4.75 apiece.

TIM COOPER: 'Think we should order a new urn to hold the ashes of the current urn. At least when Smith was playing, like him or not, we were treated to world-class batting. Root should walk over to Warner, shake hands on 4–0 and we can all enjoy the rest of the summer without having to watch this nonsense.'

England were swaying, tottering, waiting for the *Mortal Kombat* finishing move. Australia would bat again, pile on runs until it hurt, then take whatever time they needed to roll this sorry lot of damp meringue stuffed in cricket whites into the skip. Even being six down by the end of the day didn't bother Australia; these runs were all gravy. Humiliation four years earlier would become a stroll to vindication.

Unattended in my inbox that night remained a couple of emails that didn't know their own prescience.

MATTHEW FORDHAM: 'Even taking into account the dismal performance, it's the mental shift I think has broken me. At

11 am I was full of hope, trying to guess the lead and plan a sunny weekend around the cricket ending in a possible trip to Headingley on Monday.'

JUSTIN RIGDEN: 'Don't forget that England beat Australia after scoring 45 in the first innings in 1887.'

Yeah, whatever. Nerd.

Chapter 16

Miracle at Headingley

HOPE IS A virus. It spreads ruthlessly. It no longer needs physical proximity to infect new populations, it can race through them with a flicker of electrons. When England came out to bat for the second time at Headingley, the response from their own followers was mostly resignation. For a team that had made 67 in the first innings, 359 was entirely theoretical. Nine times in 140 years had a Test team chased a bigger score to win. There was nothing to do but see how long it would take Australia to bowl out England again and retain the Ashes.

But all it took was one partnership to create the thought. Joe Root and Joe Denly batted through some of the third afternoon, and little hopeful English comments began popping up their heads, delicate spring blossoms after a frost. From 15 for 2 when Pat Cummins and Josh Hazlewood continued their work with the ball, the English pair got to 50, then 100. You could feel that people were beginning to ask, in the stands, in the press box, on the internet: what if they keep going?

If you're the type who only glances at cricket it can be easy to be confused. Teams score more than 300 all the time in one-day matches, and they do that in 50 overs. How can it be so hard to win a Test match by getting 350 with north of 90 overs to do it?

The tactical and practical complexities boil down to this. One-day cricket is played with a white ball that has a heavy lacquer for its colour. It can swing early but doesn't offer much more assistance. Each bowling end has its own ball, meaning neither gets older than 25 overs. The ball doesn't get soft, so it's easier to hit long. The pitch is likely to be good for batting, with true bounce and pace, meaning you can see the line of a ball and play through it with confidence.

Test cricket is played with a red ball, dyed differently, and the Dukes brand used in England is likely to move in the air. The pitch after five days of use becomes worn, meaning spinners can turn the ball and other bowlers might get inconsistent pace and bounce. That all makes aggressive batting riskier, so fielding captains are more able to place catchers. The ball gets up to 80 overs old, and an old ball gets soft, harder to score with. The long timespan means the risk-reward equation is not the same. Batting is more circumspect, bowlers settle into a rhythm. It becomes a game of patience.

A player can go for broke as a tactic, judging that it's less risky to attack for a shorter period than be careful for longer. A lot of winning chases include a counterattacking innings that swings the game. But that's a gamble. If you do start hitting, the bowling team has the option to stack the boundary, and more latitude with short balls and defensive lines around leg stump than in short-form games.

The final factor is fatigue. Not just physical but from the mental focus that five days of top-level cricket requires. A tired team fielding last can rotate bowlers and absorb their mistakes. Tired players batting last have to play through, and one mistake can end their match. A bowling team only needs ten mistakes: bad shots, good balls, forced or unforced errors. Having to summon a final effort against those odds is usually too much. Almost every player's batting record is at its worst in the fourth innings. At Headingley, England should have had no chance at all.

But there was one other factor here that some astute observers picked up. England were chasing runs on the final day, but not on the fifth day. The beginning had been so fast that the last innings got started halfway through the third day. On the fourth day when it finished the pitch was probably at its best for batting, when its earlier wildness had settled and deterioration was yet to take effect. In short, England had been so bad on day two that they had done themselves a favour by day four.

On the third day the innings had begun as expected, with Rory Burns and Jason Roy edging for single figures. England were desperate for something substantial from Joe Root. He had long been grouped as one of a brilliant young quartet who went on to captain their countries: Root, Smith, Virat Kohli and Kane Williamson. Since taking the captaincy, Root had slid behind. Centuries dried up, his average dipped below 50. In 2015 he and Smith had each made two Ashes hundreds that won matches, with Root's coming in harder conditions and sealing a 3–2 win. Since then he hadn't defined an Ashes Test, while Smith had defined them all. Root had begun to look like a good player who didn't make the company of the greats.

At Headingley, the pressure had him rattled. His nick in the first innings was his second duck in three balls. He dropped catches, dropped his bundle, made strange bowling changes, slumped in the field. But perhaps liberated by being so far out of the match, his head belatedly seemed to clear. Australia's quicks were outstanding, working him in that channel around off stump that he had lately found so awkward, but Root started finding his balance, getting into better positions to address the ball and staying still as it arrived. His only boundaries came from the edge but he accumulated, running well between the wickets before later opening up against spin.

Denly was the opposite: he couldn't have looked more awkward at the crease if he'd been wearing one of those mascot suits. But he battled his way to an even 50 before gloving a short ball, and Root was well past that mark by stumps. It didn't fully restore his equilibrium – Root snarked at Jonathan Agnew while leaving the field about being 'too negative', as though being bowled out for 67 had offered English commentators fertile ground to accentuate the positive. But Root had at least marshalled some resistance after the crash. Ben Stokes was with him.

Root didn't last the next morning. He came down the wicket trying to whip Nathan Lyon away. Not to the pitch of the ball, it turned enough to take his inside edge onto his pad, up and back at pace over Paine's head. There was Warner, diving full length behind the wicketkeeper to pull off one of his more ridiculous slip catches. Root was gone for 77, England four down, the target still 200 away.

The dismissal brought Jonny Bairstow to join Stokes. In retrospect this is where the previous Test at Lord's was important. A draw with that much rain shouldn't have mattered, and the idea of momentum had dissipated in a trice at Leeds. But the English had carried a couple of things on with them. One was Archer doing damage bowling full, the other was Stokes and Bairstow batting.

Australia had started the last day at Lord's with a chance to win, with England 104 ahead but four down, and Stokes repeatedly edging Lyon past slip. Once he and Buttler had lasted past lunch they had squeezed the air out of contest. But when Buttler was out, Bairstow pumped it right back up again. He went after Lyon, his liberation freed up Stokes, and they smashed 71 from 48 balls like a passage of play that had time-travelled from the World Cup. Stokes went from nicking Lyon to belting him into the crowd, on one knee for that slog-sweep he'd employed against Trent Boult. He took England 266 ahead, able to declare for a gamble on a win that nearly paid off.

It was the first in a series of Stokes moments in these Ashes, a continuation from his World Cup. Having bowled nine overs and taken Labuschagne's wicket on the first day at Headingley, Stokes backed up in the second dig with 15 overs straight from tea to stumps. Archer was down with cramps and England needed someone in his place. An exercise in contrasts, Stokes has the most energy-intensive bowling style possible. He hurtles in and muscles the ball down, touching 90 miles an hour, sometimes launching long salvos of bouncers. He had Labuschagne dropped twice and caught off a no-ball. He curled a yorker through Travis Head and had Cummins splice to the cordon. He was the reason the target didn't get past 400. When he bounced out Matthew Wade he celebrated by sitting down on the pitch to rest.

He had sent down 36 overs in the match by the time Australia were done on the third day, and was back out batting himself by the end of it. With Root he only wanted to reach stumps, his score 2 from 50 at the close. He was smashed in the head by Hazlewood first thing the next morning, sending his neck guard flying in pieces. He carried on, 3 from 73 at one point, but when Root departed so did the chance of batting long to wear down the total.

After the rehearsal at Lord's, here he was with Bairstow again. They were two overs from facing the new ball. That was supposed to work in Australia's favour, with a new seam and more swing, but a harder ball also meant more value for shots. Bairstow liked playing with his foot to the floor. So the pair decided that their best means of survival was to do what they had done in London. It worked to the tune of 66 runs in ten overs, more than a few donated in wides as Australia's quicks were taken aback. When the score passed 200 the Headingley crowd went bananas. England reached lunch 121 behind.

Thus came the truly absurd final stanza. Stokes edged Lyon millimetres in front of slip, then the next ball Bairstow's edge carried easily as he tried to carve Hazlewood over the cordon. Hopes that Buttler and Stokes would reprise their World Cup work were extinguished: Stokes tapped Lyon to midwicket and stuttered a couple of steps, while Buttler responded to the movement. Head raced in for a one-handed pick-up, an underarm throw diving forwards, and hit the side stump from 20 metres. Woakes soon drove a catch to short cover. The win was 98 runs away with three wickets in hand.

Stokes had to keep focus. At each wicket he produced a counterpunch. After Bairstow, Stokes nailed a pull shot from Hazlewood to the fence. After creating Buttler's downfall, he angrily cut Lyon away. After watching as Woakes was softened up by the short ball until his wicket was a formality, Stokes drilled a gorgeous on-drive from the spinner. Archer took a lot of strike and helped add 25 runs, but always looked a liability against Lyon. After lofting two boundaries in an over, he went once too often and it was Head flicking the ball up at deep square leg, stepping beyond the boundary, then coming back to complete the catch. Broad lasted two balls, nailed on the ankle by Pattinson.

By this stage I was down in the Western Terrace, the loudest part of the ground, for the final frenzy. What stood out now was the blithe confidence. At nine down and 73 runs from home, England supporters were wandering off to the bar and coming back with rounds of pints. They fully expected to be here for a while. There was a festival mood, the sun fair and strong. A few Australian derelicts in tropical-print pyjamas tried to match it with the locals, up against those inevitably bald stocky types who look like someone put a pair of sunglasses on a knee. 'He's got no hair, on his head,' sang the Aussies to a tune that they got from a Mastercard ad rather than a hymn book. Up in the Australian rooms, the documentary cameras captured Justin Langer watching out the window. 'Ben Stokes. Absolute golden summer,' he muttered to no-one in particular.

Stokes was on 61. He needed more for the last wicket than his whole team had made in the first innings. He had the modest batting talents of Jack Leach to support him. He surveyed the field. Consider the degree of difficulty. You can't tick the runs down, because you only have one wicket left and there's too much chance your partner will get out. So you don't just have to score, you have to score fast. You need boundaries, but your opponents have eight men on the fence. This means that fours are almost out of the equation. You can score a two. You can score a six. Near the end of every over, you can score a single to keep the strike. That's it. Go.

Six months earlier, Sri Lanka's Kusal Perera had achieved almost exactly this. His team's series win in South Africa had come after he batted through most of an innings chasing 304, including 78 for the last wicket. The degree of difficulty was higher: Sri Lanka had a dismal history in South Africa. Perera was a less established player facing top-line bowling with no crowd support. He bombed sixes, hoarded the strike, and got there with 153 not out. It couldn't happen twice in a year.

When the first six of the Leach partnership came off Lyon, Australia didn't mind. It was a promise that Stokes would be caught on the fence soon enough. He was cornered, desperate, getting his front pad out of the way and slicing straight when he wanted to go over long-on. Against Pattinson he screamed back for a second run, then found a single. One ball to Leach, and Pattinson wasted it with a bouncer.

The second six off Lyon was almost the promise fulfilled. Even more of a slice, and the tallest man on the ground had been moved straighter for exactly this. The ball hung in the air just long enough to clear Hazlewood's jump. In the stands, the Aussie pyjama squadron and the kneecap men were buying each other beers and insisting that everyone skol.

In all the years that you might watch the game, you might never be able to answer this. What is the thought process that says, in a situation this finely balanced on the last day of a Test, to walk at Lyon and play a switch hit? How does a cricketer's brain make that decision? It was probably because of the shots that Stokes hadn't hit cleanly, with the line outside off stump and spinning away, so the left-hander wanted to hit with the turn. But still. Spinners are used to players charging but Stokes went sideways, outside off stump, keeping his hands in their original grip but turning a half-circle to position his left leg as his front leg. Both feet were outside off stump as he played a monstrous slog-sweep over what had once been backward point, hitting out of the rough, down on one knee as he spun with the shot to watch it soar. With a single from the last ball, it was 49 to win.

Paine went for pace from both ends: Pattinson and Cummins. Still looking for gaps and brimming with trick shots, Stokes attempted a ramp to a Cummins length ball and missed it completely. So of course he went again to the very next ball: faking a backstep to the leg side before walking the other way, timing the scoop this time over fine leg for six.

With everyone on the fence now, Stokes used his World Cup experience. He nudged to square leg softly enough to hare back for a second run. He was on his haunches and blowing after the effort. Then a single. Here Leach came into his own. With one ball left he took off his helmet, then his gloves, and pulled out a fibre cloth to clean his glasses, wiping them carefully before putting all his gear back on piece by piece. Giving Stokes time for a breather while also composing himself to block the ball. That's the over.

The moment of the day came when Stokes raised his hundred, precisely because it wasn't a moment. His shot off Hazlewood was special, hanging back in his crease to belt a not very short ball through wide long-on. The placement to beat the boundary rider was immaculate. As Leach came down the wicket to congratulate him, Stokes waved him back. He ignored the cheers, took a couple of seconds to breathe, took guard again, and faced. They needed 33 to win. His share was irrelevant. His focus was on the next two balls, raining them down on the Western Terrace, as he got under an attempted yorker then slammed through a slower ball. The pyjama men were quiet. Make it 21 to win.

Smart play continued: two runs behind point, another single from the fifth ball. In the first innings when Hazlewood bowled Leach, it wasn't by chance. He had noticed the left-hander stepping across and said to teammates that he would hit leg stump. Bullseye. Now he tried the same trick again. Missed by a fraction. Every time Leach faced a ball the anticipation was intense. Knowing there would be no running, Stokes couldn't watch. He crouched with his head down at the far end, curled up like a woodbug, hoping for a cheer. Those dot balls were greeted as loudly as any six.

With 18 to win the squeeze was on for both sides. Paine bringing back Lyon was a gamble: sixes were likely but so was the miscue required. Stokes lined up a series of hits that didn't connect and eventually settled for a single. That brief build of pressure could have been it. The first ball of the next over was a huge swing at Cummins, a high outside edge towards third man. Marcus Harris came sprinting, his late chance to make a mark on a poor Ashes debut. He couldn't time his dive, falling hard and digging a mudcake-sized chunk from the turf with his knee, getting the ball into one palm but having it jar out as he crashed. He called it the worst feeling he'd ever had. The next two balls beat fielders into the fence, one hoicked over square leg, the other rifled back down the ground with a flat bat.

Cummins got two balls to Leach, and when the second hit his pad Australia used their second umpire review. Cummins was sure the ball had pitched outside leg stump, but Paine said even a tiny chance was worth taking. Eight runs from a loss, they couldn't afford to wait. There was no jackpot from the video replay. Stokes was back on strike.

When you see sixes on television you don't really get their trajectory. You don't know where the field is. Catchers can pop into the frame like special guest stars. But at the ground you get the sound of the contact, then the strength of the initial arc. You can feel immediately when someone's got it right. You also know that when they keep hitting sixes, they're bound to get one wrong. There'll be a clunking sound, a parabola too low or too sharp. On this day, though, Stokes just kept getting them right. Eight times in all, clean contact and clean flight. Hazlewood might have been able to fingertip the last one off Lyon, but by then it was Labuschagne at long-off, seeing it drift over his fingers.

Two to win, two balls in the over. There was urgency for a single, Stokes reverse-sweeping along the ground, nailing it to backward point and Cummins. Knowing there was no run. Looking up horrified to see Leach three quarters of the way down the pitch, marooned like Allan Donald in 1999. Stokes was watching helpless, all of his work wasted, as Leach turned back, as the throw came in on the bounce and ... Lyon dropped it. Not the easiest take, flat and skipping, far enough from the stumps that the bowler had to move across and think about getting back. But there was time, Lyon snatching in his urgency.

'I was absolutely gutted, thinking I've lost the Ashes,' Lyon later said. 'But I knew I couldn't dwell on it. I had to get up to bowl this last ball. At the top of my mark I'm thinking, ok, what type of shot is he likely to play, what kind of shot do I want him to play, how am I going to get him to play that shot. It comes back to me bowling my best ball.'

He did. Landed it perfectly, beat the sweep. Hit the front pad, low. The appeal louder than any Lyon will ever give, and the umpire firm in denying it. Australian media went feral at Joel Wilson for his decision, as well as Paine for the reviews. Lyon was bowling around the wicket angled at leg stump. Stokes knelt and played over the ball. His back knee was grounded outside leg stump. So was his back foot, and his front foot was only half in line. The ball had straightened sharply but that was hard to spot with only a couple of feet to travel to the pad. With the flurry of movement across the crease, his eventual position outside the line, and the initial angle, it was reasonable to think it was sliding down the leg side.

Wilson was done a further disservice by the ball-tracking projection. The ball clipped the inside of the front pad, deflecting onto a straighter line to the back thigh. The computer didn't seem to register the deflection. The projected angle after impact changed towards the stumps with a slight but perceptible kink. Without the error it would still have been shown as hitting leg stump, but not hitting middle in the way that got Wilson panned. The suggestion by some commentators that he should have taken into account which team still had reviews available was against everything umpires are trained to do.

When the appeals had died down, it was a dot ball and Stokes had lost the strike. Cummins had the chance of a full over to Leach, six shots at a one-run win. Where Stokes looked superpowered, the skinny and bespectacled Leach was a champion of the ordinary. You could have found him in any sandwich shop in the country. He was a mere mortal just trying to stick around. Leach cleaned his glasses again, taking every second of his time. The Australian desire to go short was again a waste. Bouncers, at the body, nothing threatening the stumps. The third ball of the over Leach fended off his hip, just wide of the field, and Stokes was already streaking through: Leach's only run from the 17 balls he faced in an hour at the crease. He tied the scores, and Cummins' wide ball across Stokes symbolised a team that had been run dry. Crashed through cover to light up the ground.

The aftermath is all images. Stokes standing with arms spread wide, roaring to the heavens, as though trying to hug the ground, the stands, the summer, the sky above. Leach crashing into him, quite literally up in his grille, sweat splashing off them in a slow-mo spray. Lyon hunched disconsolate afterwards in a side room, patted and soothed by the burly tattooed arms of Wade. It had been three days of bowling brilliance from either side against pockets of resistance. Warner and Labuschagne against Archer and Broad, Root against Hazlewood and Cummins. Then the coup de grace: one of the greatest performances as part of an irresistible season. The Ashes alive, 1–1. The delirium, the adrenaline, the inexplicable forest of shoes being waved in the air, the voices drowning out the presentations.

Players on the screen can seem huge, their stardom filling them. When they walk by on the boundary it can be strange to remember that they're just people. Stokes went past with his bat under his arm, a bloke in whites looking a bit zoned out as he stared around at the mayhem. Perhaps it was like speaking in tongues, letting a spirit take you over and feeling little control of the experience. Everyone else could tell you what they had felt while watching you, but you could never explain what it was like in the middle.

Of course Stokes was pumped up as a hero. The newspaper that had published his punching spree lurched so far the other way they left their stomachs behind. 'The Sun couldn't back the call for Ben Stokes to be knighted any more enthusiastically. Nobody is perfect. Stokes certainly hasn't been – but then, who is? Since that night in Bristol he's not just delivered on his potential as a world-class cricketer but as a role model for a generation. His grace in victory is a lesson for all of us. Make no mistake, this is cricket's summer. From the World Cup to Headingley, it's been remarkable drama. Now there are two tests to go to bring the urn home. Come on England – and Sir Ben.'

There it came like a freight train: the end of the six stages of redemption, the stations of triumph and forgiveness, even though there had never been much in the way of repentance or loss.

His work that day would have moved anyone. Stokes had looked around. He saw that winning was impossible. Then he went ahead and did it anyway. His World Cup miracle had mixed skill with divine protection. Eoin Morgan called it the rub of the green. Headingley had been the bigger heist: batting far longer, and for more runs, after much more work, on a hotter day, against tougher bowling, with more fielders in the deep. There were moments of fortune, yes, but the audacity to demand them, as if luck itself had no choice but to go along. This was the Summer of Stokes, and only feats with this power and charisma could hope to eclipse the shine that Smith was on.

When a cricket match is over, even one like this, eventually it drifts away. The crowds disperse, the ground grows quiet, like some hibernating creature returning to a doze. On this night the warm breeze held as the day dipped out of itself, carrying the smell of grass and of moisture. Under the soft purple gauze of an English evening fading into night, Jack Leach led his team back out to the pitch, the only player still in his whites. As they sat and watched, he recreated his one run in its entirety: taking guard, nudging off his hip, sprinting to the far end. The ordinary among the extraordinary, he more than most couldn't believe that he was here. He did what anyone involved in such a thing might do, what those of us who only watched would do in months and years to come: try to recapture what we were lucky enough to feel, marvelling at the visitation, never quite understanding what it was.

Chapter 17

The Sliders Multiverse

IN HEADINGLEY'S AFTERMATH, the response in Australia lingered on the three climactic points. Nathan Lyon's fumble attracted sympathy – most could imagine the horror of making that mistake when the heat was on. Joel Wilson's umpiring got a scathing review, but fundamentally people know that wrong decisions are a hazard of the game. The lasting frustration centred on the one thing that was completely in the team's control, the mistake that didn't happen in a split second: the decision to use their last DRS referral. Former captain Ricky Ponting, a presence of Godfather authority over the sport, represented the consensus: 'There was no way in the world that Pat Cummins one could have been out. They burnt that one and it's cost them the Test match.'

Except, it hadn't. It didn't. It's generally not smart to argue cricket with Ricky Ponting, he of 560 matches for Australia. But his statement in this case was fundamentally not true. This isn't a case of interpretation or opinion; it's about a chain of logic that is usually partly obscured, but is no less immovable for that. Most of us who follow cricket, even its exponents touched with genius, fail to properly understand time.

Cricket is all about time. The fractions of seconds between a ball leaving the hand and reaching the bat, the smaller fractions that decide whether it finds the middle or the edge. The extra minute of making the striker wait while you host a conference with mid-on. The way the dying overs of a day can last forever when nothing is happening, or when everything is happening. The siesta hypnosis, one seagull giving voice, one distant lawnmower, one occasional punctuation of 'Catch it!'

We know our sport is made of time but we still don't account for how time works. Take the bowler who picks up three wickets, has a catch go down, then nabs a fourth. Or the batter out for 98 who follows up with two centuries. He could have had five wickets today, we say. She could have had three tons on the trot.

Neither of which is right. If that bowler's fourth chance is caught, he has four wickets. That is definite. Everything after that is unknown. In our world where the fourth chance is dropped, every delivery after that ball follows a dropped catch. In the other reality, every delivery after that ball would have followed a fourth wicket. Meaning the two realities would be totally different. He'd be bowling to different players at different times in a different state of mind. If the fourth catch was caught, he might then take a fifth wicket. If the fourth catch was dropped, he might then go on to take nine. You can't know.

If the batter wasn't out for 98, and instead made her century at the first attempt, then her two subsequent innings would have been different too. She might have played differently. She wouldn't have had the disappointment of missing out. Perhaps she would have made three centuries in a row anyway, but they would have been different centuries to the ones she did make. Different shots, different scores, different everything.

Put simply, anything that was changed in the past would change everything that follows. Any time-travel movie tells you that. Even the slightest difference can cause ripples. Which means in cricket that delaying or bringing forward a certain delivery by a second will mean that it's different to the one that would have happened otherwise.

No bowler can produce the same ball twice. You can't count the minute variables affecting a human action. We're not talking a major brain-fritz like when you put the car into drive instead of reverse and go through the garage wall. We're talking the twitches in muscle fibres and the timing of heartbeats, breeze and air pressure, the slight change in how a boot grips the ground on landing. Good bowlers can produce very similar deliveries, but there will always be millimetres of variation in where they land, how high they arc, how many rotations, how they bounce, how they turn.

Then, even if you could completely replicate the same ball to the same batter, the way they play it will be different. They might think of the same shot, attempt the same shot, but as with the bowling, there will be differences to their swing, their step, their timing, their point of contact. You might end up with the same result – dot ball pushed back to the bowler, say – but you will get it in two different ways. Or you might end up with a different result, between a boundary and a single, or a single and a dot, or a dot and a wicket. There are myriad possibilities but we can only know the one that came to pass.

So every pause can make a difference. An extra word with the captain, Jack Leach cleaning his glasses: any decision by any player will affect the outcome of the next ball. Stopping to tie your shoe might be the difference between getting an unplayable that you nick or an unplayable that you don't nick. There's no way to predict it; it's a launch into the unknown.

With that in mind, an umpire review can take two or three minutes. Waiting for the television director to come up with the goods, checking the front-foot cameras, the soundwave graph, the computer reconstruction. There's a tension during this time, an emotional effect. The fielding team might feel discouraged, the batters emboldened, or more anxious, or anything else. The delay at Leeds gave Stokes time for a breather. Starting a new over, he missed two shots against Lyon and sent the third for six. The fourth hit the field. The fifth was the near run-out, and the last was the lbw shout.

Without having taken the review, Lyon would have bowled that first delivery minutes earlier than he did bowl it, straight after Cummins finished his over. Stokes might have made a mistake to that ball, or the next. Or he might have put them both in the stands. If the review had not been taken, then the sequence that followed wouldn't have happened. The shot that created the run-out chance wouldn't have happened. Lyon's fumble wouldn't have happened. The ball that should have brought Lyon the wicket could not occur without the review that denied him the wicket. If Paine hadn't 'wasted' the review, the next opportunity to use it would never have existed.

This is what we struggle to see. It's not intuitive. In a cause-and-effect existence where each moment is a fork in the road between possibilities, we can't process them all. We imagine at best one degree of separation from reality, one junction at a time.

The most damning scenario you can muster is that if Australia had not taken the Cummins review, it was possible that some time after that delivery, they might have had a different appeal against Stokes or Leach that might have been incorrectly given not out and that they might have reviewed successfully. It's possible. On the probability of how often appeals occur, combined with the lower probability of how often appeals are turned down, combined with the lower probability of how often appeals are turned down incorrectly, combined with the lower probability of how often they're turned down incorrectly and then overturned on review, the chance of Australia using that saved review in the few remaining deliveries of that match was exceedingly unlikely.

The match was about to end one way or another. Which means that had Paine not reviewed, Australia would most likely have lost the Test anyway while keeping a review pointlessly in hand. Or they may have won the Test via an unrelated dismissal while keeping a review pointlessly in hand. Using it early didn't cost them the Test, except by being one of the thousands of temporal junctions that eventually led to the final few deliveries in which they lost. Attributing the loss to any one of those decisions makes no sense whatsoever.

Paine's logic on the punt was sensible: with eight runs to win and a batsman hitting sixes for fun, you had to take a Hail Mary chance at ending it. It was the last ball of an over, and for all that

Paine knew, it was the last ball one of his bowlers would get to Leach. It might be the last appeal he would hear against either batsman. Imagine how he would have been roasted had he failed to overturn an incorrect call and led a losing team back to the rooms with a review in the bank.

It's the same as the agonising over the many crossroads of the World Cup final. Changing any of them would entirely change the ending into something else, rather than slightly editing the ending that we ended up seeing. In a game divided into discrete contests, we can be sure about one link back in the chain. Only the last ball in a contest lets you be sure how a difference would have affected the result. The rest is guesswork, which centuries of sporting predictions have proved is pretty close to worthless.

At a quantum level perhaps things are different, multiple realities existing at once. Perhaps there are universes out there where Australia did get to review another shout and won the Test at a breathless last gasp. Perhaps there are universes where they batted more effectively in their second innings, and a much less interesting series saw the urn retained. Perhaps there are universes where the Ashes are contested between Afghanistan and Crete. Perhaps there are universes where Rembrandt Cryin' Man Brown was the star he always aspired to be. Perhaps there are universes where you can run out the non-striker without setting off a spasm of moral lamentation. Sorry, that one's ridiculous. But from our small speck in the cosmos we can see the one sequence that according to us took place. The rest lives in the vast expanse of the unknown.

Chapter 18

Don't Look Back in Anger

BEFORE TIM PAINE left the team rooms to speak to the media after losing at Headingley, he gave his troops a few choice words with an extra dollop of sauce.

'Fuck, that's gonna fucking hurt a lot, no doubt, for the next couple of days. However, as I said to a few of you out there, we've still got two Test matches. So let this fucking sting. We had our chances to win that game and we fucked it up. Shit happens. We can talk about that another time. We've got two Test matches. We've got a bit of time off. Let's take time. Stick together. Keep knowing that the process we've got in place to beat these blokes is going to work. So it's not game over. It's not toys out of the cot. It's a game of cricket. Shit fucking happens. Yeah, it was fucking important, and we wanted it. We should have fucking won it. Let's move on, and start getting our head around winning the next two fucking Tests.'

What else can you do after the most pulsating finish of your career? After you've lost the unloseable? Anguish at the missed opportunities, humiliation at being bushwhacked. The only thing more embarrassing than being bowled out for 67 would be losing to a team you bowled out for 67. Only twice in history had a team won after making a lower score, and both were in the 1880s when a hard day's bowling was tended to by medicinal leeches or a sacrifice to the Sun God. Having held the trophy in their hands and then given it back, the question was whether Australia would fall apart, or, more accurately, how they could possibly not fall apart.

Even in long-term retrospect, Paine admits the loss still bothers him. In the moment, he had to play the part of moving on to get the rest coming with him. The coach decided that before that was possible they had to stew in their disappointment. The morning after the match Justin Langer called the squad to a conference room and made them watch the winning partnership again, every ball. Nathan Lyon sat up the back with his head in his hands. Paine was spiky when Langer raised tactical mistakes: 'We had blokes come out and say bowl slower balls, so I've bowled him three slower balls and he hit them for three sixes. We didn't panic, we didn't shit ourselves. We tried our best. We had a crack. The bloke had a day out.'

Complacency hadn't been a problem. Through the third afternoon Australia's quicks had been excellent, knocking over the openers then unwavering in discipline through the stand between Joes Root and Denly. For hours they hit the seam and beat the edge and denied the width to deflect or the length to manoeuvre, giving away runs at somewhere south of a trickle.

After Jonny Bairstow's flurry on the fourth morning, Australia resumed the pressure after lunch with five wickets. The only missteps were at the end. The bowlers were taken aback by the assault, unable to switch to a one-day mindset, while having eight fielders on the fence put pressure on Stokes to get his sixes right but removed pressure around the bat. He was free to line up hits without worrying about an infield. With 74 runs in hand there was room to back the bowlers with conventional fields. But all this was easy with hindsight.

Paine's position had been vulnerable from the start. Having taken over as a caretaker captain, plenty of people only saw him in that way. They lamented his batting although his average in the low 30s trailed only Adam Gilchrist and marginally Brad Haddin, while he was one of six Australian wicketkeepers with over a thousand runs. England players had got stuck into Paine during the series with the contention that he wasn't good enough to be playing them, which was bold from a team that had nine batsmen out in single figures in an innings. It was also forgetful after being batted out of the game by Paine's 57 when choosing to bowl first in Adelaide in 2017.

The aftermath of Headingley brought his leadership to the fore. Even before the winning boundary had hit the fence, Lyon had collapsed at backward point. Paine immediately walked over to pull him up. 'He's a really important player in our side,' he explained. 'I said to him that if our players see him dealing with it really quickly and moving on then our younger players are going to do the same thing, and we turn up to Manchester or our next training session in a much better frame of mind.' He didn't dwell on the mistakes, and stuck up for Joel Wilson.

'I don't think I've got a referral correct the whole series, so I can't sit here and bag the umpires. We also had other opportunities to win the game and opportunities on other days with our batting and we didn't take them.'

Stability and calm were important. The Ashes were neither won nor lost. Paine was right that you had to be philosophical when a freak performance goes against you. But winning positions don't come easily in Test cricket, and while the Stokes miracle didn't diminish what the Australians did right, it might rattle them enough that they would start to do things wrong. After being taken apart it was up to Paine and Langer to put the team back together. Watching the match again was drawing toxin from the wound. 'Truth is, this could easily break us,' Langer told the group. 'That's what the whole rest of the world will be saying. But it's our choice.'

They were off to Manchester, the home of Oasis. 'Slip inside the eye of your mind / Don't you know you might find / A better place to play.' Bloody oath, never think of Leeds again. 'You said that you'd never been / But all the things that you've seen / Slowly fade away.' They had to. Don't look back in anger, said Liam Gallagher, the only man alive who liked a night out more than Stokes. Even in his most addled state Liam knew there was no point looking anywhere but forward. A win and a draw to start the series had given Australia three shots at retaining the trophy. They'd only blown the first. They were still the team with the advantage – if, and only if, they could keep from getting themselves down and letting England up.

If there was ever a time to have a tour game against Derbyshire, this was it. Derby is the kind of English town that you don't remember existing even while you're in it. Low-rise, Midlands, grey sky over brown brick. Existences curled in the corner of small pubs where the pork pies sit menacingly at room temperature on the bartop. It's a place where you can switch off almost every part of your thinking, concentrate only on what you need given the lack of external stimulus. Once in a while you might find yourself in an aisle at Tesco, contemplating a box of frozen fish fingers or a jumbo packet of Twix, with no idea how you got there. Time doesn't really flow in Derby, it's more of a lagoon.

Everyone came along. Cameron Bancroft led yoga classes on the field. They played touch rugby, had dinners together. Mitchell Marsh had set up a tour-long habit of taking a morning stroll for a coffee, bringing anyone with him who wanted a break. In Derby teammates trailed him like baby ducks. He had named his ambition for the tour to be the best team man possible, and without having played he was doing exactly that. Pat Cummins did a *Final Word* interview with us for an hour, relaxed as can be. Paine came to do media at stumps even though he wasn't playing. They smashed the local team with Mitchell Starc's bowling prominent. They looked content.

For all the motivating talk, nothing would be as valuable as having Steve Smith back. In the Derby match where he was supposed to find his groove, he came out to bat when Afghan off-spinner Hamidullah Qadri was partnered with part-time leggie Matthew Critchley. There was a sense from Smith that this was beneath him when he needed to be preparing for seam and swing. He hoicked at every ball, smearing a few boundaries before holing out for 23, then marched off to pick up his bag at the boundary line and walked straight into the nets. With Marnus Labuschagne having made himself indispensable to the Test team, Smith would replace Usman Khawaja, a senior player who never quite delivered against England making way for one who never failed.

So to Old Trafford, where Paine chose to bat. This was where it became clear that Warner was really gone. He had kept saying that he'd just 'got a few good balls', perhaps convincing himself of the idea, and his runs in the first innings at Headingley had raised the prospect of a change of fortune. But his innings to follow it had been a second-ball duck, and in Manchester he made another. Stuart Broad bowled wide and curling away, back of a length. Warner was trying to leave, but had shaped to come forward, and that lunge wafted his bat towards the ball. For the second time in the series he'd edged while in his backlift, in three or four minds at once. Marcus Harris followed. All of England's elation from the third Test, into a perfect start to the fourth. And Smith stopped it right there. A wall went up. From 28 for 2 he would help add the small matter of 410.

Pundits had been asking how Smith would cope against Archer, whether he would lose his nerve. The two faced off from Smith's first ball. There was a sense of proving a point as Smith immediately walked across to get in line, defended down the pitch, ducked the short ones, then smoked a wide ball for four with a particular flourish of the bat and no attempt to keep it down. The open expanse at cover, with the short leg and the leg slip in place, abruptly looked a bit silly.

Smith carried on, driving Stokes twice to the fence before pulling through fine leg. He went past 20 at nearly a run a ball, and lashed Archer over backward point with an uppercut to reach 42. For the first time in his breakout summer, Archer was a player diminished. As cold winds swept across the ground he huddled in the field with hands in his pockets. There was dullard commentary about his upbringing making him unused to the temperature, as though he didn't spend his Aprils playing county cricket in the frigid sea breeze of Hull. He was still a new bowler who had just turned 24, and who had delivered astonishingly through 14 one-dayers and two Tests. There had to be a moment when it caught up with him.

Broad's early storm blew over. Squalls from the sky filled in. After lunch and a long delay, both Smith and Labuschagne reached half-centuries. If you were England, that combination must have felt especially unfair. Here's this guy who just keeps making runs against you. He walks out early and never goes back without at least fifty, often a hundred, sometimes a double. You can't get him out. You try being patient, you try getting funky, you play on boredom, you play on ego, you try desperation, you try mimicking birdcalls to lure him into the reeds, you get Tony Soprano to ring from a payphone and say that Silvio will pick him up to visit a sick friend in hospital. Nothing works.

Finally, after years of this stuff, you find a way around getting him out. You knock him out instead. Not something you would plan for, but it gets you a break. A few minutes for a breather. Except in his place another one arises. Not him but a good enough analogue. Another player who thwarts victory, defuses situations, can't be got out without fifty to his name. You're Mickey Mouse cleaving a magic broom in half to stop it carrying pails of water. What does that create? Two magic brooms. Four pails. Because now Smith is back. Both of them at the same time, marching up that spiral staircase to continue the slow flood.

Labuschagne's three innings in place of Smith had been about patience and simplicity. Dodge short balls, defend good ones. He had left alone more deliveries by per centage than anyone in the series, while scoring whenever the ball was full or on his pads. Now Smith had a chip off the old broomstick who helped him salvage the score to 144 for the third wicket. The wind was so strong that it kept blowing the bails off and sending rubbish across the ground. The crowd's highlight of the day was Labuschagne chasing a plastic bag that kept eluding him. Finally Smith began stalking it. 'Whooooooooooooah ...' ascended a thousand voices as he got close, then cheered as he trapped it with his bat. Later a beach ball rolled across the pitch. Smith knelt and played a sweep shot, sending it on the wind to square leg for four. The symbolism was perfect.

Labuschagne fell late for 67, Travis Head and Matthew Wade didn't make many the next day, but none of that helped England at all. Smith was absolutely on one. His idiosyncrasies are much discussed, but there was never any sense at Old Trafford that his game was anything but what he wanted it to be. To raise fifty he stretched absurdly wide to a full ball from Stokes, not taking a step beyond his usual shuffle. He overbalanced, toppling over onto one padded knee, arms stretched out toward the return crease. He still hit it cleanly out of the middle, almost one-handed by the time it connected. Four.

The default Smith still stepped across to defend or work singles, but was joined by a Smith who came for the bowling savagely. His wind-up looked bigger, his bat swooping from gully around through the line. There was a real whip of the ball, striding into shots like he was wielding an axe. Cover drives flew as he splayed his grip. He drilled the off side with absurd skill off the back foot. Pulls were helped to fine leg. His drives through long-on were proper rasps, flayed through a full length with his front foot staying put to leave space. His shots to spin had a swaggering thwack, blotting rather than stroking. From Stokes he used a horizontal bat easing on the bounce between gully and slip. From Root, a lap-sweep into a sabre swing. Everything had a flourish, a follow-through ending in elaborate circles, like kids writing their names in the night with sparklers.

It wasn't even that line about playing a shot with contempt. There was no contempt because Smith doesn't care about bowlers. They're a mechanism to provide him a ball. This was some more basic need, the order of the world not being right. The ball was not where it should be. A swat through the field was him sending the ball to its home.

Chances were few. Archer couldn't snatch a return drive that was past him before he saw it. Smith was well past his century when Leach turned one away to have him caught at slip, but the spinner had overstepped. The embroidery on Smith's shots drove England mad. He shadow-batted as intently as the real thing. He pointed the bat at bowlers after defending, spoke to himself, gesticulated at the field where he might have aimed. On driving a single through cover he stopped to do some gardening on his way down for the run.

His company through much of the day was Paine. After a group send-off from England's huddle at Headingley, the captain would have especially enjoyed his archetype innings: digging in, quietly assembling runs, supporting a premier batsman as the two of them took the game out of reach. Paine was derided for having one first-class century, but with his rebuilt fingers he wasn't there to be Gilchrist. He was there to stitch innings together when required. He arrived before Smith's century and took it close to the double, staying with his own score on 49 for half an hour. They put on 145. He let Smith drain England before making way for the tail to batter them. Paine's 58 didn't become a hundred, but by then it didn't matter. He'd done enough.

Again, the story was Smith and the power of resumption. Past his double ton, past Steve Waugh to 11 Ashes centuries. That left only Jack Hobbs with 12 and Bradman with 19 ahead of him. Smith had been able to do what Warner and Stokes had not, to plug back in from the first moment. Long break, short break, didn't matter. After every pause Smith had resumed exactly as he had wanted to resume. He disregarded fine-tuning. He paid no mind to rust. He wasn't interested in momentum or mental blocks. Short ball? Left-arm spin? Leg-side trap? Do what you like. 'I was hungry for it. I think I went through a period of batting where I lost concentration for maybe twenty minutes,' he said at stumps. 'After that I switched myself back on.' You could not stop him until he was done.

He ploughed on to 211, until with Starc bombing fences for a fast 54, Smith was caught reverse-sweeping off a part-time off-spinner bowling a leg-break. It was formally party time. Root was the bowler, the two golden boys who had lost some shine since 2015. That series had also seen Root have Smith caught off a reverse-sweep: golden boy turned golden arm. Having used up every possible question about his batting, I asked Smith if he knew that his only career dismissals to the reverse were both off Root. 'Both to Joe Root, and both over 200,' he shot back without missing a beat.

Australia declared at 497, then the squeeze from Cummins and Hazlewood ahead of late wickets from Starc kept England to 301. With 55 overs left on the fourth day, Australia could bat long enough to rest the bowlers and come back for a few overs at England before stumps. The lead was already 196, but the 359 chased down in Leeds might have played on Paine's mind.

The lone and undying hand of Smith was soon back at it. He might have expected to be cut some slack, but Australia fell to 44 for 4. England's quicks were firing. The huge temporary grandstand that stabs its sharp angles into the sky was heaving in all its *Hunger Games* intensity. If England could run through the visitors they might only be chasing 300.

Except ... Smith. Where Broad had blown up the openers, Smith defused every ball with no doubt about whether to cut the red wire or the blue. Up until tea he calmed the situation. Afterwards he started taking bowlers down. He swept Leach, slapped and glided Archer. When Broad tried to cramp him by bowling short down leg, Smith backed so far away that he could drag a pull through midwicket. When Broad responded by going wider again, Smith stood still and watched it go for five wides.

Everyone watching, everyone playing, was still trying to come up with a method to dismiss him. I received a single-line email to *The Guardian*. 'A bouncer or two, then reverse swing yorkers for Smith, to get him out.' Perfect, I'll pass that on. At one point Smith got in a tangle against a full ball from Broad, squeezing out a ricochet that rolled past his leg stump. 'That's the spot to bowl to him I suppose,' said Jim Maxwell on the BBC. 'Just keep bowling yorkers.' The next ball, Broad's repeat was on-driven to perfection, wide of mid-on and straight of midwicket, leading the fielder into the fence. Just keep bowling yorkers, Smith might have muttered. Please.

If his first innings was oddball, this was a new level. We saw Smith the absurdist: cantering, chuntering, walloping, a slew of rubberised elbows and knees as he lashed through cover, over the bowler, between the sweepers. Delirium tremens via interpretive dance. He crab-scuttled sideways, spun in circles. The bat swished like the tail of an angry cat. At times when he hit the ball you swore you heard a comedy ooga horn. When Archer bounced him, Smith got under the ball by falling forward onto his knees outside off stump, then by falling backwards outside leg. When he wound up flat on his back, he practised an uppercut from his spot in the dirt.

He looked a dead cert for another set of twin tons, motoring to 82 from 90 balls, and fell short when doing the team thing by continuing to go large with five overs until the declaration. The only way England could get him was when Smith decided he was willing to risk being got. It didn't matter. Australia's lead reached 382. Smith had faced nearly a thousand balls in the series, making 671 runs from five hits. The combined efforts of Warner, Bancroft, Harris, Khawaja, Head and Wade was 683 from 38.

There was a final facefull of dirt for England with half an hour to stumps. They got through two deliveries before Cummins forced a leading edge from Rory Burns with pace. Root had spent most of the day as the traffic cop outwitted by clown cars, and now had to walk out at the number three spot that he didn't want, to get possibly the best ball that Cummins will bowl in his career: angling slightly in, seaming slightly away, the ideal length to stop Root getting forward, drawing his defensive shot down one line before slipping past it to take the very top of off stump. Golden boy to golden arm to golden duck – before this series Root had never been out first ball in his 82 Tests. Now Cummins had bagged him first ball two matches out of three, either side of Hazlewood getting him for a second-baller. Before this series he had five ducks in 152 innings; during the series he made three ducks in five hits. He walked off looking exhausted, deflated, defeated.

Cummins was already Australia's bowler of the series, the only quick to have played every Test. His first three overs on the fifth morning monstered Denly and Jason Roy, constantly cutting in to take them on the body in between moving away to beat the edge. He came off to give Starc the newer ball, but his third spell after drinks did the job. Roy lost his middle stump when the ball jagged once too often. Stokes got a standing ovation all the way in. Trying to get himself set as he had in Leeds, the left-hander wanted to leave a ball angled across him. It was just too close, too accurate, moving back off the seam. It cut through him and took his inside edge.

Cummins ended up bowling ten overs in a row either side of lunch. Four maidens, two wickets, 23 runs. It matched the ten-over spell he had bowled either side of tea in the first innings. First time around, his hostility and line built the pressure that saw Josh Hazlewood grab three wickets straight afterwards. This time, the tail end of his spell saw Lyon pick up Denly at the other end.

'They're extremely consistent, that's why they're good,' Paine would say of Cummins and Hazlewood. 'What I love about those two fast bowlers is that from day one in this series to this afternoon, the same effort has come in all the time … They run in hard, bowl as fast as they can every time they get the ball in their hand. For me that's a real weapon to have.'

The final stanza got closer and tenser than Australia wanted. Bairstow lasted nearly two hours before Starc blasted through him. Jos Buttler batted past the tea break, then Somerset teammates Overton and Leach – promoted ahead of Broad after Headingley – saw out 14 overs to get into the last hour. The draw was becoming a chance with the risk of bad light. As time ticked by and the sky darkened, the Australians could have panicked. The prospect of letting slip two Ashes-clinching wins was circling. It was Paine's inspiration to bring on Labuschagne.

For the left-handed Leach, with footmarks outside off stump, Paine put five catchers around the bat. The part-time leggie was spinning the ball into the batsman. Short leg soon claimed an edge. At the other end, Hazlewood's class told: having previously bowled Buttler with one that jagged in a mile, he did the same to trap Overton in front of the stumps. Of course at nine wickets down Overton reviewed the decision, and the visitors gathered for the verdict. The Spidercam that usually zipped around overhead dropped to ground level. When the big screen confirmed the dismissal the players erupted. Hazlewood raised his arms among his tiny batsmen, a tree where the kids were building a cubby house. Paine ran forward, punching the air while holding his gloves in his other hand.

The celebration wasn't just of this performance, but producing it from such a low. Afterwards Paine wondered whether a previous ordeal might have helped. 'I think potentially it did. A lot of the guys in that change room have been through what happened at Cape Town. It's times like that that you find out what sort of people you've got. People can roll up and give up, or they can keep fighting. We've got a group of guys that will keep fighting, keep wanting to be in situations like we were in at Headingley. Because those games, when you win, make why you play really special. Headingley's loss makes today sweeter, after a lot of people wrote us off.'

The Ashes were theirs, the long wait since 2001 when an Australian team had last come to England and taken the urn home. The classic of 2005, the deflation of a fifth-Test loss in 2009, the fortune and misfortune of 2013, the implosion of 2015, had come and gone. Two of the 2001 players, Langer and Waugh, were coaching this team. It had come from an uncelebrated bunch of players, through brilliant bowlers and one exceptional batsman. At Old Trafford, where some of the most remarkable contests of the 1800s had been played, this was Smith's sepia moment. With the dressing rooms one floor below the press box, we could soon hear the celebrations rumbling, ready to spill out onto the ground.

Chapter 19

Anticlimax and the New Australia

HEADING BACK TO London for the fifth Test at The Oval, there was already a sense of anticlimax. Had England held on for the draw in Manchester, the Ashes would have been up for grabs at 1–1 in a headline final. Instead, the primary point of the series was decided. The match still mattered, because Australia badly wanted to win a series in England, and for all their efforts they could still be denied to draw 2–2. But after the energy that had gone into Manchester's comeback and the celebrations that followed, there was a good chance the Australians would be emotionally and perhaps still literally hungover.

Tim Paine's decision to bowl didn't help. Captains are pilloried whenever this doesn't work, which is often illogical: if they bat first and fail then people blame the batting, not the captain. The win-loss ratio between the options is pretty much even across the history of the game. Batting second is theoretically the simplest way to win a Test: you bat once and bat long, probably on days two and three with the pitch in good shape, and give your bowlers lots of rest. Batting first can mean a rushed third innings and a declaration with less recovery time for your arsenal. But the match pressure of putting a score on the board first has its worth, and it avoids the chance of batting last. That's enough to sway most captains.

In this case though, rest should have been a primary consideration. Pat Cummins and Josh Hazlewood had bowled on the last four days in Manchester, had three days off, and now had to bowl again. Add to that Smith's outstanding first-innings record: 16 of his 26 tons, and an average of 94 compared to 65 in the second. Smith was coming down with the flu and was nearing exhaustion, so perhaps Paine wanted to rest his batsmen rather than his bowlers. Perhaps he was worried about a team being off the boil. A bad first day batting can lose you a Test, a bad day bowling is more likely to leave you a path back in.

Paine's public rationale was that with clouds overhead and grass on the pitch, his bowlers might get more help on day one. It was a gut decision, leaving Justin Langer and the other coaches taken aback. It could have worked, but plenty went wrong. Peter Siddle tore a muscle in his hip early on. He bowled through the rest of the match but was hampered. Mitchell Starc should have been retained after useful work at Old Trafford, with pace that might have helped on the flatter Oval track. The team lost wickets to dropped catches and no-balls. Joe Root was put down three times in six overs. After one, sprawled on the ground,

Paine had the presence of mind to scream into his gloves so he wouldn't be captured on camera.

That they kept England to 294 was due to a surprise package – Mitchell Marsh. Extremely likeable in person, he was especially sunny in England on his mission to keep spirits high. 'I try and have a positive impact on everyone I meet in my life. Not just cricket. Not just me the cricketer, but every single person I come across I like to have a positive attitude, get the best out of myself and make people happy.' In the final Ashes chapter he was upgraded from the coffee stroll, batting at six but mostly there to support the bowlers. He responded with the most outrageous display of swing, pitching the ball full and moving it an average of 2.5 degrees. The series average for everyone else was 0.7, and the closest individual spell was Ben Stokes with 1.7.

Marsh had always been a holding bowler, back of a length with an older ball to limit scoring. This time he was let off the leash. 'JL came up to me before the start of play at lunchtime and just said go for it, attack. Bowl the way you want to bowl. I was a little bit – well, not shocked, but it gave me great confidence to go out there and give it everything I had. Maybe it changed the mentality to allow me to bowl more attackingly as a player. It was fun.'

He mixed inswing and outswing to harvest lbws and slip catches, his first five-wicket innings in Tests. His smile lit up the ground. As recently as October 2018 he had been a vice-captain and senior batsman, then was soon out of the squad. In London he was frank about why. 'You bat at four for Australia, you need to make runs. Last year was a range of stuff. I lost a close friend to suicide at the start of the summer. When things like that happen – I didn't probably handle it as well as I could have. That transitioned into my cricket at times as well … You know when you do anything and you badly want to do well and it doesn't work out, it's very easy to get down on yourself. I was certainly at that stage. I did a lot of work with our sports psych Matt Burgin at Western Australia about detaching myself from the outcome.'

By the end of the domestic season he had started to get his game back, and aimed for an Ashes spot. He and his brother Shaun had long been contentious. Being sons of former Australian batsman and coach Geoff Marsh got them a lot of leeway from selectors. Criticising that was reasonable, but plenty of onlookers (and I'll put my hand up) directed frustration at the players. At The Oval, Mitch was asked about it.

'Yeah, most of Australia hate me,' he said, a little heartpunch. He was still smiling, but it flickered. 'Look, Australians are passionate, they love their cricket, they want people to do well. It's no doubt that I've had a lot of opportunity at Test level and haven't quite nailed it. Hopefully they can respect me for the fact that I keep coming back, I love playing for Australia, I love wearing the baggy green cap, I'll keep trying. Hopefully I win them over one day.'

Marsh had kept England to 294, but the change in line-up didn't change Australia's batting fortunes. Openers gone quickly, Smith batting long, support from Marnus Labuschagne with 48. Aside from Nathan Lyon slapping 25 at the end, no-one else reached 20. By this stage of the series David Warner was so toasted by Stuart Broad that he came out wildly against Jofra Archer, swinging at balls so wide they barely hit the strip. Even

Smith was battling. 'I was loading up on the Codral Cold and Flus throughout the day, and just tried to stay as focused as I could.' You could tell he wasn't himself when he actually missed a ball on his pads, leg before to Chris Woakes without having been concussed. He had still made 80, and it was his lowest total of the series. Every time he had batted he had top-scored.

Archer was back on song with six wickets and England had a lead of 69. Nice. They made it swell. Joe Denly had fought through the series, sometimes with himself as much as the bowling, and was rewarded with 94 in a long partnership while Stokes made 67. Buttler added 47 to his 70 from the first dig. Three more catches went down, two lbws weren't reviewed. Lyon had a lonely battle, getting Burns, Root and Stokes despite a bad cut on his spinning finger. Siddle pushed through injury to remove Denly with a special over and to bounce out Buttler. Cummins took two tailend wickets, Hazlewood none.

That last pair had bowled through the first day in London, into the second morning, a burst on the second evening, and all through the third day before finishing on the fourth. England set 399. They formed a huddle before the chase, geeing themselves up, but the visitors were never likely to rally from that far down, that deep in the season. It was the middle of September and the Australians had been in England since May.

For all his feats, Smith has never made a fourth-innings hundred. It wasn't going to happen in his current condition. He'd had the wherewithal to take a stunning slip catch, full stretch with one hand, but another long innings was a different matter. He played like he had in Derby, airborne clouts landing short of onrushing fielders. When Smith is out of juice he goes after the bowling. Even along the ground he was trying to hit the cork out of the ball. His summer of complete control had ended.

For interminable hours across two Ashes series, England had placed a leg slip for Smith with the idea of bowling at his body. That fielder had grazed like a Jersey cow. Until now. Broad bowled an innocuous thing back of a length, Smith glanced, and Stokes around the corner dived low to his left. Impossibly, Smith was out, for 23. One talisman of the series had cancelled out the other. The cheer of the crowd was less celebration than disbelief.

As Smith left The Oval to complete his season, those who had just cheered his dismissal stood to him in a full-voiced ovation. 'I guess I'd shifted them, perhaps,' he later said. Parochialism aside at the last, people had to appreciate what he'd done: 1196 deliveries faced across the series, seven innings, six dismissals, 774 runs. Three centuries, three near enough. The defining presence. 'He's just a genius,' said Paine.

Between Archer and Matthew Wade, the closing exchanges included fireworks. Neither of the Hobart teammates wanted to cede ground. Wade does his best work when expressing his combativeness with bat rather than chatter. Once Smith was out, Wade skipped down at Jack Leach to carve the spinner through cover, down again to drop-kick him over midwicket, then back to cut a third boundary in a row behind point. He even managed to hit the spare helmet behind the keeper for five penalty runs. Root asked Archer to quell the threat, so Wade hooked him for four, goaded him into wasting a review for a ball pitching outside leg, and hooked him again for six.

It was on. The speed gun was back above 90 miles an hour, the deliveries above chest height. Wade ducked, chirped, pulled for four. Archer sent through some nostril-trimmers and others that whizzed past the edge. At one point they ended an over with a theatrically long staring contest, and you felt like both of them were struggling not to burst out laughing. Amid the barrage Wade still got forward to crash an errant full ball through cover. Archer's response was to hit him on the shoulder and get the radar past 96 miles per hour, 155 kilometres. An edge went through slip, a gorgeous on-drive to the fence. Archer had bowled four overs before the tea break, and followed it with eight overs straight. Wade moved to 96. The contest ended with neither party diminished.

There was a moment, eight overs later, with Cummins defending stoutly and Australia needing 155, that yet another outrageous finish looked a chance. It would have suited the series. In the end, probability had its day and Wade's 117 was a consolation ton. Had the trophy been on the line, had Australia got another 80 in the first innings, it could have been a belter. Instead, the day was entertaining but the result was flat. Australia retained the trophy but had already celebrated. England won the match but didn't feel festive.

The home side could still say that no Australians had won a series in England since 2001. That wait continued. A drawn Ashes was unusual, and 2–2 had only happened once before, in 1972. The scoreline was fitting. Neither team had been good enough to deserve to win outright, and both had been bad enough to deserve to lose a couple of matches. Both required acts of greatness by one player to fend off a series loss.

Both sets of bowlers were outstanding. Home advantage looked to have been levelled by James Anderson's injury, but his absence gave Archer a clear run at four Tests and 22 wickets. Across the ten innings Broad took a dozen wickets within their first ten overs, a record for a series. Woakes was the weak point, chronically underbowled. One Australian advantage was a complete set of quicks in every match until Siddle's injury. The other was that Lyon was a different class to Leach.

But for both teams, the bowling quality created a mismatch. It was the third innings of the fifth Test before either set of openers made a fifty partnership. The highest Australian opening stand was 18, while only twice was their second opener still there with the score above 50. Burns was the only one who found a way, building from his Edgbaston edge-a-thon to contribute scores across four of the five Tests.

Across the board there were 92 scores in single figures out of 207 attempts. Jason Roy, Cameron Bancroft, Usman Khawaja, Moeen Ali and Travis Head got dropped. Root batted out of position and struggled. Wade's lack of runs between his hundreds was reflected in a series average of 33. Denly kept his head above water but would be sunk within a year. Buttler had one good match when it was too late, Paine made one good score just in time. Bairstow forgot how to play anything aimed at his stumps. Warner lost the plot, Marcus Harris never had it.

England mustered just enough support for Stokes to push for a win at Lord's and complete one at Headingley. Australia eventually found Labuschagne but the results were all Smith. Without him Australia would have been rolled on the first day at Edgbaston and that would just about have been that. First time round he saved the day, second time he set up the win. He averted another disaster at Lord's, as well as soaking up

Archer's most vicious spell. He was missing at Headingley when Australia didn't get enough, then came back to set the terms at Old Trafford before anyone could think differently.

Smith's tally of 774 wasn't just a tribute to the iconic ABC Melbourne call sign. Nine players in history had scored more than that in a series. Smith had done it in seven innings, which only Bradman, Viv Richards and Everton Weekes could match. More than anything, Smith's numbers echoed the work of another unsupported genius, Brian Lara: an England tour in 1995, a tally of 765 runs, a 2–2 draw.

But Australia had the Ashes, and England their first World Cup. If you'd looked to apportion the spoils by desire, that's what you would have come up with. Seven England players had contested the Ashes after the emotional work of winning the other trophy. That they had even dredged up the effort for a draw was admirable.

The other thing for Australia to take away was an improved public image. That had been one of the aims: a team seen as cheats and bullies needed to be rehabilitated under the brightest spotlight. The spirit on the field had been manifestly better and redemption was explicitly invoked. 'What I'm most proud about is that Australians are proud of us again,' said Langer.

The broadcaster Gerard Whateley, fond of big sentiments, gave this summary: 'From the deepest scandal where people were repelled by the national cricket team, to the collective embrace of accomplishment when the Ashes were retained, that's the journey of redemption in sport.'

There was and remains scepticism about whether an Australian change would last, which is fair given the history.

Within this team, at least, the values had a strong founding in Paine. Remember it was he who named the problem when the sandpaper story broke: 'We've maybe had our head in the sand a bit over the last twelve months – that if we continue to win, we can act and behave how we like and the Australian public will be ok with that.' He knew that changing a reputation would take years of work. Some opinions would never change, but that was more reason to be steadfast. Whether his motivation was about ethics or public relations didn't really matter: Paine pursued it, and his players had to meet the standard. Langer might have been comfortable with a more abrasive style, but backed his captain.

The celebrations at Old Trafford were the only reversion to type. Most of it was in good spirits, like revising the tedious ding-dong doorbell tune of 'Same old Aussies, always cheating' to become 'Same old Painey, always winning'. The best scene in *The Test* is when the entire squad crams into the narrow confines of the dressing room to re-enact the final wicket. Marsh plays the role of Craig Overton, Hazlewood is himself, spin coach Sridharan Sriram the umpire. Delivery, appeal, dismissal. They even acted out waiting for the third umpire.

It was less cute on the ground for the team song. Reporting on the huddle has always seemed a bit off; it should be the players' moment to themselves. It was their choice though to park themselves right below the press box, which has open balcony doors and was full of people working. It was Lyon's choice while praising Smith to point up at the box, loudly announcing, 'This guy's probably the best cricketer I've ever played with. To come back like that, after all the shit talked by these cunts up there ...'

It was the old siege mentality from when Smith and Darren Lehmann ran the show, as though media workers were the ones who induced players to cheat.

The story that got reported was about Smith impersonating Jack Leach in the huddle when he put on a pair of glasses and shaped up like a left-hander, amid the spray of beer before the team song. Leach's post-match fun at Headingley would not have delighted the Australians. The response was harmless too, but some outlets wrote about graceless Australians, to which Langer and others insisted that Smith had been giving a 'tribute' to his bespectacled and left-handed former teammate Chris Rogers.

Having watched it all in person, all I can say is that the huddle spent a good few minutes beforehand screaming, 'Come back, Steven! It's a no-ball. It's a noey, Steven! Back you come!' Leach had overstepped when having Smith caught in that match, and a viral video from the crowd had featured a lubricated Australian shouting that line. During the no-ball chat, Smith was handed a pair of specs. He asked if he should clean them first, as Leach had done. He polished them on his shirt and put them on to more shouts of 'No ball!' and a few shouts of 'Leachy! It's Leachy!' Only at that point did someone say, 'Bucky Rogers is back!' which prompted a new round of shouts about Rogers. None of it mattered, or should have mattered. It just seemed odd that in the era of elite honesty, this minor story was worth a response that came across as less than elite.

Anyway, the only truly offensive thing done by Australian cricketers that night was to play the same John Williamson song about sixteen times in a row, by which point you could cheerfully strangle all of mum, dad, and a cockatoo. They had at least spared the world from England having a World Cup and Ashes double that could have been waved around by mad jingoists as the spirit of Empire brought back to life. The backdrop of the entire summer's cricket had been the political turmoil of the land in which it was played, an era of anger and waste. Theresa May gave up as prime minister in the second week of the World Cup, Boris Johnson cornered the job just before the Ashes, and the night before the fourth Test he lost his majority in the Commons with mass defections over a no-deal Brexit.

The World Cup wasn't much use to racist nationalists, given its defining image was Archer, Buttler and Adil Rashid locked in a joyful embrace. It was a trophy secured at the last by a Caribbean British cricketer under a government that a year earlier had been aggressively and illegally deporting Caribbean Brits of the Windrush generation. Rashid went home to Bradford for a hero's welcome from a northern Muslim population so often vilified as not wanted and not British. Their captain Eoin Morgan was an Irishman whose nation of birth would stay in the EU, and who expressed how he valued diversity of thought and experience. These were the themes of that team, not of much interest to people who support Eton failures wearing tweed and carrying braces of pheasants while rorting the Chancellery and blaming migrants.

The world was not in a good state, and all of it rolled on. But this English cricket season, at least, was winding down. The 2020 edition would take place in a vastly different world, but for the last days of 2019 we got to enjoy a season when magic wove its way through everything. The Ireland Test had been part of that: a cricket country that had fought for so long to get a chance on the big stage, bowling out England for 85 on the first day at Lord's. Somerset had claimed the last one-day final to be played at that ground after coming second a million or so times before. Meg Lanning had set the highest women's T20 score. In the fortnight ahead, the county championship title would go down to the final day of the season between the two contenders, ending with the veteran Marcus Trescothick on his knees at slip in the last season of a career that had started back in 1993. Essex would prevail in that contest, and would make it a double with their T20 win led by players with a sprinkling of fairy dust like Ravi 'Careless Whisper' Bopara and the Netherlands' finest Ryan ten Doeschate.

As Langer had said, a golden summer, and not just for Stokes. There had been the rain but then there had been those afternoons, the sort that bring England to life. In the cities, ancient buildings stretch their stonework up to a blue sky. In the country, everything blazes green. Glory, when you can sit outside in the perfect temperatures that make you think that in these moments at least, England is the best place to watch cricket in the world. The World Cup final had teams evenly matched in their mistakes, the Ashes evenly matched in their shortcomings. Sport audiences say they want to see the best standard, but really they want a fair fight. Modesty ensured equality. And the series draw was no dull stalemate, it was a spectacle of audacious good cheer.

Within it came those performances worthy of any era. Smith on the first day, walking back into the hardest format of the game after so long, taking on a swinging ball and a heckling crowd and a collapsing team to make the best hundred of his career. Stokes at Headingley, three words that will long evoke the mayhem and glory of his trademarked final day. Cummins and Hazlewood, never letting batsmen draw breath, tireless despite the aches, finally dislodging England in the shadows of a fifth-day dusk at Manchester. Perhaps most of all, Archer, his lithe run and casual menace in one of the game's most memorable debuts, when Smith looked set to make another match his own, shocking a Lord's crowd to silence under dramatic skies. They were what remained – the moments of awe. Sport is slow-motion electricity, the crackle of defining moments from the present down through the years to come. We're all wires to the future.

Chapter 20

Bancroft and Bankrupt

A T THE START of the Ashes, the story was all about the
return of the three suspended players. Steve Smith, David
Warner, Cameron Bancroft, in triumvirate as they had been
in South Africa. 'Getting the banned back together' was the
headline on Peter Lalor's story when the squad was announced.
Heading back to Australia a couple of months later, Smith was
the primary story for his success. Warner was second for his
failure. Kicking back on the Qantas flight with his headphones
on, Bancroft was entirely an afterthought.

No-one was posing his name in water-cooler conversations
about the likely XI ahead of the 2019–20 summer. He would end
up making a squad briefly but wouldn't get a game. He would
fade in the Sheffield Shield and finish the season dropped by
Western Australia. Come April when the next year of national
contracts was announced, he didn't have one to lose and wouldn't
gain one.

Bancroft's flirtation with the Test squad was due to two players taking mental-health breaks. In October his Shield scores were 30, 0, 10, 6, 0 and 11, though he made some runs in the one-day comp. He wasn't initially picked for Australia A to play Pakistan in November and didn't think he was in good enough form. He was included when Nic Maddinson withdrew late, and used the chance to top-score with 49 during a rout for 122. Then Will Pucovski took a break when he was likely to be the spare Test batsman, letting Bancroft hop into that spot. This time though, Joe Burns got his tilt at the team and made a solid if unspectacular go of it. Bancroft was downgraded to standby and went home.

His innings of 30 to start the Shield season would remain his top score for WA until he was dropped in February. He spent the summer not merely getting caught in the leg-gully trap but bringing a bedroll and setting up camp there. In a streak of six innings out of seven he jabbed the ball off his hip to that catcher. He looked out of kilter. It had been an intense few months with a lot of scrutiny and precious little to show for it: four Ashes innings that must already have seemed a lifetime ago.

Cumulatively, the Ashes openers were a sorry tale. Warner had his worst series and neither Bancroft nor Marcus Harris filled the gap. Bancroft's scores were 8, 7, 13 and 16. It was worth considering though that Bancroft's occupation of the crease had at least been some contribution. His tally of balls faced was 25, 31, 66 and 40. His second innings at Edgbaston lasted three quarters of an hour, helping Usman Khawaja stabilise the innings for Smith to come in and do his work. In the first innings at Lord's, Bancroft batted close to two hours either side of stumps on the second day to hold back Smith's entrance until the 23rd over. In the second innings that ended with Australia at risk of being bowled out, six wickets down in 47 overs, he batted for over an hour to get Australia past the tea break after Archer had started like a steam train to dismiss Warner and Khawaja. The fact that Australia batted out that draw could in part be put down to Bancroft.

Dropping him for Headingley must have been a close-run thing. The day before the game Justin Langer told journalists there would be no changes. His protege had been picked in difficult conditions against excellent new-ball bowling in a series where every opener was struggling, and his team led the series 1–0. In honesty Bancroft got burned: two chances then cast aside, when the failure rate of Test batting would suggest that at least a third match makes a fairer sample size. His original selection had been dubious, but once that was done it was equally dubious to punt him early.

When Marcus Harris came in it was free lunch at the carvery. Stuart Broad and Jofra Archer had perfected bowling to Warner, and a flaw of the squad from the start had been that Harris was an off-brand replica. Short, stocky, left-handed, belligerent outside off stump but less likely to middle it: he was Warner in the two-cylinder hatchback model. In home conditions Harris was a fair substitute; in English conditions he was a liability. His best score for the series was 19, his best partnership 27. He couldn't match Bancroft's contribution of sticking around. He was out early each time, facing fewer balls in six innings than Bancroft in four, 121 to 162. His shortcomings were evident early but it would have been too chaotic to recall dropped players in his place. Harris rode out the series, ran out his luck, lost his place in November and his contract in April.

By the terms in which public forgiveness is granted, Bancroft had failed his redemption story. He ticked off the first requirement, attaining another shot at the big time after his shot at his own foot. In the team's documentary he spoke of the significance of returning at Edgbaston. 'We all make mistakes, and I reckon it was almost a great metaphor for the fact that we have a choice whether we want to live in the suffering of what that is, or we want to move past that and be better and be great.' The only problem was that he wasn't talking about himself. 'Steve Smith did that,' he went on to say.

Meaning that Smith was the one who got to move past it. Bancroft didn't. 'I wanted the perfect story. The perfect outcome. I wanted to walk off with two hundreds next to my name. The welcome back. I wanted that.'

That's how it works. Loss, shame, punishment, repentance, triumph, forgiveness. Players are morally cleansed by their feats letting them become something new. Smith was now the Ashes champion, conqueror of English fields. Warner had enough credits for a further chance back home. Bancroft was the one who hadn't changed. He had the double hit of still being the ball-tampering boy while now being held solely responsible for his fate. He would no longer be seen as the kid whose career had ended after being dragged into a debacle; he was the player whose career had stalled from a lack of runs.

It's worth remembering that Bancroft was Australia's leading scorer on that South Africa tour despite missing the last match, a tour on which Smith and Warner fell apart and three other senior batsmen delivered far too little. He played lengthy innings and defended in a way that has deserted most Australians for decades.

He had plenty to offer before he was derailed. His involvement in the 2019 Ashes was analogous to Cape Town: pulled into something he shouldn't have been part of, quickly expendable when it didn't work out. Afterwards he was left behind. There is time and ability yet for a third coming of Bancroft, but nothing is written.

Nor was he the only player left dislocated by that long season in England. Smith and Warner coming into the World Cup squad threw out the rhythm of everything that had begun working well. Shaun Marsh had settled at first drop, four centuries in eight games. For the World Cup he subbed in twice for injury, batting five and then six, broke his wrist in the nets, and that was that, his last appearance for Australia. Marsh wasn't short of opportunity over his career, but was pushed out at the most consistent he'd been for his country. Peter Handscomb didn't make the squad at all, then was called back when Marsh was injured. Straight into a semi-final, where he predictably failed and hasn't been seen in an Australian shirt since.

Then there was Khawaja. At the time of writing his last match was the third Test at Leeds. Being dropped for Labuschagne at number three was fair enough based on runs. But Khawaja had a great record as an opener. If Bancroft had been retained for that third Test and failed a third time, Khawaja could have taken his place for the fourth. If Bancroft had succeeded then there would have been no doubt about dropping Khawaja. But with Harris coming in for the third Test, Khawaja couldn't push him out for the fourth despite being the better player. Khawaja's three Tests to that point had been ordinary without being disastrous, but he sat out the series watching Harris complete three that were.

All of this came after a World Cup that trashed one of the most productive periods of his career. Preparing for the tournament he made 655 runs in ten matches, only three scores below a half century. He went into the World Cup with more ODI runs that year than anyone in the world. Yet once it started, his successful partnership was broken up and he was pushed down to bat at three, four, six. Things never clicked, though he saved Australia against New Zealand and ended up with similar returns to Smith: 316 runs in nine innings versus 379 in ten.

He didn't guess that his Test sacking would also see him out of the one-day team. When Australia next picked a 50-over squad in December 2019, he wasn't in it. He'd scored 1089 runs that year averaging almost 50, with a strike rate of 85. The strangest moment came at the Australian Cricket Awards in February 2020, when the contenders were announced for ODI Player of the Year. Montages rolled of shots cracking off the bats of Finch, Warner and ... Khawaja, whose time in the format seemed like years ago. Finch narrowly claimed more votes, a relief for some and a disappointment for others. As he's someone who speaks his mind, it would have been memorable had Khawaja taken the stage.

As Australian cricket headed into 2020, not knowing that troubles far greater than scandals lay ahead, these were the examples that comebacks are not all glory. The big names were back, sportswashed, dressed up in their tuxedos, cleansed by success and the passage of time. Their teams would benefit from their abilities, and their presence would come to be seen as only to the good. It was less so for the others who got burned along the way.

Chapter 21

Trial and Triple Elation

THE 2019 ASHES will follow David Warner for life. Even the most extensive careers get remembered in dot points. Warner's will include his three sets of twin tons and his century in a session. It will include his sandpaper adventure. And it will include one of those rare sets of stats compelling enough to stay in the minds of the broader public: five Tests, ten innings, ten dismissals, 95 runs. You can work out the average.

Of that slender total, 61 came in an innings. The rest of his series read 2, 8, 3, 5, 0, 0, 0, 5, 11. The three zeroes in a row was when people really started losing their minds. That's the emergency services number in Australia. Stuart Broad was the duck hunter, sniggering like a Nintendo dog every time he got another one on target. The three times that Broad didn't get him there was Jofra Archer to mop up. What was happening to a guy who had just made 647 runs in the World Cup and had 21 Test centuries, a guy who had made fifty in every Test on his previous tour of England?

Players have horror stretches. That's a fact in a game where failure is the statistical norm. Warner was in an especially difficult bind. He was at a dead end, questioning everything about his game, but had been too successful across the rest of his career to be dropped. Missing a match would probably have been a relief, but he kept being backed on the basis that he might come good. In the end it only gave him more chances to fail.

The storied West Indies all-rounder Learie Constantine scored 72 runs visiting Australia in 1930–31. Plum Warner, known for being England's tour manager for the Bodyline series, went to South Africa as a player in 1906 and totalled 89 runs. Those two are the only non-tailenders in history with a smaller harvest than David Warner from ten innings in a series.

Plum Warner still got a grandstand named after him at Lord's, and by the end of the 2019 series England fans would have been ready to add David's name alongside. They relished every minute. Warner had long been Enemy No.1 for the terraces, ever since he threw a blancmange punch at future captain Joe Root in the Birmingham Walkabout in 2013. He was the cliched Australian of their fevered colonial dreams: rough as guts, on the piss, bereft of self-control, built like a clenched fist, bristling of character and of chin. He was a lot more fun to jeer than Smith, who serenely got on with the job of making England lose Test matches. For years Warner had invited the fight, invited the opprobrium, so his epic freewheeling failure was the sweetest plum of all.

As for Australian supporters, sympathy was less prominent than frustration and disdain. Everyone understood that the comeback players were in this series for atonement. Smith was getting it, Warner was not. As his dismissals came to seem inevitable, each was greeted with sighs and groans. People muttering in the stands or the comment sections lamented the waste of a spot. With his years of Test brilliance far behind in the memory, the mood of the moment was frank. Warner? No good.

Among the gloating and the angst, one thing was totally overlooked: David Warner almost sealed the Ashes for Australia. It was Warner's half-century at Headingley that staved off what would have been a disastrous collapse. Getting Australia to 179 was worth gold when England got done for 67. Not to mention his five slip catches, some of them stunners. After two days of that match, 999 simulations out of a thousand would see Australia go on to lead 2–0, and then win the series. Warner would have been pivotal and more kindly remembered. Instead he set up the opportunity and saw it squandered.

It's also forgotten how good that innings was. For hours, against extreme lateral movement and bounce that sizzled past the edge, Warner kept a compact shape, playing straight to protect his pads. He was beaten constantly but didn't let it bother him. He played as late and softly as possible, and rewards came. Bowlers erred and he directed them away with minimal backlift or follow-through. He ran sharply enough to draw two boundaries from overthrows. He got the run rate to 4.5 an over without a risky shot, and it took a perfect ball from Archer to end his stay.

Perhaps there was more danger when the ball was moving less. It didn't miss the edge anywhere else. Broad's method was to come around the wicket, varying the angle, cutting the ball in to threaten the stumps or away for a catch. Warner would be done one way or the other. But pointing out the dominance is wisdom after the event. Warner started with two unlucky dismissals and a couple of pearlers. Runs in his fifth innings supported Justin Langer's belief that he was an hour away from coming good. England supporters enjoyed his dismissals so much partly because he was always seen as a threat. It was only by the fourth Test that the extent of Broad's hold over him was clear. By then Warner had tinkered with his stance, changed his approach, consulted everyone within range. In the aftermath of the fifth Test his coach addressed the problem. 'Talking frankly I thought he let Stuart Broad get into his head, and I think he thought way too much about it,' said Langer.

'I've seen it before, even with the great players. Every now and then they have a series. And I'm talking about the all-time great players. I'm talking about Gilly with Andrew Flintoff. I remember seeing Steve Waugh sit on the team bus in South Africa, and the guy had been a run machine for so long. He got out just before stumps, and I actually in a sick sort of way thought it was the best thing I'd ever seen. Because I didn't think great players had lean runs. Even great players have lean runs. I've learned over a long period of time, you never write off champion players. It doesn't matter what sport. You never write off champion players. They tend to come good, don't they?'

Any speculation about Warner being dropped was out of touch with reality. His near-decade of Test cricket was worth 6458 runs in 79 matches, 51 scores over 50. It would have taken an extended failure at home to see him gone, especially after the goodwill CA had expended bringing him back. Still, his wait between seasons would have been uncomfortable. He knew he had to succeed. So he steamed into the new season as a T20 locomotive. The perfect start against Sri Lanka, his first century in the format while posting a huge team score. The next two were chases and he was not out for 60 and 57. Against Pakistan he was rained off, got out for a fast 20 in a winning chase, and was 48 not out in another.

Then the Tests. The last time Warner had played Pakistan he had carved a hundred before lunch on day one, the fifth batsman to achieve the feat. That was in Sydney in 2017, but his 2019 Brisbane effort could not have been more different. Starting on the second day after Pakistan were bowled out, he was careful all morning, circumspect outside off. His first pull shot didn't come for more than an hour. His off-side runs were steers. Only dross was cut, only the fullest balls were driven. When Imran Khan bowled a wide line across Warner, he waited. When Naseem Shah bowled short he swayed and smiled. Partnered with recalled right-hander Joe Burns, they hit gaps, trusted one another's calls, kept the field switching and the scoreboard rolling. Australia began the innings at near six an over, and within half an hour it felt like Pakistan had lost their grip on the match.

Through much of his career Warner had played under a charm. He pulled off audacious feats by having the gall to try them. His four-leaf clover had wilted through his suspension and his Ashes, but now it was green again. He was caught off a Naseem no-ball before going on to a century, the fourth such reprieve before a Test hundred in his career. Imran hit his stumps without dislodging the bail. Yasir Shah's direct hit from the deep trailed him home by a millimetre.

But luck was Warner's garnish, not his substance. His 154 at the Gabba was his 40th international ton, second for Australia behind Ricky Ponting. Resuming on the third morning, he added three to his overnight score but batted for an hour in doing so, soaking up the fresh bowling while Marnus Labuschagne scored freely. In the end Warner faced 296 balls across 444 minutes, a record for the longest innings of his career in both respects.

That record would last for one hit. Next up Australia batted first on a true Adelaide pitch. One teenage quick on debut in Naseem was replaced by another in Muhammad Musa Khan. His bowling was rapid, short and wide, and Warner went hard over point knowing that the first two sessions would be the most profitable in a day-night Test. He threaded drives through cover, not even looking to the leg side until deep into his innings. Again his running forced overthrow boundaries, bringing up his fifty with a rare six along the carpet. Eventually he began lofting the spinners. He only got twitchy before his hundred under lights, losing his bat coming through for the final scrambled single.

Warner ended the night on 166 and ploughed on the next day. He sprinted down the wicket emitting a howl on raising his double hundred. Such was his control that the triple seemed to arrive soon afterwards, coasting into existence. One of the grand feats of batsmanship, and he greeted it with a series of Super Mario jumps before offering a deep bow to the grandstand. The crowd there cheered as he moved towards the famed Australian mark of 334 held by Don Bradman and Mark Taylor. The declaration came with him on 335. He had faced 418 balls in just shy of 11 hours.

This was truly a comeback, from the depths of his batting to the peak. Among the cheers though was a different response, one of resentment rather than acclaim. In Brisbane plenty had enjoyed a smirk about Warner's first innings at home being worth more than his ten innings in England. But a triple-century? To go past Bradman? It was received as poor taste. The tone was censorious. People lambasted the flat track, home comforts, beating up an outmatched attack – how could that score mean anything at all? It was flaunting wealth after an austerity program. His celebrations were the showboating of a pretender who couldn't deliver when it counted.

Wrapped up with that response was the contention that Warner wasn't a real Test batsman because he couldn't do it overseas. That too had started after Brisbane but it tripled down in Adelaide. If you set up a false equivalence of ability in one context to inability in another, then greater success in the first context will amplify the claim. The better he played at home the more he could be hammered for it.

Unsurprisingly, the assumed wisdom missed a lot of nuance. Foremost, all triple-centuries suck. Without wanting to disappoint anyone, none of them have been made on raging greentops or turners against bowling attacks stacked with menace and variety. They get made at St John's in Antigua or the Sinhalese Sports Club in Colombo, where the ghosts of bowlers roil and groan in the blameless turf. They get made in matches where teams pass 900, matches where there are five other centuries and 14 total wickets, or two double-tons before the triple.

Nor do they come in quality contests. Out of all 31 triples, 18 have come in draws and 11 in wins by an innings. Brian Lara's two world records, Bradman's masterpieces at Leeds – bore draws. Only two triples were fightbacks from disadvantage: Brendon McCullum in the third innings while 152 behind India and five wickets down, and Hanif Mohammad with history's longest vigil to hold off the West Indies of Garfield Sobers. Two other triples came in close matches: Azhar Ali in Dubai setting West Indies 346 that they nearly chased, and Lawrence Rowe getting West Indies a lead of 200 only to see England cling on for a draw.

The other matches wouldn't be on your repeat-viewing list. Huge scores come in bad games. By their existence they kill contests. Then they fall behind in history until the context fades, leaving the figures with an aura of authority in the stats columns.

It's also true that the feat of the triple-century in itself is incredible. Batting is a cumulation of probability: each ball you face is another chance to be dismissed. Compounding those odds is fatigue. Even peak Lara against a team of schoolkids would miscue a catch after a few months. So the level of fitness and focus to face Test bowlers for two days without making the mistake that gets you out is astonishing. On the evening when Warner stopped batting there had been 94,951 individual innings in men's Test cricket. He had made a bigger score than all but nine of them. This is the temple of the triple, the magnitude and the pointlessness of the achievement.

That Warner played better in Australia was obvious. His record of 17 tons at home and 6 away was tabled as Exhibit A. But numbers can mask more information. They didn't do justice to the Warner who made twin tons at Cape Town against a superb South African side, the Warner who saved Australia in Bangladesh with two of his best. Most players are more prolific at home, and Warner wasn't much more lopsided than lauded names like Greg Chappell (16 home tons out of 24), Matthew Hayden (21 out of 30) or Mike Hussey (14 out of 19). Warner's Ashes average that year of 9.5 was parlous, but Jason Roy opening for England in the same series averaged ... 9.5. Marcus Harris got up to 9.66, replacing Cameron Bancroft who went at 11.

The focus on Warner's trouble overseas also obscured how fully he had mastered conditions at home. By Adelaide he had more Test centuries in Australia than anyone but Bradman, Hayden and Ponting. Combine all formats and only Ponting was ahead. In 2019–20 Warner elevated his game another level. Previously he had tended to reach a hundred and assume licence to bomb the crowd. He scored as big as his patience or fitness or fortune allowed. In eight years he had batted through a full day once. In this season he did it twice in a week, and the second time batted most of the next day as well.

Warner had made work crucial to his scoring. Throughout his back-to-back centuries the sharp single was his release shot, usually patted to point or cover, or dropped to midwicket. His hustle on the first run often set up a second or third. The bowler searching to quieten him would make mistakes. Laced through his innings were boundaries that capitalised on them.

The simplicity of his game and the level of his fitness made it a highly repeatable style, supported by the mental application to keep carrying it out. In Adelaide he spent a *Lord of the Rings* movie marathon at the crease, but had as much control when the Elves began sailing into the West as he had when Gandalf showed up at Bilbo's birthday. It was notable even when Warner was past

300 how hard he ran for his partner, at one point sprinting back for an overthrow despite having overshot the crease by 20 yards.

'I think early days, I didn't really have changing the gears in the right sort of context in the game. The only way I knew was to sometimes throw the kitchen sink at it,' was his explanation after that innings. 'But over time, the last two Tests, it's the best I think I've ever batted. The most disciplined I've ever batted and the most patient I've ever batted. I just felt at ease, especially batting with Marnus, we were really talking about the game. I think sometimes I get carried away with talking about where I'm looking to score instead of what the bowler's actually doing and how he's trying to get me out.'

Up until Adelaide his streak across T20s and Tests was 776 runs in eight innings, six of them not out. He would finish the Test season with another unbeaten hundred against New Zealand in Sydney, score another in a one-dayer in India, a couple of T20 fifties in South Africa, and 67 against New Zealand in an ODI before coronavirus shut down the season. All of them were scored with fundamentally the same method. What stood out was how consistent it was across formats, only shifting up or down in urgency as required.

With a longer view, it became clear that the home summer was not a turnaround. It was a continuation. Warner's comeback had started in the Indian Premier League the previous April, where he had been the top scorer by a mile with 692 runs – a century and eight fifties from a dozen innings. This consistency came from moving past his early style of ransacking the bowling. Rather than the four or six, his currency was the two, hitting a gap neatly enough to give space for a second run. He scored from nearly every ball and took boundaries when they came rather than hunting them. His method still left him with a healthy strike rate of 143, while doubling or tripling his average from other seasons to 69.

This was the approach he brought to the World Cup, overcoming his harried beginning, nearly topping that tournament too. From April 2019 to March 2020, the Ashes was the anomaly rather than the trend. His whole body of work could have been very differently received but for one game. Had Australia won their World Cup semi-final, he might have been lionised as the one who drove them to a trophy. Instead they lost and his work was brushed aside. As ever, it was easier for people to whack the player they didn't like. Warner had long had a knack for being dislikeable, which had partly been held back by a dam wall of runs. When the sandpaper story broke, all that was latent had been activated. Now people thumped him for his failings as a batsman because his sins as a person gave them cause.

Smith, on the other hand, had earned all the leeway he liked. When he walked out to bat in the Gabba Test against Pakistan, the score was a million for two. I could check the exact number but it doesn't matter. Smith by his own description hates being on the sidelines, still relating to cricket like a seven-year-old, so it must have been a special kind of pain for him to be kept waiting into the third day. Pakistan had batted through the first, Burns was the only wicket on the second, and Warner lasted 14 overs after the resumption.

Finally Smith arrived, the Ashes glutton, the man for whom too many runs were never enough. On a friendly track against tired bowlers, away from menace and barracking. He blocked a few, left a couple, skipped down to deposit Yasir Shah's leg-break over midwicket for four. The next ball was flighted, full, landing almost on the popping crease. Aiming for the same panel on the fence, Smith was left digging it out from under himself. He fell over his stiff front leg, his foot marooned where it had started rather than stepping to the line, as the ball skipped inside his bat and onto his stumps.

Smith, ten balls faced, bowled for 4. It just made no sense at all.

Except for the ways that it did. Australia was way on top, a lead of 111 with eight wickets in hand over an opponent unlikely to challenge. The remaining batsmen had licence, if not expectation, to hit. And Smith rarely produces his best from positions of dominance. He rejoins the mortal batting realm when situations ask him to breezily swing rather than save the day.

He had played a couple of excellent recent T20 innings against Sri Lanka and Pakistan, at ease with the simple mindset of the shortest form. Through the Test summer though, his team kept dominating and Smith kept not. The score was 369 at Adelaide when he came in. He got 36, nicking an ungodly leg-side slog. Against New Zealand he came in at more reasonable scores of 75, 131, 61, 100 and 95, but Australia were very much ahead in those matches, and soon ahead in the series, while Neil Wagner put the clamps on Smith with a concerted bouncer attack. Smith had made at least two centuries in every home summer aside from his first in 2010–11, when he only got three Tests batting at six and seven. In the current season he was kept to a couple of fifties.

Nobody minded much. These series did not excite a great depth of feeling. It was interesting, though, that all was not in good repair with the formerly faultless machine. The reason being the human on the inside.

Smith's game works best under pressure. Away from home, in the toughest climes, he had saved the team time and again. Six tons in England, three in a series in India. Centuries in South Africa, New Zealand, Sri Lanka, West Indies. As captain he saw collapse after collapse, trying to sandbag as fast as the water would rise. He made a couple of gravy hundreds beating India at home in 2014–15, but most of his big innings have come from disadvantage. What sets him apart is seeing the situation then summoning the powers necessary to deal with it.

These powers come at a cost. Like the telekinetic Eleven in *Stranger Things*, using them exhausts him to the point of helplessness. On that epic India tour in 2017 he started the fourth Test in a blaze of shots, scoring twice as fast as Warner until well past his fifty, and out soon after his hundred. He knew he only had a couple of hours of concentration in him. 'At one point I hadn't made ten and I hit Umesh Yadav over cover for four, something I wouldn't normally do in a Test match,' he said later. 'I was so mentally drained that I just didn't have anything left.'

The 2017–18 Ashes in Australia did a similar number on him: another three hundreds in the series, crying in the dressing room after the trophy was secured. It wasn't elation, it was relief. He admitted mental fatigue but said he felt fine after two weeks off. His next engagement was in South Africa, where burnout was a big part of both his worst tour with the bat and his decisions that ended with his suspension.

In 2019, same again. Smith was baked before the series was over: at The Oval 'it got to day two and my mind was saying keep going but my body had shut down and wouldn't let me do anything'. Again the proffered tonic was two weeks off before a Sheffield Shield season began.

An interesting statistical line shows this pattern within series themselves. One thing that Smith had over almost every other player was concentration. So it made sense that he was a player who got his centuries, not spooked by the approaching milestone. From his first century at The Oval in 2013 through to his Ashes double in Perth in 2017, Smith got past a score of 71 on 24 occasions. Once there he was dismissed short of a century twice. Otherwise, those 24 opportunities yielded 22 centuries, a conversion rate beyond belief.

The change came after that double-hundred in Perth. His next dismissal, he chopped on at the MCG for 76. On a pitch deader than the Wicked Witch, a guaranteed hundred evaporated. He made a ton in the second innings, then was out in Sydney for 83. With his record, two slip-ups in three was astounding.

The pattern recurred in 2019. Out understandably at Lord's for 92, at Old Trafford for 82, and at The Oval for 80. In his biggest performance of the subsequent Australian season, 77 not out on the evening of Boxing Day, Smith was snared at gully for 85 the next day. The man who at one stage never missed a hundred had now dropped a bushel of them. The plausible explanation was being out of juice.

If there was no crisis, Smith's otherworldly powers weren't invoked. If there was not much on the line he wasn't sure how to proceed. Smith was the rarest anomaly in the modern game, as the player who could do it anywhere, and the most valuable commodity, as the player who could do it when it mattered. His greatness on those measures was indisputable. The part that was missing is that for a player to make the most of their potential, they have to be able to cash in. Bradman became the statistical Everest because he never let up, thrashing the weaker early South African and Indian and West Indies sides as remorselessly as he did England. Smith has let pass some opportunities to get closer to Bradman than anyone.

None of which matters much. It's about what spurred Smith to great heights. Wanting him to dominate in lower-profile series is the greed of the stat-fanatic, the desire to see him racing up the centuries list, feeding that obscenely swollen average. But Smith's record was already a wonder. If a quieter series here or there helped him recuperate, he was due whatever he liked.

Given the gulf in how Smith and Warner were received, the 2020 Australian Cricket Awards night was the most interesting in the event's uninspiring history. In early February, with Australia still smouldering from a summer of bushfires, a crowd of shiny people came in from the smoky air to Melbourne's Crown Palladium. Towards the end of the night the event felt more like the 2017 Academy Awards, when Faye Dunaway was handed the wrong envelope and announced *La La Land* as Best Picture instead of *Moonlight*. The Australian version, to a rather smaller global audience, was for the Allan Border Medal, covering matches from January 2019 to January 2020. The winner read out to the black-tie assembly was: David Warner.

What? First of all, the fact that your contenders were both guys who hadn't played until June was silly in itself. But of the two players who had missed 13 matches in the voting period due to suspension, how could it be Warner? How could Steve Smith, the gold-plated home-feted true-blue Aussie Ashes champion, have lost to the bloke who spent that series forgetting how to hold the bat?

This, at least, was the reaction of a substantial part of the cricketing public. Some of them tried to be reasonable: 'Warner's win means it's time for an AB Medal rethink' ran one of a number of similar headlines the next day, with one article going straight to Allan Border himself. Others were angry. Now Warner was pitted against Smith directly.

The anger wasn't helped by learning that a single vote had been the difference, 193 to 194. To Australians, the Ashes were what mattered. Smith had been heroic in cricketing terms, standing alone against rising tides, and to spectators was undoubtedly the player of the year. Had a panel judged the award they would have made that choice. But votes are allocated across a year, and Smith had a limited impact outside one series. Marnus Labuschagne picked up votes in his Ashes wake and dominated the home summer, pipping him as Test player of the year. Warner was the consistent performer across both white-ball formats as well as the home Tests. Smith's concentrated effort was so good that it still nearly beat them both, but he needed one more performance.

Allan Border Medal votes are awarded in sets of three, two and one for the best three players in a match. Teammates collectively decide a set of votes; the other set is combined from the votes of umpires or match referees, and a member of the media in attendance, who is randomly asked by a CA official.

Some decide their votes solo, some consult the press box for a consensus, either way it's done quickly. This is not a scientific process, Your Honour, it's about the vibe.

The final step is to add a weighting: multiply votes by six for a Test, three for an ODI, and two for a T20. It makes for big disparities: if all the judges think you've topped a Test match, that's worth 36 votes; if one side puts you third in a T20, that's worth two.

Smith got full Ashes votes at Edgbaston, Lord's and Old Trafford, and second behind Matthew Wade at The Oval. That was a haul of 132. But his only outstanding white-ball matches were the World Cup semi-final when everyone bombed, and a T20 at Manuka when he bossed Pakistan. If we do some reverse-engineering from his final tally and his performances, he must have come third in the votes against Sri Lanka at the Gabba, third in the World Cup against the West Indies, and had his only split decision against Sri Lanka in London with one vote for second and one for third. A single vote in a single Test at home would have sealed the medal but he didn't land one from six attempts.

Warner did get votes in the Ashes. Headingley, of course. Third behind Labuschagne and Hazlewood for a dozen to his tally. He hoovered them up in the World Cup: best on ground against Afghanistan, Pakistan, Bangladesh and South Africa, 18 votes apiece. Best on ground through the home T20s in Adelaide, Brisbane and Melbourne, with what must have been a split decision in Perth for a solitary third-placed vote in a small chase. Through the home Tests he was behind Labuschagne in Brisbane, on top for his triple in Adelaide, and third for his century in Sydney. The very last hit of the qualification period earned him the dozen points that squeaked him home.

All of the above confirms the idea of Smith being best when the going was tough. But while there's a weighting for format, there isn't one for subjective qualities. There's no ranking for pressure or expectation. Which meant that Warner's win wasn't unlikely. The bookies had him paying under $1.50 and Smith over $4. It's mostly a batting award: by force of habit a fair batting day of 60 gets valued higher than a fair bowling day of three wickets. Specialist bowlers have won four times in its 21 years. In the 2020 period Patrick Cummins played the most matches, took 103 wickets and bowled twice as many overs as the next quick. He came third. Among batsmen, openers have an advantage because of short games, like when Warner's T20 dominance meant that Smith wasn't required. Warner batted 34 times in the voting period, Smith 27. Cummins bowled in 47 innings and batted in 28.

Those with a certain sense of humour couldn't help but laugh as the winner walked to the podium while others across the country scowled at their televisions. It felt like the ultimate bit of Warner trolling. One vote the difference between the crowd's golden boy and the villain, and the latter had triumphed without having made a convincing heel–face turn. Warner had always liked riling people. He got a boost out of it. He was stubborn and punchy and would push on regardless of situation or consequence. No matter how badly people didn't want him around, he couldn't help defying it. Centre stage again.

Still, the Warner who stood up in front of the plastic veneer glitz of the casino ballroom was a more hesitant variation. He probably anticipated the blowback. He must have been aware that he had to come across the right way. He wasn't sure what to say. You could read as much from his body language: invisible on the cameras, but below the frame, he spent his speech with one leg tucked behind the other, pressing hard together in an attempt to hold steady. Tension radiated off him. A couple of times he seemed close to tears, the catch in his voice more natural than in his confession of 2018.

'I couldn't be any prouder to stand here and receive the award,' he said. 'I'm extremely grateful to be accepted back by Cricket Australia and the peers, and also be accepted by the fans. I had mixed emotions of how I was going to be received back here at home. I definitely knew what I was in for in England. Standing here today, I'm extremely proud to have that opportunity again and extremely grateful.'

His suspension was still referred to elliptically, and Cape Town wasn't mentioned at all. But he addressed the consequences in surprisingly direct fashion, as well as his own performances.

'The way that Finchy and Painey accepted us and were always in contact with us, we really appreciate that. I want to thank my club team at home, Randwick-Petersham, for giving me that opportunity to go out there and play grade cricket. I realised a lot of things in that time off, that we don't actually understand when we're in this bubble – the importance of this game, and the smiles on the faces that we bring to a lot of people. Having three daughters at home looking up to guys like Smithy, Cummo, we're playing cricket in the backyard and they're yelling out Virat Kohli's name – these are the smiles on kids' faces that we put on. To go back there and be able to be reintegrated in the grassroots, it really helped me get to where I am today. Because without that, getting cricket taken away from you, something I've always dreamed of, it really really hurt.

'It's just been remarkable to come back, and have a good World Cup. To not go the whole way was disappointing, the Ashes were retained and that was fantastic. I obviously didn't turn up and I apologise for that. But I really had the hunger and determination to come back and put my foot forward and do the best for our team. To come back and have a summer like that and just contribute, it really put a smile on my face and I hope it did for you guys as well.'

The closing thank-yous were when he started to pause for composure.

'First of all my mum and dad: I know I've let you guys down in the past but you guys always stick by my side, and I really appreciate that. And my brother. My wife ...'

There was a catch in the throat as he turned to the ceiling and breathed out 'Fuck,' just loud enough to make it through the microphone.

'As I said before, my rock. You are absolutely amazing. I don't know what could ever break you. You're absolutely fantastic. You're an inspiration not just to me but the girls. It's hard for a man to stand up here and say a lot of nice words about people, but you always seem to bring the best out of me and the kindness of my heart. I can't thank you enough for what you do for me and our family. I love you dearly.'

That ending felt hugely significant, given that Warner's adoration of Candice had played such a part in his behavioural meltdown in the sandpaper series, enraged as he was by South

African players, officials and crowds denigrating her. His personal combativeness was very different to his protectiveness of those he loved. She had been his support through the suspension and his stability for the comeback. There was vindication in her work that night, and there was something to admire in his: a changeable man with a head always full of ideas, for better or for worse, to whom eloquence didn't come naturally, but who had to compose these thoughts and deliver them. Perhaps more surprising than his win was his frank and moving response.

Like Warner, Ellyse Perry had clinched the women's prize with one Test performance. She hadn't beaten Alyssa Healy to the T20 or ODI gongs, a double which in non-Ashes years would by definition win the Belinda Clark Award. But with the loading for Test votes, Perry's runs at Taunton vaulted her to the top. She stood for photos in a long dress, tall and at ease, next to Warner, shorter and squarer, awkward with his white dinner jacket and his strained smile. His triple hundred, now his triple in the Border medal – his third win which nobody in the previous couple of years would have thought possible. The world can change in the time it takes to draw breath.

Chapter 22

Won't You Help to Sing

O N 8 MARCH 2020, a set of giant numbers came up on the MCG screens. They read 86,174. The Women's T20 World Cup final had pulled the biggest crowd for any women's cricket match ever staged. The local contingent got their money's worth: Australia's opener Alyssa Healy blazed from the start with 75 from 39 balls, clean as can be hitting sixes over cover. Beth Mooney finished on 78 not out.

India's chase began with one of those moments when a plan comes off. Megan Schutt's style was to pitch up for swing, but Shafali Verma usually boomed anything full back down the ground. She had towelled up Australia in the opening match of the tournament. In their last two contests Schutt had bowled a dozen balls to Verma for five fours and a six. So this time Schutt held back the length, denying that drive while giving room to deviate. She drew an edge to Healy. India's main hope of chasing 185 was gone.

Public engagement with the tournament had been big. When Australia had won the previous edition in the Caribbean it barely registered. But this year, that first loss to India had filled the comments and the talkback lines, arguing about selection and tactics and attitude. The investment and effort put into the women's game over five years was working. Cricket wasn't confined to the dramas of the men's team anymore.

Cricket Australia wanted to top the crowd record for women's sport, which was just over 90,000 at a football World Cup final in California. On the night the MCG's capacity was 91,000. Every ticket was distributed but 5000 people didn't show. Perhaps this talk of a new virus had them spooked. Those of us in attendance were almost dismissive of the concern. In the next few days the situation blew up. A week later that match wouldn't have been allowed to go ahead.

As it was, people surged onto the ground after the game to watch Katy Perry sing, with the Australian players joining her on stage. Eighteen hours later I would run into off-spinner Molly Strano in a bar, still in her kit, carrying the trophy, wearing a pair of Perry's white high-heeled boots. On the night itself, sitting up on the second deck to watch the show, everything felt joyous. I had started covering women's cricket as recently as 2013 and even then nobody wanted to know. Now it was front page, back page, booking out the biggest house in the world. We'd seen a spectacle saying that girls could have these dreams.

It felt like the start of something, not the end. But it was just about the last cricket for months, with postponements imminent across the world. The game would resume in biosecure bubbles: no spectators, no spit on the ball. The sport would become a series of comebacks, setbacks, pushbacks. After all their time on the sidelines, Steve Smith and David Warner faced another 11 months between Tests. Nostalgia for the English summer of 2019 is not just for what was extraordinary, but because it might have been the last of an old normal.

While Australia's women had their moment, the men experienced the other side of the coin, ignored on a white-ball tour of South Africa. It would normally have won attention as the first trip back there since the sandstorm tour. 'Walking into the hotel at Sandton, just initially I was like, last time I left here it wasn't pretty,' said Smith.

His captaincy ban expired at the end of March, though Warner was blacklisted for life. You could be sure that as long as Tim Paine was in the job there would be speculation about his successor. Ex-players would give soundbites that would be written up online, one more scoop of grist to the content mill. The Australian misconception that your best bat is your best captain would never change, though Smith had already provided an unrebuttable closing argument as third speaker for the negative. The media itch for the redemption cycle would never be fully scratched. As to whether Smith was thinking about it, he invoked the Australian version of pleading the Fifth: 'Yeah, nah.'

By June a different leader was gone, the pandemic finishing off CA chief executive Kevin Roberts. He had responded to the pandemic by declaring an emergency within the sport and insisting everyone follow his austerity lead, much as he had when trying to bullock the players' union into a new pay structure in 2017. Like that time, he failed, eventually overthrown by the state associations who said his numbers didn't add up and his communication wasn't clear.

The men's players and coach went on learning how to be themselves in the public eye. Video interviews from home were endearing. So too the documentary about their England trip. Said Justin Langer, 'my third daughter Sophie watched the first two episodes and she got this look on her face, and she said, Dad, that's the first time in my life I've ever seen you angry. In one way it's a compliment to me as a dad I guess. But when my daughters see that, they see another side of me at work. But that's ok, that's what it is. I've got nothing to hide, we're human, we've got our frailties, we've got our vulnerabilities, and we just go about our business. It's a taxing job, it's an emotional job, and sometimes you smile and sometimes you're growling.'

In the new world of crisis, past scandal seemed a long time ago. Smith and Warner were back to being part of the furniture. When Joe Root missed a match, Stokes was picked to ascend to the ranks of England Test captains. There were few objections.

These sorts of cycles rolled on. Four days before Stokes led out his team in Southampton, Australian Football League player Jordan De Goey was charged with indecent assault in Melbourne. With no court date for months, he sat out one whole match for Collingwood after the charge was announced before being treated like a returning hero. The club posted a saccharine 'Welcome back, Jordy' message online. Commentators pumped him up with every goal, including the esteemed Bruce McAvaney describing his absence as 'a hiccup'.

This kind of response is the norm, not the exception. Take a previous Collingwood case with Dayne Beams and John

McCarthy, or Port Adelaide with Peter Burgoyne. Take a squad's worth of National Rugby League players from Canterbury and Cronulla. European footballers from the top like Cristiano Ronaldo to the low divisions like Ched Evans. Take New Zealand cricketer Scott Kuggeleijn, Irish rugby players Paddy Jackson and Stuart Olding, basketballer Kobe Bryant. That's just a handful. All were accused of rape. All were supported to play on in the colours of professional teams.

Innocent until proven guilty, right? Few were charged, fewer were tried, none successfully. But that means little given that courts are largely useless for sexual crimes. The threshold of proof is correctly high for all criminal convictions, which makes them rare in cases built on conflicting testimony. So police don't lay charges and prosecutors don't advance them, though we know how prevalent such assaults are.

The presumption of innocence becomes misused and misunderstood. As a cornerstone of justice, it rules on the state's right to punish a citizen. It doesn't rule how fellow citizens should respond. Being pretty sure that someone committed assault is not enough to jail them, but it's enough to warrant keeping your distance. As ever, what's more likely: lying to deny an assault, or lying to invent one? Pretending this isn't real takes a wilfulness that is plentiful in sport. Fans, teammates, administrators, all use legal formality to dodge grim likelihoods about players they want or need, a convenient way to avoid taking a stand.

In doing so they create a binary: the accused is either convicted or spotless. But that's not how life works. The accuser of Beams and McCarthy said she was having sex with another man when the pair let themselves into the room and joined in.

Evans' accuser said the same happened in a hotel. The Cronulla and Canterbury stories were similar but with half a dozen men or more. Burgoyne's accuser left a pub with him but two other footballers followed them. The Irish plaintiff said Jackson grabbed her when she was isolated at a party before Olding came in to join him. Ronaldo's accuser said he ambushed her while she was changing clothes. He was already a global star; her medical records showed sexual injuries from violent penetration. Bryant was similarly famous, his accuser a young hotel worker who also documented sexual injuries. Kuggeleijn's accuser repeatedly refused sex while he kept attempting it.

None of those men denied the above. They didn't dispute their acts, only an interpretation of consent. All their cases involved abruptly putting people in situations likely to be intimidating. The women in all these cases were young and in most cases intoxicated. The athletes had all the power: physical, social, financial. Cronulla player Matthew Johns summed it up inadvertently: 'she gave no indication that she did not want to be there,' he said of his accuser, rather than being able to say that anyone had made sure she did. In each of these cases and a million more, men put a burden on women to prevent sex, rather than women being able to choose it. A legal interpretation of that behaviour matters at trial. But to the world outside, it's the behaviour that matters – or it should be. Decency is not bounded by the criminal code.

This was the all-or-nothing reasoning applied when Stokes was tried. As soon as his verdict was returned, those supporting him held that it wiped clean all that had gone before. It's quite the stretch: because a court couldn't be sure about rejecting his claim of self-defence, there was magically no problem with him punching people in the head 15 times. Fifteen months after the event, when he finally faced his ECB disciplinary charge, the fight itself was not addressed. Not a crime, not a problem.

And in the end, even convictions are ignored if there's incentive. The Seven Network and *The Age* newspaper still employ former footballer Wayne Carey, convicted of three assaults and accused of a raft of others against strangers, partners and police. The boxer Floyd Mayweather makes a fortune despite years of battering women, with the convictions and testimony from his children to prove it. Mike Tyson served half his sentence for rape and fought a bout billed as 'He's Back' that made US$96 million. *The Irish Times* wrote about Conor McGregor's relationship with the US, as a fighter who too often took his work outside hours: 'luckily for him sports fans there have short memories. Most don't care about his appearances in the courthouse dock or the newspaper allegations; all they are interested in is what he will do next in the boxing ring or the octagon, and it takes a lot for an athlete of his stature and with his ability to generate revenue to become persona non grata in the sports and entertainment worlds.'

You can say that sport is a job, and athletes should be left to earn their living. But players represent teams, and employers can decide that someone is a risk to the project or the people around them. The nature of celebrity will give athletes rewards, open doors, and most importantly give them access to people who will trust them and to people whom they could harm. There is a responsibility to meet. In a field where participants will be held up to be praised and emulated, they need to be worthy of emulation and praise.

It's curious how off-field violence is brushed off in sport where far lesser offences are not. Bad sportsmanship on the field or sniping someone at a press conference can draw greater censure. Australia's ball-tampering prompted more unified and potent condemnation than any athlete's criminal charge. Partly it's because these actions happen in the open, in front of the audience. If there are accusations of cheating they don't need to be proved to the standard of a court. There is little punitive risk beyond disdain, so the lower stakes mean a free-for-all.

In some ways the response to roughing up a cricket ball was surreal. There were any number of factors, not least undermining the perceived ideals of sport, the constant striving to be better. Within a team, cheating comes across as systematised deception. Warner and Smith were held to have committed spiritual harm to the game, something that injured those who loved cricket by injuring what they loved. The offence was against something vast in its entirety, not someone unknowable in their specificity.

On their return, then, perhaps Smith and Warner had more claim than most to be absolved on the field. Having sinned against the game, performing astounding deeds within it could be direct recompense. It had more logic than the joking talk about Sir Ben that will definitely be made real before long by some invertebrate prime minister.

This is always the part that makes no sense: that a person good at sport can compensate for non-sport behaviour by continuing to be good at sport. Stokes' cricket and his punch-up had nothing to do with each other except an enthusiasm for swinging hard until it was over. But forgiveness is a convenient way to go back to enjoying what we enjoyed before.

Thomas Patrick Oates writes that there are always 'discrepancies in the path of redemption and the erasures they require'. Perhaps rather than religious ideas of salvation, a pardon is pragmatic and primal: reintegrating someone to our group who still has value. Separating art from artist tends to depend on how much you love the art. In a general public view of Stokes, of course an increasingly hazy wrongdoing was surpassed by concrete delivery of a World Cup and a Test classic. Perhaps it's as simple as this: when someone is tawdry, they make you feel bad. When they produce a grand performance, they make you feel wonderful. In the emotional equation, recency wins. You take their act as a gift to you.

True redemption though, the real thing rather than the spin cycle, is possible. It first needs remorse, then it needs penance. It's not that all wrongdoing must be carried in shame for life. It's that resolving it requires acknowledgement of the harm done, work to make amends, and a genuine will to change. It's progress rather than punishment. This remains the missing part for our cricketers. Neither Smith nor Warner has given the full story, as trivial in some respects as it would be. They edge around the subject like it's a hex that can't be named. Evasiveness is a block to resolution. Stokes never conceded any problem with his violence. He could have demonstrated growth, drawn from his case to encourage others to be better, but that potential good was wasted.

In the story of 2019, there was one distinction between our three comebacks and the standard outline of sporting redemption. Normally a player just has to resume. Score a goal, get a win, there it is in the papers. But Smith and Stokes in opposition to one another raised their games. They didn't resume, they ascended. Feats more extraordinary than they had managed before, despite in the interim having trashed their careers, their preparation, their equanimity. The contests they played in were full of comebacks. Stokes in the World Cup: almost against Sri Lanka, almost against Australia, there for the final. More absurd still at Headingley. Smith from the collapse at Edgbaston, the injury at Lord's, the trough before Old Trafford.

Warner too came back a better player than he'd been. His prolific World Cup despite his struggles, his Australian season at a consistency and reliability that felt impossible. His real comeback was from his Ashes, under scrutiny that would have broken many a player less insanely fuelled by self-belief. That's his thing. Once corona hit, Warner spent his lockdown on TikTok every day, beaming as this happy dancing dad with his three little girls and Candice, doing music videos, magic tricks, choreographed Bollywood numbers. After all that has happened in his life, he'll put himself out there, day after day, a real person next to the personas. Warner has his moments of doubt but surges through them, no embarrassment, no fear, just joy.

Joy is the only point of sport. Those moments from the huge to the small. It doesn't have to be twin tons at Headingley. It can be the rare feeling for an ordinary player of hitting it sweetly: a lofted cover drive, a dead ball curled into the box, a jump shot from beyond the arc. It can be clinging on when you've never held a catch. It can be watching while a second-tier player like that Marnus kid jumps a grade. It can be diving for a frisbee when the grass is soft. The swoop of Healy's swing, Ash Gardner's smile getting her cap. It's the collective second of freeze when we see something so good that we don't think about whose team it was. It's when the crowd finds voice with a whump like kerosene igniting. It's when you leave after the magic and you realise that you were there.

That creates the power of sport, and the power creates money, and the money creates celebrity. Players become part of a pantheon, and it's dicey up there; it's crowded and changeable and there can be a long way to fall. The shameful things they do are on display, while our shameful acts live unseen closer to the earth. But only minor divinities lose their spots; the bigger idols are forever caught and restored, keeping their power no matter their wrongs. The sporting Olympians were named for dangerous gods, after all.

Perhaps in part Cameron Bancroft was right, and our response to public wrongs tells us about ourselves: the audience, the subscribers, the massed jury. There are reasons that we condemn people or cover for them, reasons that we rush to forgive. We rarely challenge ourselves about what is right or how to get there. It all happens on this side of the television screen, before we flick our channels endlessly on. So too the lure of stories, of being cleansed to start anew. We'll keep hearing them, regardless of how attentively the six stages are observed. We'll keep absolving selected others of their wrongs, even as we keep walking into confessionals, hoping to find some way to make ourselves pure. The impulse behind it can't be eradicated. You could say it's a comeback. You could settle for redemption. You could call it resurrection. It never dies.